Enjoy the Journey

of Women and their Horses along the Snake River Plain

Enjoy the Journey

of Women and their Horses along the Snake River Plain

W. Lenore Mobley

authorHOUSE®

AuthorHouse™
1663 Liberty Drive
Bloomington, IN 47403
www.authorhouse.com
Phone: 1-800-839-8640

First published by AuthorHouse   06/01/2011

ISBN: 978-1-4567-6954-3 (sc)
ISBN: 978-1-4567-6956-7 (ebk)

Library of Congress Control Number: 2011908029

Printed in the United States of America

Table of Contents

Acknowledgment and comments..vii

Introduction...1

History...7

Rodeo 17

Golden Girls 31

Endurance Riders 39

Pony Club..43

Ranch Women of the North..49

Women who Raise Horses...55

Ranch Women 69

Pleasure Riders 89

Mule Riders...95

Team Drivers 105

Thursday Sage Riders 113

4-H: Leaders /Members...137

Back Country Horsemen..145

Dressage/ Warmbloods..151

Specialty Riding 157

Drill Teams...165

Friends 171

Working Horse...183

Family 189

"Blessed are the peace makers, for they shall be called the children of God." Matt: 5:9

Acknowledgment and comments

I received so much support in writing this book. I wish to say THANKS to the following; My husband, Bill, as he has been a darling putting up with all this, two years of book work and helping me with the computer.

Ben & Janell Pearson for their editing helps, without them I would be lost.

Renee Maher who jumped in and "composed" the picture pages which was weeks of work.

My friends—Greg & Peggy Peasnall: Karen Majerus: Freddie Hopkins: Karen Ambrose: Carol Sobotka who worked with me in many areas of writing.

Lisa Moore and Susan Haney the Photo experts: Mike Edminster, photographer (H. Ruby), photo and Linda Anderson, Photo(Jo Heiss)

Yes, hugs to you all.

And of course, thank you to the "Women of the Snake River Plain," who gave me their memoirs. They were so patient and encouraging.

Also those who worked with me at Authorhouse—you were so helpful, patient and kind.

And most of all, thank you, my precious Lord God for opening these opportunities for me to meet all of the special people that are featured in <u>Enjoy the Journey</u>.

W. Lenore Mobley

All scripture is taken from the King James version of the Bible.

Other fiction books of The Journey Series by W. Lenore Mobley are;
The Dangerous Journey
The Lost Journey
Star Dancers Summer Journey
Calypso—Dark Horse (a children's story)

<u>Enjoy the Journey</u>, is a work of nonfiction. Most of the spoken words that appear in this book were uttered in my presence; some were recounted to me. Others, who sent me their memoir in complete form, I left much of the manuscript as they wrote it, as I felt it had a rhythm of its own. I have attributed thoughts to some of the characters, as most all of them were plausibly described to me when I met with them.

Please note; some of the women gave me a quote that was meaningful to them and it was placed at the beginning of their memoir.

Please keep in mind that a memoir is—a story of their life, spoken as best they can remember it and may be slightly mistaken in very minor details.

I apologize for any margins of human error. I did not write this book as an intellectual or detailed study. However, I alone am responsible for any errors.

The places and towns are in Idaho, unless otherwise stated.

Introduction

Idaho's Governor & First Lady, Lori Otter

Sacajawea

Bruneau Dunes State Park

ENJOY THE JOURNEY

In our stories we have **not** told you how to train or gentle a horse. Perhaps you, like me, learned from the **school of hard knocks** as many of us were not great horsewomen when we first acquired a horse. These women **tell of their love for their horses** and their experiences as they go out and enjoy them. A great passion is shown in each of the memoirs written. It may be from many months of gently working with a young horse, or from a thankful heart that **their equine bonded with them**. And some women have offered thanks for being able to return to riding as they recovered from a serious illness or injury.

The following chapters tell about how a horse came into someone's life at the right place and the right time, as if carrying with it a purpose or fulfilling a dream. And maybe horses are able to help people make some of their **dreams come true** and in return the beloved equine only desires to be given proper care. Horses do inspire many of us, and you might say wherever a horse is, so is your dream.

Come make yourself comfy and join in a celebration of warming moments in the tales of these women living along the Snake River Plain of Southern Idaho and its northern reaches of the Salmon River Valley. Learn what they did to refresh their souls.

Many of the women in this book, I met through the Thursday Sage Riders of Magic Valley and some of the group inspired me to write about them and their horses. I found their history with the equine in their lives unique, entertaining also learning, and I hope you do also.

+++++

Idaho's Bird Woman

In the following chapters, I do not mean to imply the following women were famous women like Sacajawea, but they were just as courageous. The other thing they had in common with her was their **love for their horses.** Whether they were out on the prairies or mountains, riding their horses down a trail or competing in races, shows, rodeos, drill teams, cutting, reining and roping events, driving their teams or raising them—this is what made them happy. I would call them independent, strong and adventurous; most of them are my mentors and friends.

+++++

Janey:
There was a woman who graced Idaho, whose nick-name was Janey. In 1805, she was less than twenty years old. When she rode one of her many horses, it was often said of her, that everyone noticed. And in those days and under those circumstances, it was unheard of for a Native American woman to even have her own horse. This woman was described as "independent as a hog on ice and a stickler for her rights."

In her travels, a river was named after her by the explorer, Captain Clark. He called this tributary of the Missouri River, <u>Bird Woman River</u>—or Sacajawea, (as the Shoshone people called her). Lewis and Clark often paid tribute to this small, brave adventurer because she wasn't a quitter. It was very fortunate that she managed to return to her homeland as she had ventured with these explorers all the way to the Pacific Ocean, **half that way on horseback.** She loved to travel and see the western countryside. Some say she lived a long life, and died in 1874 at her home in Oklahoma, but this is not known for sure. The one thing is known with certainty is that Sacajawea was responsible for raising the Native American woman to a new level of respect and admiration. No other Indian woman before was able to meet at Tribal Council with the Chiefs as Sacajawea did. She spoke several languages and seldom complained about her circumstances.

There is a Sacajawea Memorial Area one forth mile south of Lemhi Pass in Montana. It has a lovely picnic area with wildflower trails in the area. **The Idaho monument is 120 miles east on Hwy 28** (out of Salmon) commemorating the birthplace of Sacajawea the Lemhi, Shoshone woman who accompanied the Corps expedition. (www.sacajaweacenter.org.)

+++++

Lori Otter: First Lady of Idaho
2010

Pursue Your Vision

Stay Fit for Life.

Our First Lady of Idaho, Lori Otter, at an Empowering Women Conference made the following statement. "Listen to your own voice to find direction in life." She was speaking from experience as she found herself in changes and much was expected of her. That day Lori encouraged the women to discover things that they too, can be passionate about. She said, "**Empower yourself by pursuing your vision of life**—not everyone else's. For me time is the enemy in this decade of life and I have many a tight schedule as the wife of our Governor. Balancing priorities is very important to me and difficult for me—my family, fun, work, home . . . it's a lot."

Lori has enjoyed horses for many years. **She and Governor Otter often ride on their ranch** sometimes for pleasure and often to help with working the cattle.

"I usually ride Cooper, my pretty Quarter Horse—a bay with a star in the middle of his forehead. He is quiet, but willing to move out when asked."

"I'm a lot nicer person if I get my horseback rides in and I found just being outside helps with stress. Yes, horseback riding, jogging and working out calms and energizes me; therefore **I try to get out on my horse three times a week.**"

"You too can be fit for life with low impact workouts and maintain your energy levels, a healthy weight and a healthy emotional and social life. You are either working to live or living to work; and I much desire working to live." Lori grew up playing basketball, baseball, volleyball or just about any other team sport you can name. So it was only natural for her to become a physical education teacher. She was a good example in these activities that she asked her students to participate in.

Lori wishes you to have happy trails. And I am proud of you Lori for your example to us. Thank you for your encouragement. May you always stay 'fit for life.'

Lori and Governor Otter's 'Code of the West'

Live each day with courage.
Take pride in your work.
Do what has to be done.

Be tough, but fair.
When you make a promise, keep it.
Ride for the brand.
Talk less and say more.
Remember that some things aren't for sale.
Know where to draw the line.

+++++

Nancy Merrill: Eagle
Idaho Department of Parks Director

11-21-2009, Caldwell, ID. Nancy was the dinner speaker at the Idaho Horse Council State meeting; this is part of her story of her association with horses. Even though Nancy hasn't been on a horse in several years, she told me that their appeal to her had not faded. The following is her story.

"As a Young Girl, I too was in Love with Horses."

"I go way back to loving horses. Even their smell is something I will never forget and it is not offensive to me as **it evokes many memories** one I will tell you about."

"My first horse was named Jewel, and she was a jewel of a Quarter Horse—a pretty bay, dark with four white stockings and I thought beautiful. She let me and my cousins ride three astride bareback on her at the ranch and up the country roads. I loved brushing her mane and dark tail and taking care of her. At twelve years old, after the chores were done, I was able to swing upon her by grabbing her mane then taking charge of the reins, we rode everywhere. **I share the same love today as then to horseback riding."**

I also learned that Nancy's two daughters were a part of the Eh Cappa bareback riders for several years as they performed for many events and parades.

Nancy's speech continues.

"And it was not just the one million dollar impact the **1.9 million horse owners in Idaho** made to the state that we talked about (although I felt that was worth mentioning), but as Parks director, my desire is to partnership with all groups. I will continue to make many riding trails such as you find at Bruneau Sand Dunes, Eagle Island Park, The City of Rocks and Farragot State Park, along with thirty others. I will plan to keep many areas open for our use. We will also have the **Trail Rangers** help us keep the parks open as well as clean the two hundred miles of trails."

"We are looking for partners and I hear over and over, that equestrian people are so polite. I believe in 'can do people'—not can't, as I know that if most of you had a wall to climb over that you would go around or throw a rope to each other and make that climb—so just remember **we can't do it alone—It takes partners**. Thank you for having me come to speak to you at the Idaho Horse Council and let us keep in touch."

Thank you, Nancy for you sharing your love for horses and keeping trails open in our Idaho parks. I wish you good success in all you do and I feel you serve the people of Idaho well. I hope your plea brings response to acquire the needed help.

April

The roofs are shining from the rain,
The sparrows twitter as they fly,
And with a windy April grace
The little clouds go by.—Sara Teasdale

History

Jerome, ID

Three Island Crossing

Bev Stone

7

2 Chapter

History and Historians of Idaho

The Snake River Plain covers a third of Idaho with many geological features from the volcanic lands of Craters of the Moon that covered several hundred miles to the Shoshone Falls that falls over two hundred feet into the Snake river. It is a unique land with Sawtooth National Forests on both the north and south of the boarders. Most of the land is green with vegetation which is irrigated from the Snake. Beyond the sage, sand and scrub, resides the soul of a land that the Snake River waters.

The Horse;

There is just one of many historic places about horses I recommend you to visit here in our Valley. It is the **Hagerman Fossil Beds National Monument** to investigate their collection of equine fossils (which looked quite modern—like 3000 years, to me.) The historians claim they are millions of years old. In 1930 excavations by the Smithsonian Institution began. Paleontologists discovered a large concentration of fossils of an extinct species of horse, which became known as the "Hagerman Horse."

Horses that once existed in large herds here in Idaho and Oregon are believed to have originated in the Bering Land Bridge to Asia and the continent beyond. Most horse lovers know that horses once existed in North America and it is believed that many died out, and were reintroduced by the Spanish explorers. This explains the many wild herds that run free on our high plains.

The Mustang Horse, as they are known, is a hardy, free roaming horse of the North American West. The hardiness, grace, speed and independent image of the wild horse is well known for high-performance produce and for sports mascots. Mustang, an English word, comes from the Mexican Spanish word *Mestengo*, derived from the Spanish means "wild stray." This Mustang is the living symbol of the historic and pioneer spirit of the West that contributes to the diversity of life forms within the Nation and enriches the lives of the American people that now own many of the breed and have tamed them for ranch use and pleasure.

Back to Idaho by: G. Allen; American Falls

I have traveled o're the country and I've seen most everything
Alaska in the fall, California in the spring
But there's a place of beauty and that's where I long to go
That's back to good old Idaho.
That's where I wanna go—back to ol' Idaho,
Out where my friends are true, I'll build a house of dreams,
There by the mountain streams, Underneath the sky so blue
So today I'll **start my journey,** I've a long, long way to go
For I'm a native son of Idaho.

I went to see people like Virginia because we're going to be gone one day and we must work hard to **make the memories stay.**

Pioneering farms homesteaded the irrigated land of the fertile Snake River Plain as the steep canyon walls framed the setting. Yes, the Snake River Canyon is at once a familiar part of our landscape. These 57 miles are a geological wonder—a scene that for many of us who were born here, never cease to wonder over its beauty. One of these persons is Virginia Rickets our own local historian who I visited at her home east of Jerome in **2009.**

Virginia Rickets grew up Virginia Eastman living in Berger, Elmwood area, South of Filer. She graduated from high school there in 1943 and moved to Jerome after marriage.

Writing about the Part of Idaho that Virginia Loves

This is her story.

"In my life, horses were a way of going to neighbors to visit; unless the snow was as deep as it was in 1939 and we had to be careful we did not get caught at the neighbors because we could not get the horse home. Sometimes the only way to town was down the railroad tracks. After we were married we moved to Jerome. I didn't have a lot of chances to ride horses for pleasure. I **did enjoy wagon rides** at the Jerome Fair time often being in the parade as well in the opening of the rodeo. I enjoyed watching the women's events at these rodeos. **I would like to have done more with horses,** but raising kids, work and my research in Idaho history, took up a lot of my life."

Virginia showed me it's the stream, and not the clashing boulders that make up life. She has written the most detailed and interesting history book of South Central Idaho that I have ever read. It is titled <u>Then and Now in Southern Idaho</u>. Congratulations on this great document Virginia, because of this book you make memories stay.

+++++

Idaho's Snake River

America's far west offers pristine waters that look silver in the morning light, dwarfed by the expanse of forest and mountain. I have seen an evening mist transform **Idaho's rivers** into a fantasy world. These rivers rush into the Columbia through thick forests and eventually cut through an arid desert. The rivers in northern Idaho gave explorers a westward route for canoes and rafts just as the **Snake River** gave the early settlers water for stock and gardens. We are blessed to have many streams in Idaho that begin in the wilderness and twists through the rugged land to empty into the **many tributaries of the Snake River.**
History Trails:

One of the Western historic trails our wagon trains journeyed on was a place called the **Three Island Crossing** at Glenns Ferry. Here they attempted to safely cross the treacherous Snake River The reenactment that I have written about in this chapter is one historic event that made Idaho the state that it is today.

The Oregon Trail: In 1836, two couples, Marcus and Narcissa Whitman and Henry and Eliza Spalding, felt the call to go to the Oregon Territory as missionaries. They were sent by eastern churches to be missionaries to the American Indians of the Oregon Country. There are several good books telling about their lives in the early settlement in the vast reaches of this western interior. The letters they sent home publicized the opportunities and advantages of this western country. I could not mention the Oregon Trail without giving them credit for their **step of faith.**

2009   The Three Island Crossing

As I looked into history, the first organized wagon train trip to Oregon was made in 1842. The journey began in Independence, Missouri from there it was more than 2,000 miles to Idaho where the wagons crossed the prairies, towering mountains and parched deserts. But the impossible trip, as some called it, was completed. As they blazed the trail it kindred the hopes of many that desired a better life. Within just two years, almost 900 people made their first trip on the **Oregon Trail,** as it was the main road of westward expansion, a corridor of western history.

This re—enactment of the Three Island Crossing **in Glenns Ferry** is a picture of "how the West was won." There is an Interpretive Center here that the **Idaho Parks Department** has for viewers to enjoy.

Today in the Three Island Crossing re-enactment, I would like to feature, **Julie Jeffrey,** a courageous horsewoman**,** who has made many trips crossing this dangerous Snake River in her horse pulled wagon**.**

It was a warm, but overcast August day and the crowd of over a thousand people watched breathlessly as the horse drawn wagon and the outriders entered the water on the south bank of the Snake River. The Jeffery's were driving the partially covered wagon that was being pulled by their team of **two white Percheron horses.** The Percheron horse is one of the most elegant draft horses and today their unusually free-flowing and active stride was particularly noticeable. I recognized two of the six horseback riders that accompanied them. Vic and **Janine Jaro** from Buhl led the group down to the Snake River. I later found out that this is **Janine's 10ᵗʰ year to do this out riding with the wagons.** She is a very adventurous horse rider, and later told me, "**I wouldn't miss it for the world,** and this participation hasn't been easy as we have to attend many practices for this enactment in an effort to make it safe."

It was very exciting watching the wagon pulled by the Percheron team, as well as the five horse riders as they come down into the canyon and entered the green waters of the Snake. The horses, now knee deep in water, walked downstream along the sandy strip until the water came to their bellies. There, they turned toward the island that was located in the middle of the river. They walked their horses to the islands' point and that brought them half way across the river. When the horses left the island they were quickly in the main current that was the deepest water that came up to the belly of the large team. Then **to keep the wagon behind the big team,** the outriders put ropes on the wagon and secured them to the horn on their saddles. The watching crowd gasped as the horses got in deeper and swam for about twenty yards until the team again began walking on the river bottom. At this distance the procession rolled on buy giving the large audience full view of the beautiful enactment from the early days of Idaho's settling. Those of us who are here can appreciate what we just witnessed. I asked a college girl who was sitting next to me why she came today. She replied, **"I can build on what we are as I rob from the past—it's important to me."**

The unit safely arrived on our side at the landing; **Julie Blackwell Jeffrey,** and her husband**,** drove the team pulling the wagon up to a level place as the crowd surrounded them. Julie was asked what she thought of this enactment of the Three Island Crossing being completed. "This event is something to be appreciated by the people. I just thank God **we all made it,"** said Julie Jeffrey of Glenns Ferry.

"Yes, just happy it was uneventful," Julie said with a sigh.

I asked Julie, "What do you think of this historic event?" She replied the following.

"Their legacy is our challenge to keep it alive. This tradition of this enactment here in our valley, began in 1985 and until **I got the challenge to ride in a wagon across the Snake**—it was the hardest thing for me to do. But I'm glad I did, it is a way to learn history and I enjoy history. The pioneers had heavier wagons loaded with their precious supplies and it was more dangerous for them," Julie smiled as she is a very personable person that is willing to talk to most everyone today who had any question.

I wish to thank Julie for her participation.

+++++

Bev Stone: Historian/Author
From the Desert of Idaho to Washington D.C;

"When the going gets tough, the tough get going."

Bev Stone of Kimberly loves to look into her and our history of how Idaho was settled and write about many of the pioneers who made history. Her historical book, *Stone by Stone on the Oregon Trail*, is an account of just this. Written as a personal tribute to the thousands of emigrants who trekked West, Bev attempted, in her book, to bring those unknown heroes to life by using their own words from Oregon Trail diaries. Bev's lovely manuscript **won three special awards** and I recommend *Stone By Stone on the Oregon Trail* to anyone who is looking for a wonderful gift to give whether they were raised in the west or not. It is **beautifully illustrated** by, Gary, her artist husband of 51 years.

As a result, she and Gary **were selected to represent Idaho for the Oregon Trail Sesquicentennial, which included a trip to Washington D.C.** where the original paintings created for the book's illustrations were displayed in the rotunda of the Senate building for a week.

At that time, Bev and Gary made **a presentation to Congress which was featured on C-SPAN**. As a result, they were interviewed the very next morning by all major TV news networks, as well as featured on many radio shows and several Oregon Trail documentaries. Bev has also been **listed in Who's Who, was a featured Young Author** speaker many times, as well as a speaker at numerous school assemblies across the northwest, and keynote speaker at many conventions. Bev has also written many stories of the horses that have been a part of her life.

Bev's story . . .

"I actually began writing after my kids were grown, at the request of a local newspaper that wanted a weekly history column. I wasn't sure I could do it, but said I would try. **It was fun, interesting and I loved it.** I continued that column for nine years, as well as several history articles each month for Idaho Events magazine covering all areas of Idaho. I began free-lancing here and there, and wrote three children's books, two of which are in print, one ready for press, and two more well outlined. I am working on a family history book, and a book about Rock Creek area."

As a child Bev had a fondness for horses and began to ride at an early age. She was the oldest of four and was called Slugger—(I imagine because she stuck up for her siblings.) When her mom divorced, she moved the family to Twin Falls where they lived just two blocks from where Gary Stone lived. There were lots of kids in the area, they all played together, graduated from high school and are good friends with many classmates today. Bev continued to ride until her health would not permit; however, she loves to go to the corral and care for Licorice. This registered Paint mare's name is Idaho Red Wine, but she loves to eat licorice, hence the name they call her now. **Bev has enjoyed riding her for about 25 years** but like Bev, she is now is retired.

"My first horse really belonged to my dad, who paid very little for her at an action. I was about seven and we were farming in the Cedar Draw area northeast of Buhl. I attended Cedar Draw country school where there were only two rooms; Grades one through five in one room and six through eight in the other. I rode a friend's horse to school or walked the three plus miles in nice weather and by sleigh or wagon when there was a lot of snow."

"I had no idea Pa was bringing home a horse until I went down to the barn when he backed the horse trailer up to the open corral gate next to the barn. When they opened the trailer door, **all fury broke loose.** They had loaded the horse by physically pulling her into the open trailer, and then fastening her with chains like hobbles. The moment they undid her legs, she went more than wild and tried to climb out of the trailer."

"I was scared to death at such fury, so I ran into the barn and watched. By the time she was freed into the corral, she was bloody and so were the men that were helping. My Dad had scrapes, blood and bruises everywhere, and his shirt was torn. What a sight. Pa said she was explosive, so he promptly named her Dynamite, and she had the run of the 40 acre pasture where we kept the milk cows. It was my job to go get the cows for milking twice a day, and the dark, bay quarter horse filly with the black mane and tail stayed far away from me."

"I began talking loud enough for her to hear me and leaving a trail of apple pieces as I walked. Eventually she came for the apples while I tossed them. We had sugar cubes at that time, and I began taking them along to add to the bait. It wasn't long before she **was literally eating out of my hand,** one cube at a time and nuzzling for more."

"One day my dad noticed her come to me and became interested after he had left her unnoticed for months. He had me coax her up near the fence where he quickly roped her and snubbed her to a post. She put up a horrible fight and I was crying at him to let her go. He wanted to break her for riding but after numerous attempts, he put out the word that anyone who could ride her could have her. There were many who tried. No one succeeded as at the mere sight of a man made her run and go crazy."

"One of my Uncles was eight years older than I and he wanted that horse. We were hunting and fishing buddies, as I followed him everywhere. He convinced me to help him catch her. We had a game plan and it worked and **we were able to ride her after being patient**."

"We changed her name to Dina and rode her all over. It was while we were riding on one of the country roads right where the Oregon Trail crossed, (as I later learned) that a pheasant suddenly flew up right under her feet and she shied. We were riding bareback and I fell off hard and broke my arm near the elbow. The horse took off."

"My frightened Uncle scooped me up and carried me some distance to the nearest farm house and we went in the farmer's truck to the doctor in Buhl. It was a bad break, and I spent most of that fall in a cast."

"Dina was rounded up and my Uncle took her home. It was one of the last rides I had on her, since we moved off the farm and out of Buhl area to Twin Falls."

"Dina became such a gentle animal and lived to a ripe old age. She had lots of foals and threw the best colts. My brother got one from my Uncle years later. He named him Cherokee and he became a Wonder Horse, but that's another story."

"After I married Gary, we had many horses over the years, all of them were characters and worthy of their own story. **We used them for hunting and riding in the hills**. Occasionally, some of the neighbor children would show them at the fair, but we never did. **They were just our friends and we treated them as such.**"

And being a friendly person describes Bev 'to a T.' I have enjoyed getting to know you, Bev, and good luck with your stories in the future.

+++++

There are many historic rides a person can take with wagon trains—if you have a good horse, team and wagon or are a good hiker. The following is a story of a day's ride a friend and I had the privilege to take.

Our history sings of centuries
Such varying songs it sings!
It starts with winds, slow moving sails,
It ends with skies and wings.—*Catherine Coblentz*

GIFT OF HERITAGE

My tribute to women and their horses had its beginning when in grade school I read of Sacajawea's journey with the Lewis and Clark expedition. I'll never forget the feeling when I learned that these explorers crossed Idaho on their way to the Pacific Ocean. The more I learned the more I give much of the success to Sacajawea. I felt she had a desire to know more about our unexplored west. I dreamed of all the things they experienced while horseback riding and decided some day to be as adventurous.

One June morning when I answered my ringing telephone it was Karen Majerus calling. She said, "I told you I'd let you know when the Snake River Heritage Wagon Train was coming our way. Next Tuesday they will be traveling on the old Kelton Road and leaving a camp near Picaboo on their way to Richfield. We need to be there by 8 a.m. and be ready to ride with them." We decided to meet at the fairgrounds in Richfield at seven where we could leave a truck and trailer for our ride back to get the other outfit.

I learned that this heritage ride was started by Karen's brother, Jay Ward. He told us the following day why he began the occasion. He said, "I wanted to create an event to understand our heritage and keep history alive. So, in 2004 we began looking for history events to celebrate in our own way. Besides this one, I have participated in five other historical trails rides—such as the Oregon Trail. Often these have been done with speakers who studied the history. I learned there are more trails in Idaho than any of the other western states. As many as 50,000 pioneers traveled this Kelton trail even after the railroads came this way."

The Kelton Road covered nearly 300 miles just across Southern Idaho and like Jay, Karen and I had a desire to renew the history of this land, as well as being eager for the spirit for adventure. We didn't have to be asked twice to be a part of this Snake River Heritage Days Wagon Train celebration. This was a journey that had begun on May 29, 2009, near Burley on the old Kelton Road.

We planned to join them on the eleventh day of their return trip; at this time they had traveled as far north as Hailey. The six wagons, fifteen mules and one horse along with their drivers. was spending the night before at Silver Creek campground. The next day we arrived at the beautiful camp as the morning sun was gleaming on the creek. It was a sky blue day unlike most of what we had experienced in early June. The Mules and horse were munching away at their hay paying no attention to the intrusion we made driving in; however, the two cow-dogs barked and greeted us happily.

Karen took me over to meet the team drivers beginning first with the assistant Wagon Master. "This is Glen Beck and his 6 year old grandson, Derringer, from Burley."

"Glad to meet you. What a nice day to come out," Glen greeted me.

"Thank you, Glen, nice to meet you and Derringer. I understand you have had a lot of rain that has created some muddy roads for the wagons."

He replied, "our first week on this journey was spent dodging in and out of hail, rainstorms and some snow. My wife, Myra, rode in the snowstorm and never complained once. We were slowed by mud and took some detours, but keeping the heritage of our Wagon Train Days is important to us and we continued. It is good to have some out riders with us today to alert us to any road danger along the way."

I told him that I was so glad to be there and hoped to be of some help.

As we moved on to introductions I met the head Wagon Master, Lloyd Warr, from Burley. Then I met Bob Fosnot and Joe Adams, both from Montana, Frank Adams from Paul and Monty Smith from Soda Springs.

They each had well built wagons and beautiful teams. The drivers were putting the harnesses on their mule teams and in front of his smaller open wagon, Monty harnessed his black horse—a big, quaterhorse-draft cross.

They were as anxious as we were to continue their trek on the old Kelton Road. This road was also used by freight wagons, stage coach lines as well as cattle drives. I knew it was going to be an exciting day for us to be the out riders for this wagon train on this 18 mile journey through the desert.

They began to roll at the designated time. The noise of the moving wagons alerted our riding horses that something was happening.

It was time to quit the jawing and get mounted. I put my foot in the stirrup and swung upon my Peruvian Paso horse. "We had better get in the saddle or we'll get left," Karen said.

We hadn't ridden alongside of the Wood River for more than a mile, when Karen said, "Look! There are two elk over there in the tall bushes along the river."

"Yes, I see them. Wow," I exclaimed pulling out my camera for a shot. And this was only the beginning of a beautiful day that Karen and I continued to enjoy.

Many travelers on the main highway that was just 50 yards from the dirt road we traveled stopped to take pictures of the wagon train. We waved at them and yelled, "Happy Trails." They waved back.

A little way down the road, we began to admire the mule teams' energy. For most of the way they trotted a relaxing gait and our horses had to keep a fast pace to be alongside of them. We were glad to be mounted on easy riding steeds that enjoyed this speed. I did not see any mules attempt to slow up pulling these 3,000 pound wagons.

Riding along side of the first wagon I asked Joe the names of his mules. "This smaller one is B.J. then Jenny and Hollie. They go together real well," he said with pride. And pride is what the owners showed in the good treatment of their animals.

"Tell me more about the reason you use mules to pull your covered wagon?" I asked Lloyd when I caught up to his team.

"Over the years mules have been used for a variety of different jobs ranging from being the preferred mounts of the clergy, pulling fire fighting equipment, being used by army pulling the artillery and removing the wounded from the battlefield, as well as working at the mines, and doing agricultural work."

"The mule is the offspring of a cross between a male mammoth Jack and a female horse. As a general rule, the mule has a front end of a Jack (head with long ears), an upright mane, strong legs and horse-like hind quarters with a long tail. And mules are more popular today and are more commonly seen. Although the numbers of mules declined 30 years ago, they are now enjoying a revival in America where they are used for pleasure riding and even jumping competitions," They're exceptionally strong and have lasting stamina," Lloyd added. I also learned from Glen's grandson, Derringer, that they usually have a quiet temperament. I watched him that evening go into the pasture where the fifteen mules were put up in a temporary wire fence. He easily caught their two and led them to their wagon for some grain.

Karen was riding a mare named, Mickie, a spotted Fox Trotter and the mother of the two mules that she had at home. Karen planed on riding one of these mules when we joined the train on Thursday.

In the early afternoon we out riders and the wagons rolled into the country town of Richfield. Our horses swelled their dusty sides and blew great breathe as we slowed down to ride through the streets. Karen and I waved at the many town citizens that came to see the wagons. We tied up the teams on Main Street and Karen and I tied our horses alongside. After a cool drink, Karen and I said good bye to the drivers and thanked them for their great hospitality. We were so proud to be a part of this heritage ride.

Rodeo

Lana Brackenbury Parker

Cali Jo Parker

Tanish Adams

Janeale Dean

Jackie Buckley

Rodeo

Shirley Ankrum

Patti O'Maley

Timi Lickley

Cowgirls

A Dale Evans Rogers quote; "Cowgirl is an attitude, really. A pioneer spirit—a special American brand of courage. The cowgirl faces life head on, lives by her own lights, and makes no excuses. Cowgirls take stands. They speak up. They defend the things they hold dear. A cowgirl might be a rancher, a barrel racer, a range rider, or an actress, but she's just as likely to be a checker at the local Winn Dixie, a full-time mother, a banker, an attorney or an astronaut."

Rodeo Contestants:

The world of rodeo and the women involved in the sport have seen a lot of change through the years. Who would have thought that what was called the sponsor girls, would be replaced by rodeo queens and Miss Rodeo America who continue to preserve the grace, beauty and tradition of the rodeo? But a few aspects of the rodeo remain the same—like **the cowgirls' integrity, grit and determination.**

+++++

Lana Brackenbury Parker: Wendell

1971 MISS RODEO AMERICA—Hats off to Rodeo Royalty

"The road to success is always under construction!"

Lana turned her love for horses into a rodeo career that included being crowned Miss Rodeo America. After graduating from college she went on to form several clubs that promoted rodeo events for girls. She is much too modest to tell of the many awards she won personally—as well as she taught what she knew and it was used to a good advantage to those who crossed her path.

Today I call her **a promoter for other cowgirls** to help them reach many of their goals and promote the traditions and values of rodeo events.

I knew Lana B. when she was in high school (well, who didn't that had a horse). Lana was an experienced horsewoman and at an early age she often competed in many events of 4-H, rodeo and horse showing. I was impressed by her success in barrel racing and when our daughter, Sara wanted to compete, I believed Lana was the teacher we needed. It proved to be successful and I thank her for her help.

Lana's talent, beauty, friendliness, kindness and hard work took her to top awards in rodeo circles. She is an accomplished promoter of the sport of rodeo. And she showed outstanding performance and leadership skills in equine activities. As **Miss Rodeo America** she served as a goodwill ambassador to promote the Professional Rodeo Cowboys Association and other western traditions. However, I believe it was her winning smile that really won me over.

When I called her last year, after she had not heard from me in years, I got a warm welcome and an invitation to an event she was sponsoring. The following weekend, Bill and I went to the Shu Fly arena north of Gooding, to attend the American West sanctioned, barrel racing competition and there I found the Lana that I remembered. She was taking charge of the competitive events with quick responses. It was her idea to plan clinics and events, for the spirited cowgirl to come and get the experience they need. Today I watched thirty girls compete with quickness, and even if not in the winning money, they came out with a smile.

I asked one of the mothers what Lana has that makes her so successful, and her answer was, **"she loves what she does, she seems to understand every student, and has the knowledge to help every child with her horse."**

Lana's story is at the beginning and her daughter, Kali Jo's story follows.

"Horses have been a rewarding part of my life. I think they taught me a lot about life in general. They taught me love, compassion and responsibility. I was fortunate to have had many successes and rewards from my love of horses."

"My first horse was an old rodeo pickup horse that my sister and her husband purchased to use on the ranch in Fairfield, Idaho. His name was Sparky and he was the first horse I competed on and used in high school rodeo. When I was a sophomore in high school, Sparky got the colic and I held his head while he died. But I was fortunate as a friend named Mr. Bud Roseberry adopted me as his rodeo daughter and became my rodeo dad and therefore I used his horses. Scoot Nick and Filly Sheru were my high school horses the next two years. I was a high school and **collegiate rodeo champion in barrels, poles and breakaway roping**. My horses harnessed me several scholarships that helped my family put me through college. I'll always be thankful for Bud and his wife, Verta's, role for helping me at this time in my life and for the opportunity to get to ride such fine horses as if they were my own equine."

I asked Lana to tell me about some of her most memorable awards. She replied, "In 1971, I was crowned Miss Rodeo America, an opportunity I still look back on with awe and gratefulness. What a great year. It was a chance to travel the USA."

"I was a member of the WPRA for many years and **qualified for the Wilderness Circuit Finals several times on several different horses that I trained myself.** This was very rewarding to me."

"It was through rodeo that I met my husband Tim. We have been happily married for thirty-four years. It is also through him and his ability that our children have been able to ride champion horses competing in high school and the Wilderness Circuit where they placed very high."

Lana told me her son, TW, was a champion at steer wrestling and calf roping through school and today his wife and son love to ride as much as TW's sister, Kali Jo does.

Meeting Kali Jo at the Shu Fly arena was like seeing Lana ride again. She is in the top fifty in barrel riding standings on the Wilderness Circuit. She traveled to Texas one winter where she stayed in Sonora with friends so she could continue to participate and learn more of this event. She had been awarded 12th in Pendleton, Oregon and watching her and her horse work, I know she will reach most of her goals this year and it is exciting to write about a second generation horsewoman.

That fall, I watched Kali Jo ride in the barrels competition at the Centennial Rodeo Celebration in Burley at the Cassia County Rodeo. What a ride she had in the top money; then she left that evening for another run in Utah.

Lana writes more about her daughter, Kali Jo.

"She is a former **high school and collegiate champion in barrels, poles and breakaway**. She has competed in the WPRA since she was nine and qualified for her first Wilderness Circuit Finals at ten. She has chosen a life of training, competing and selling nice barrel horses after she has proven them. I have a lot of fun and reward at this time of my life helping her with these horses and traveling with her, when my teaching permits. We have traveled throughout the country to rodeos and barrel racing events."

Good luck Kali Jo. You are very pretty and friendly as well as a talented horse-woman.

Besides being a mentor to her daughter there's a long list of accomplishments that Lana has completed. Today she still rides the younger horses to make many top competitors as barrel and roping equine. I understand she receives many personal rewards today as she rides these horses. She teaches at least one clinic a year, and has had multiple opportunities to help young riders come together with their horse.

"I, along with Shawn Davis, developed the SURA, where many young competitors in Idaho got a tremendous start in learning how to compete in the rodeo arena. Although the SURA has changed in format from a junior rodeo association to **a family oriented timed event venue**, we still ride under and believe in the same motto—SURA—*Making today's contestant-tomorrow's champion.*"

Just as daily horseback rides gave Nancy Reagan time to think through problems and enjoy God's creation, Lana also sees being on a horse as a privilege that she said, "I never take this for granted."

+++++

Patti O'Maley: Gooding

"No life is wasted that is spent in the saddle."—Winston Churchill

I was Hooked on the Sport of Rodeo

"A horse named Par was the greatest horse I ever owned as she had a lot of heart for a small horse. **Par took me to the National Intercollegiate Rodeo Title in goat tying** my senior year at Idaho State University. My competing on the women's rodeo team helped send me the four years that was needed to get my Bachelor of Science degree," Patti told me with warm enthusiasm. "I have experienced ranch life the best way possible—on the back of a horse."

Her cascade of brunette hair complimented her dark eyes that sparked when I asked Patti to talk of her love for horses.

"For ten years at our ranch in Shoshone, I got the experience needed to be the working daughter of a rodeo stock producer and supplier of bucking horses and bulls."

"I began riding horses the summer when I was six. We moved to the ranch near Shoshone from Nampa to begin a life long commitment to ranching and rodeo stock contracting."

"My pony Captain Crunch helped me learn I could also ride burros, calves and my dad's big palomino ranch horse we called Sam. But, I wasn't finished with the pony business and my great aunt often told the story of the day she watched me head north on my pony. It wasn't long before she heard screaming and had to race outside to find out what all the commotion was about. To her surprise, all she could see was a cloud of dust, Captain Crunch running towards home and a screaming kid hanging on for dear life. To this day I do not know if I was screaming out of fear or from the excitement of my first runaway!"

"My first horse was called Cowgirl, a horse I participated with in 4-H, learned to gather cattle, rope and run barrels. This mare was a great learning horse, but lacked speed, so at the age of ten my dad found a barrel racing horse called Tink. He could run a barrel pattern at such speed that could set me on the back of the saddle."

"One of my most horrifying riding experiences happened one late spring day, (when) my sister and I rode out to where Dad was fixing fence. My sister stepped off her pony Apache and he bolted and ran toward home. I volunteered to catch him and bring him back. It had been raining and was slick and my dad warned me not to run. I guess Tink did not listen for he must have had a flashback from his racing days and run he did. He was out of control as far as I was able to stop him. He failed to make a sharp turn into the corrals and went cross country and attempted to jump a five wire fence. He cleared it only to land upside down on the other side, in a ditch. Needless to say, God was keeping an eye on me as I survived with just a few stitches and a sore body."

"By the time we started producing rodeos and supplying bucking horses and bulls; I was hooked on the sport of rodeo—roping and riding. I rode more specialized horses and upon entering high school, my parents gave me a choice—'a car or a horse for rodeo competing'? **Of course I wanted a horse.** This horse was a four year old mare named Barbie. Over the next four years of high school, I spent hours riding and training Barbie to run barrels and poles. It was good learning for me too. I have experienced ranch life the best way possible—on the back of a horse."

"When my dad traded a grey Brahma bull for a grey Appaloosa named Fred. He was an ultimate all around horse. You could gather livestock, do breakaway and rope steers on him. I hauled Fred to Rapid City, SD and finished third at the **High School Rodeo Nationals in breakaway roping** during my sophomore year."

I learned Patti was awarded the Lurline Whittaker award three years in a row those years she was competing. The award is given each year to the high point All-Around Cowgirl in District 5.

"After Fred, came a little rope horse I called Wilson. Wilson was my Houdini, a horse we have all probably had one like. He could untie himself and go into the shed to munch away on dog food. **He loved candy bars and potato chips.** He probably ate more junk food during the summer rodeo season than I did."

"When I was home during the summer, **I would often ride some of the bucking horses** to gather and sort stock. Believe it or not, two of my favorite horses to ride were Cherry Creek and Whiskey River. Several times I remember packing the American Flag at a rodeo, dismounting and unsaddling Cherry Creek so he could be used in the Saddle Bronc Riding at the arena. I don't think the cowboys who drew him were too thrilled to be bucked off the same horse that I rode during the Grand entry."

Patti is still active in the family stock contracting business called the Slash T Rodeo Company. When she can find the time from her teaching career, you will see her helping with the gathering and sorting of livestock during the rodeo season. And often she competes in the roping events riding a horse named Boots. Watch for her there. Patti is a giver, and with her teaching attitude she was placed in a training program called **EAGALA (Equine Assisted Growth and Learning Association)**. Several years ago she had the opportunity to run an equine therapy program for an adolescent drug and alcohol treatment program. Patti called it a great experience.

Patti concludes, "I have ridden many great horses and could probably write an entire book about my experiences growing up in Southern Idaho. I am extremely grateful to have been blessed with the opportunity to live in the countryside. I often saddle up and head out the back gate of the ranch onto 1,000 acres of BLM ground. In September we take a number of the horses out to the range and re-gather them in December. **Fairfield area is also a favorite place for me to trail ride** on my equine partners."

"As a Spanish Proverb goes, '*a horse is worth more than riches.*' And so it has been for me! Happy Trails!"

Yes, Patti, the Fairfield area is our next date to get together riding. See you there.

+++++

On the Oregon Trail of the late 1830's the town of Soda Springs was put on the map when an experimental trail cutoff was made. It extended to the north to Pocatello and the Fort Hall area.

Nathaniel Wyeth, a fur trader, was angry at the bigger fir trading companies and decided to start his own trading post. In 1835 with his fur monies he built a **post along the Snake River that he named Fort Hall.** It was there for the wagon train immigrants to re-supply their stock, and to do repairs in the blacksmith shop.

One of the first wheels into the area was the missionary, Doctor Marcus Whitman and his wife Marissa.

This beacon of safety, closed after the big fur dealers bought him out. It is recorded that in 1862 many travelers stayed there, camped in the abandoned buildings and grazed stock in the pastures. It became a good stopover for many who were preparing to continue on but some feared the crossing of the Snake as they considered it a torrent from other rivers they had crossed thus far. This caused many to consider staying and helping themselves to the free, rich soil with lots of water. Thus, the area began to be settled as a farm and ranch area.

This Bannock County area is where Timi grew up.

Timi Ankrum Lickley: Jerome

In the fall of 2010, I kept reading about Timi Lickley placing in the top three in the barrel competitions at the area rodeos. Anxious to meet her, I phoned a friend who I knew would introduce me to her. Thank you, Timi for taking the time to write your memoirs for me and good luck to a second generation rodeo gal.

This February, I went to the Shu Fly arena to watch Timi and Shirley perform. I was not disappointed for Timi did take home the **first place prize money** as she, riding Rock, scooted the barrels in record time. The big surprise to me was getting to meet Shirley, her mother and I had a nice visit with her as well as getting to see her perform and get her story also.

This is Timi's story in her own words.

Horses are the Glue that Keep our Family Close

"My name is Timi Lickley and I was born and raised in **Pocatello**. My parents are Brent and Shirley Ankrum, and I have an older sister named Buffy. I guess you could say **I grew up on a horse's back.** My mom always rode horses and ran barrels in jackpots and rodeos, so that is what my sister and I did while growing up."

"My dad used our barrel horses to chariot race in the winters when we were not using them. It was pretty exciting for us when he would win races against those high priced race horses! It seemed that our lives revolved around our horses, and it helped to keep our family close. We still do so much together with them. My mom, sister and I still barrel race, and we often go to these rodeos together. My dad has always been very supportive, and he will still drop everything to go with us. **Horses are truly the glue that binds us all together**."

"We never had the money to buy finished horses, so from a very early age my mom started teaching us to **train our own horse.** We used our horses for everything such as—Buffy and I showed our horses in 4-H and at open horse shows, we used them in the reining patterns for rodeo queen contests, and we used them for the various rodeo events we competed in."

"But most of all, we used them for transportation! We rode our horses everywhere. My mom felt that we were safe, as long as we were on our horses. People were not surprised to see the "Ankrum girls" ride up to the drive-in window at the Bandito Burrito or ride across town to the library. We even rode them down to the local fish hatchery to do some 'fishing'!"

"Growing up I had two very special horses. One was a beautiful chestnut gelding named Lucky Town. The other a little sorrel spitfire gelding named Arimo. My parents purchased both of these horses as two year olds, and I had the privilege of using them throughout my entire youth. "Lucky" was given to me when I was in the second grade. He was the first horse that was really and **truly all mine**. I loved him with all my heart. He became my best friend, and when times were tough, Lucky was who I sought out to help me through it. We had a very strong bond until the night he died in a trailer accident when I was a senior in high school. That was devastating to me, but when I think of Lucky, it is always with joy in my heart."

"Now, Arimo was a completely different story. That horse **bucked me off** more than any horse really aught to be allowed to buck someone off! One time, during my rein as the **Princess of the Pocatello Frontier Rodeo**, he bucked me off right in front of a huge crowd, Miss Rodeo America (a complete goddess in the eyes of a ten year old), and Bob Tallman (rodeo announcer extraordinaire)! Arimo was so athletic and yet so full of spunk and personality that you just couldn't help yourself but love him. I think **he made me a much better rider, too."**

"The first time I remember actually competing at a real rodeo (not a jackpot or junior rodeo), I was eight years old. It was in Jackson Hole, Wyoming. All the "toughs" of the time were there, and I was in awe. I don't remember if I even won any money, but I do remember the loud roar of that crowd when I ran. It was amazing to me, and **it gave me a rush like I had never known.** Needless to say, I was hooked! That rush is still the same and just as exhilarating. In both of those instances, I was given a great opportunity, and it was given to me by a horse named Prince. He was the first horse that I learned to ride on."

"This year I had the opportunity to run barrels at the Reno Rodeo. During the Final Round, it was a little like deja vu. All the big names were there, and I was in awe again. That run was so exciting, and amazing, and well, a little overwhelming, but the rush was the same. I am still hooked!"

I learned that at this rodeo Timi and her horse Rock, ran fourth which allowed her a chance to compete in the 'short round' and here they recorded a 17.0 time. She was awarded silver spurs and interviewed in front the rodeo audience. Timi said it was an exciting time for her and her horse. Her plans are to attend the Houston, Texas Rodeo in the spring. They are qualified to compete in The Super Shoot Out. Good luck, Timi!

"Rock, is the horse that I now ride, although I have had several horses in between, and I have learned so much from each one. I feel that each one helped me to become the rider, trainer, and person I am today. **Without those horses I wouldn't be me.**"

"Through horses and rodeo I have met so many wonderful people. They have been willing to share their knowledge, expertise, and most of all friendship. One very special person that I met through rodeo was my husband, Ryan Lickley. We met while attending college at Idaho State University. We both competed in rodeos and shared a strong desire to become better competitors and people with horse knowledge. Ryan was raised in a ranching family near Jerome. (I had the fortune to know his grandmother, Lois Lickley for many years.) That is now where we live, work and ride. Yet, most importantly it is where we are raising our boys, Christian and Samuel."

"Ryan is a calf roper, and although I may be biased, he is one heck of a horse trainer. Ryan and I travel to rodeos together with our children. I have seen so many wonderful places while traveling to rodeos, and now Ryan and I get to experience all of that with our kids. **It doesn't really get much better than that."**

Thank you, Timi, for your friendliness it was my privilege to meet you and get your story.

Happy trails to you and your fine family.

+++++

Shirley Ankrum: Pocatello
Barrel racer and an equine therapy provider

So many Horse Problems are People Problems

I watched Shirley run the barrels on her big Quarter Horse, Angeluma, where she had a great run. I could tell they enjoyed the event, although not placing in the money. Later Shirley told me her mare got ahead of her. To a novice like me, I let Shirley explain what she meant, by getting ahead of her. She said, "I did not wait for my horse to get into position—I should have trusted my training." The registered Quarter Horse she rode is eight this year and one she trained herself.

Shirley's story continues.

"I have been riding since I was a kid; I did not get into the barrel racing until I was in my twenties. I have been training horses for over thirty years and giving clinics for twenty.

I am a certified Acuscope-myoscope technician. Both are certified to control chronic pain and aid in healing by as much as 50% in equine, which are non-invasive and drug free."

Shirley told me often dealing with lowering a horses pain, can give a person the head start in helping it recover with the proper follow up. I know I would have been interested in this form of treatment for a stifle with one of our horses.

I asked Shirley how she felt being able to enjoy this sport competing with her daughters.

She replied, "I feel that having my daughters share my passion for horses has been a blessing in our lives. We are a very close family anyway, but I think having similar interests keeps us even closer. With the rapidly changing demographics taking place in our country, a horse is a gift with my family as well as other horse lovers and is truly a blessing."

Nice to meet you, Shirley, do have a great year and keep on riding.

+++++

Third generation Rodeo-girls

Cindy Adams and **Tanisha Brook Adams**, daughter: Albion

"*Sharing* What You have is More Important than *What* You Have."

The quiet community of Albion is a picturesque Cowboy Country. This is the Old West as it was meant to be. Before the 1900's Albion was the county seat of Cassia County, a cow town, but at that time, a state normal school was established there. Today only 350 people live in the town. The first Cassia County Fair and Rodeo was held in Albion. Declo is just eight miles away.

It was a cool morning in January with a fine sheen of frost lying on the fences that sparkled bright as I drove along the country road north of Gooding. At the **Shu Fly arena** there were more than a dozen trucks and horse trailers in the parking lot with horses that were saddled and tied to their trailers.

I wondered who I would meet today that loves the competition of the sport of rodeo events enough to brave this cold weather. Just inside the open door there were several horses that had been warmed up as the steam was rising from them.

It was cold in the enclosed arena and I immediately went to the viewing stand and stood next to the warming heater provided by **the owners Stan and Colette Born**. Several people offered me a seat by the fire. I thanked them and sat next to Jeneall Adams and we began to visit. I found she was from Albion and was there to cheer on her granddaughter, Tanisha, as she 'ran the barrels.' Curious why this family would come so far to compete here, I learned that Tanisha had a new Quarter Horse/Thoroughbred cross that she was getting ready for the spring rodeos that the high schools put on. With new interest I watched the young teen round the barrels with confidence and skill and placed high for a good prize. I would have never guessed she was riding a new horse.

Tanisha's mother Cindy said this about her,

"Here is one young girl who would rather clean a stall than her own room . . . .
Here is one young girl who would rather wear chaps than a party dress . . .
Here is one young girl who would rather go to the barn than the mall . . ."

This is Tanisha's story.

"I always had a love for horses. My first horse I worked with to ride in competition was a small black mare I called Ebony. When she was young she had an attitude. My 4-H leader told me she was afraid I (or someone near me) might get hurt if I continued with this horse. I was nine at the time, but I knew I could work with Ebony and make her into the good horse that she is today. Most every day I would I put her through the patterns—at a slow trot first then to a smooth lope. Ebony and I have **won many ribbons and trophies** and even going to **District rodeo level**," Tanisha said with pride, thinking of her older horse.

Tanisha's mother Cindy told me that working as a team, Tanisha riding Ebony, also won the Cassia County Princess one year and the next won Teen Queen at Oakley.

"I love to hear the roar of the crowd cheering for you and this is a great feeling while buzzing the arena. I get chills talking about it." Tanisha said smiling.

I found she was persistent for two years competing for this honor, before the award was hers.

She looked relaxed and confident when I watched her ride her new horse, Diamond. To get Diamond in shape for barrels as well as her roping horse, Ed, she is now traveling to jackpots in the area for that faster mark. This practice paid off as Tanisha that spring, won first place in the 6th district competition of the barrels. When I asked her how often she rides, she answered, "My mother and I try to ride an average of two to three nights a week during the winter and Julie Ann has helped me a lot, going out with me to work in the arena. I really appreciate her."

I then asked her if she would change anything in her riding experiences.

"I don't think that I would change anything. I didn't start riding a well trained or 'push button' horse and it was okay, because I had to learn to ride well, and as I did this my horse seemed to understand what I wanted out of her. It has made me a better rider and less intimated when having to draw a strange horse during some queen competitions."

I wished Tanisha good luck and I planned to see her at the rodeos. The following summer, **Queen Tanisha was reigning at the Cassia County Rodeo** that I attended. She wore the crown well by showing a lot of friendliness to all who wished to talk with her. Her friendly smile won many 'Hello's' as she rode her new palomino gelding, D.J. in the arena, at the celebration of the 100th anniversary of Cassia Rodeos and Fairs.

"D.J. is a wonderful well mannered horse for me. I've only had him two weeks as I bought him for my last year's high school competition in break-away roping. He likes to chase calves as you could see when we helped at the roping contest during the rodeo. I still use Diamond in the barrels and poles but it is a lot of fun to have a nice horse like El De Jay and I really appreciate the honor to be his new friend," Tanisha said with her sweet smile. She was dressed in a pretty maroon shirt, white broad-rimmed hat and pink trimmed chaps (for dare to wear pink Friday.)

Yes, dare to ride, work, and play—this is Tanisha. When I visited with Cindy she told me that Tanisha's work day starts at 4:30 am feeding her stock; she rides most every day, and also enjoys playing volleyball with her teammates at school. I could tell her mother was very proud of her . . . and so was I. What a cowgirl!

+++++

Her mom (**Cindy Adam's**) story;

Picked up by the Britches

"I grew up on a small farm in Declo and began riding at a very young age. My first pony was not the nicest to handle but I was not discouraged. Because my parents both participated in rodeo events, so later growing up **I had a variety of horses I could ride**. My mother told me a story of what happened to me when I was just a toddler. While she was busy feeding, I crawled into the horses' corral where one of them picked me up by my britches and carefully carried me over to the fence. Mom saw what was happening, but just quietly stood there not to scare him so he wouldn't take off. The horse walked over to the fence and quietly set me down. So began my 'closeness' with the equine. In my grade school days, my friends in the neighborhood would come to our arena and we would ride bareback and play cowboys and Indians, trotting around trying to see who we could knock who off their horses and be the last one still riding. Believe it or not no one ever got seriously hurt; probably the worst was landing in a pile of cow manure."

"My great experiences were competing in 4-H and **High School Rodeos**. I was very serious about keeping the horse I rode in good condition and at this time I would ride mornings and after school as weather permitted. The hardest thing I had to deal with was loosing several horses I had grown up with."

I learned Cindy placed high in many events during these years.

"After I married, I did not ride in competitions but still enjoy being on horseback so I often ride with my daughter Tanisha, to help keep her horses in shape—besides I enjoy her company. All our family enjoys riding when we go on our hunting trips (the boys and my husband.) But I wouldn't have traded these horse related experiences for the entire world—for **when I ride I do not have a care in the world.** If I could go back and had the money, I would have liked to have competed more and traveled other places with my horse," Cindy concluded with a smile.

I certainly enjoyed visiting with the Adams, they were friendly, courteous and quoting Cindy, "Sharing what you have is more important than what you have," and this does fit this kind, western family.

+++++

The Women's Professional Rodeo Association (WPRA) that was formed in 1948 by twenty-eight women rodeo riders is the oldest organization of female professional athletes in the United States and the only one controlled and **managed entirely by women.**

Carol Short and **Jackie Buckley**: Wendell

Mother Daughter Team

In the fall of 2009, I met Mildred Fritch and at eighty-seven, visited with me as if we were old friends. She was the mother/ grandmother of Carol Short and Jackie Buckley—a mother daughter team from Wendell. I really enjoyed getting to know them and I know you will also.

Barrel racing is their forte' these days. In fact the women have been doing this for several decades. Jackie was so excited about this sport that she went to work for rodeo pros like Martha Josey at her place in Texas a few years back. She said she really enjoyed being with this winning team where she hauled to the Pro shows all over that state. Today, the mother-daughter team travel to Arizona, Oregon, and Nevada. The big program was at Reno last year in October, called the American West 5th Division Finals.

"You might say **I was born on a horse,** Jackie said. From the **Pony Club** days of riding English, to this date, **I think and sleep horses.**" She smiled remembering those early days. I learned even injury didn't stop Carol from going back to the love of her life.

"When I woke up in the hospital, all I could ask was, *where's Jackie?* (At the time Jackie was only three years old) At least that is what they told me—I didn't remember a thing for more than a week." Carol related. "When the horse threw me, it had happened before."

Did you keep the horse? I asked.

"No, I didn't keep her, she had an attitude, but it happens," Carol replied.

So your broken neck kept you off a horse for six months—only six months? I asked thinking *it's the broken ground that produces . . . . it shapes vessels of good* and Carol certainly seems to have great ability to ride most any horse.

"Yes, **you can't let fear keep you from something you know and enjoy** so well," was her reply. "No," Jackie chimed in, "recently, my knee was really torn up for most of a year, but I was really anxious to return to the schedule."

"I've been fortunate to have a horse as soon as I was old enough to ride by myself. It was a POA-Welch pony. I did pony club, 4 H, rodeo clubs, you know all the active programs. It gave me enough experience for this competition the American Barrel racing gives me," Jackie said with a gleam in her eyes.

I learned that Jackie and her mother were doing well in the America West running. They both had many finishes in the top ten. And Jackie's last finish placed her fourth.

This information gave me a desire to go to the Shu-Fly arena the next Saturday where these talented women would compete. While there I met Jackie's new horse, Danny, a part thoroughbred black gelding off the race track. At nearly 17 hh, I figured this Danny might just stride out of the arena and have the best time. She also rode a nice horse named Bonz. You didn't want to stand behind him as he rounded a barrel and took of for the next; the dirt he threw up landed twenty feet away. Then I saw Carol with her good looking twenty-one year old mare—Tully Lily ran the indoor arena barrels at 15.9. What a run. She was in the money that day!

"We were excited that we had the American West Classic held in Filer last June as it is an important event to gain more points for finals," Carol said.

Another attraction to me that day, was meeting Carol's mother, Mildred Fritch, who has lived in Idaho for most of her life. We visited a lot that morning and as we watched Carol compete, she said, "I can remember Carol loving horses since the first grade when she rode a lot by herself in the summer months. She would have to stand on a stool to get on. Yes, Carol **has always loved to ride.**" Mildred laughed at the memory.

I had a warm feeling about the mother-daughter team. I know they will do well in the future and have a barrel of fun trying. Good luck Carol and Jackie.

+++++

Janeale Dean: Jerome
Age 17 2009

Approve the things that are excellent Philippians 1:9

We wrote a lot about the past 100 years in our excitement of the Centennial celebration Jerome had in 2007—but that year, I was inspired watching young rodeo participants knowing that many of them will be the future leaders, teachers, parents and business people of Idaho. In my opinion the rodeo team from the Jerome and Valley schools represented "OUR TOWN," with pride.

This story I wrote in 2007 highlights Janeale Dean who is a **4th generation Idaho citizen.**

This is an account of what I reported; "A slow drifting haze of dust rose up as, Janeale Dean, riding her mare Sky, finished her successful run on the barrels competition at the high school district rodeo in Jerome. I watched with awe as the pretty cowgirl reined up the fast moving horse then reached down to pet Sky's neck, praising her until she settled down to a walk. It was obvious to me that the two have great respect for each other in the five years they have learned together.

Janeale gives credit of her knowledge of horse riding to Megan Millican, Jerome, who taught her in her younger years. She attended a rodeo camp her last year, and has been coached by Lyn McKinzie. Janeale praises her team sponsor, **Pam Smith,** Jerome**,** for so much help and encouragement as the Jerome school system choose to drop the program. Janeale also enjoyed working with many of the competing students such as, Jill Georgio and Kaycie Smith who were also **top winners** in the barrels. "I have fun participating with the Rodeo Team," Janeale stated.

One classmate stated that, Janeale's good run should put her in third place for tonight. By the sixth evening of the district event in Shoshone, Janeale received more points as she completed an excellent run in the poles taking a third place that evening. "With four more events, anything can happen," Janeale said. Janeale's riding ability is not her only talent. She loves art work and is an excellent piano player and her music goal is to win a gold cup at the spring music festivals.

Janeale plans after graduating to attend an art school and she hoped that there may be a way to take her horse, Sky with her.

Janeale's parents are David and Linda Dean her best supporters—and I got a glimpse of her grandparents, Jerry and Betty Doughty on that cold and windy night in May, sitting in the bleachers wrapped in blankets as they supported their very nice and beautiful granddaughter." Janeale gave me more of her story.

"When I was five I knew I wanted to ride and was allowed on my sister's horse Tabasco as that is when I began to ride. I wish I had practiced more at a young age and the other horse I had the opportunity to learn on was a quaterhorse I called George. We got along OK doing some roping—then I got Sky. I have enjoyed participating in rodeos since the fifth grade. My junior year **I qualified in the barrels to attend the State High School Rodeo**. It was a fun time although I was full of mixed emotion. First it was the excitement in looking forward in competing as the adrenalin rush was always there when I ran the barrels. The speed and unpredictability always made me nervous. I knew we'd be fast but never knew if Sky would be cooperative and not buck or stumble. I had to be on top of making immediate corrections. But it was a great experience and I would do it again."

Today Janeale is attending an art school in Washington and does not get home as much as she would like to. She said she misses the riding, especially the spring, in Idaho. Thank you, Janeale for giving me your story.

Golden Girls

Marge Brass Heiss & Bert Brass Garrettson

First Miss Rodeo Idaho, Bert

Bert Brass Garrettson

Idaho Horse Council

The Idaho Horse Council has issued some rules to adhere to when you travel down the state roads of Idaho as well as most of the other western states; for 2009, they are as follows:

1. Carry an Idaho Brand inspection certificate (if the animal hauled has a brand)
2. Purebred Registration papers with your name on it.
3. Bill of sale if less than 10 days purchase made.
4. You must stop at all Port of Entries if transporting livestock and your Gross Vehicle weight is over 10,000 pounds.

*Call your local brand inspector at least 24 hours before your trip. Lifetime certificate is $26.00. State information is 800-884-7070

+++++

Pioneering Women

The following memoir is of a special pioneering woman who for nearly four decades was active in the Idaho Horse Council. Marge Heiss worked hard to see to it that many of the trails we enjoy today remain open to horse travel.

The sleeping Wood River Valley has always been a favorite of the humans who found it and loved it for many reasons. The base of the valley is 6,000 feet above sea level. However, the Sawtooth Mountains, looming over 11,000 feet, protected the upper valley from the northern gales. In the winter the sun is warm and the snow is deep.

Trappers and minors loved it as it provided what they came for, however the cattle and sheep ranchers appreciated it for the economical summer pastures. Many moved in to stay in the early 1900's.

The big railroad barons loved the Wood River Valley because they loaded up family and friends to enjoy the hot springs, the scenery, the gold and silver mines and the beautiful hotels. E.H. Harriman had acquired the Union Pacific railroad that ran into Ketchum. His son, Averill in the 1930's shook the quiet Valley when he built the Sun Valley Inn—complete with a nice ice skating rink. This brought in a new class of the rich and famous to enjoy the skiing on Baldy Mountain.

+++++

My tribute to **an early ranch woman who fought for good trails** in the Sawtooth Mountains.

Marge Brass Heiss: Ketchum

Grand Marshal Wagon Days Parade

A woman of Passion for Preserving Trail Riding in Idaho

I honor you, Marge, in your work to keep us riding on the wilderness trails in this great state we all love. **She took leadership in establishing the Idaho Horse Council** when she saw the need for this organization. This tells us much of her love for equine, as well as being one of the **founding members of the Idaho Trail Council** in which her daughter, Cheryl, got her involved. Thank you, Marge, for working with many user groups that encouraged us to work together for all outdoor enthusiasts. This accomplished, we could preserve the beautiful trails for future generations to enjoy. Marge was a woman who lived her adventurous life in full color—a real role model to many who loved people, horses and outdoor Idaho. She was honored as Grand Marshal when she rode in the Wagon Days Parade in 2004.

My husband and I have been fortunate to know Marge for more than five decades. We often stopped by to see her at her home in Ketchum. We always received a warm welcome—she was always the same to everyone. She had no fear of death, for here was a lady who **believed in God** and often talked about **His beautiful handiwork** on this earth that we have had the privilege to see as we rode together in the Idaho Mountains and high desert areas. This gave her the passion to be a good steward of the land and she joined others with like mind. These were the traits that I admired in Marge. I wish there were more western women like her.

This is her story.

She was born Marjorie Brass, one of five children and by the time she was a toddler her family moved to a ranch with a three bedroom log home near the mining town of Ketchum. She was one of the oldest daughters and much was expected of her. In the early 1900's, the children did the housework, garden care, and helped with the meals. Yet at this time in her life, during the long summer hours, Marge began riding one of several ranch horses. **Thus began her lifelong passion of riding horses,** trailing cattle and blazing trails. Later, for her and her sister, Roberta, (called Bert) her father bought two pretty Quarter Horses. She rode one named Doc and her sister rode Nix. Their picture with these horses was in many publications including a calendar the year they were older teens. She **helped with the trailing of cattle** when she was older. When Marge was a teen, she and Bert rode these good riding horses which gave them much freedom. They rode them to town, up the canyons, at the fairs and rodeos as well as on their ranch.

This early experience gave Marge the expertise to continue to be the ranch owner she became with her husband, Clark, as owners of the Heiss Charolais Ranch in Jerome. This is when I met Marge as my husband and I often trucked their prize-winning cattle to special sales or shows.

They raised three daughters, Cheryl, Lynette, and Glenda Jo—all who love to horseback ride today. They are very congenial and fun "cowgirls".

+++++

The following is a ride we Thursday Sage Riders enjoyed—details are taken from my diary and I hope you enjoy going along with us.

One day Marge called the Thursday Sage Riders and said she would show us a new riding trail up Deer Creek near Ketchum. When we met Marge it was a brilliant blue-trimmed sky with white, puffy clouds. We felt extremely lucky to be there as our horses climbed to the top of the ridge. We could see the ski mountain of Baldy and down into the valley of Wood River. All around us we registered in our minds every breathtaking vista of all the new sights that added to the magic of our adventure.

Marge was one to exclaim, "We ride for the adventure that each mile brings. It comes through faith for with complete faith there is no fear of what faces me in life or death. And it is also a time

33

to renew old friendships as well as make some new ones." At lunchtime we stopped under some tall pine trees for our break. At this time Marge welcomed new riders and asked their names. She often complimented them on their horse and told them she was glad they came. She was very friendly to all. I remember her being impressed with my new horse an Arabian named, Macho, as he could keep up with *her* fast paced horse, Macho. He was a beautiful horse with a soft pace and had accompanied her for many years into the wilderness areas. At the end of the ride her quote in my book was, **"It doesn't get any better than that."** This area was one of Marge's favorite places to ride and she continued riding there and at Greenhorn for many years. Marge rode even into her eighties.

She often told us **not to lose sight of the sense of freedom** we have to enjoy our great outdoors and she was always asking us **to get involved in keeping our right to ride the wilderness trails.** She served on committees in the Idaho Trails Council for years, working to save our horse trails. That Thursday we finished the day embracing the time we had together. Marge lived her life, as she said, "I give thanks for God's beautiful handiwork on this earth in the Idaho Mountains and the privilege I had to see it." There are many stories she could tell; however Cheryl told me she was writing some of her mother's memories and I am looking forward to reading more about this gracious woman.

You might question—are we just powder puffs? Or did we have something of the pioneer women buried in us? Well, compared to Lewis and Clark, we were doing this the easy way however, the mountains are still as high and jagged, the wind blows just as hard, the rain is just as chilling and many of the rivers we cross are just as deep and deceptive. Those of us who rode with Marge did see very much of the **pioneering spirit in her** as she was out there riding the high ridges at an age when most would have quit, yet, she was climbing the mountains, enduring the weather and finding new trails to share with us.

Our riding safety depended on our well fitted horse and us keeping watch on the trails for obstacles. Now we also have our guardian angels. We of the Thursday Sage Riders are fortunate now to have one more angel added along with our deceased riding friends, Frances, Eva, Virginia, Bert and Marlene, and her name is Marjorie.

It has been my pleasure to have known Marge. She has indeed been a role model to many of us riders of the Idaho wilderness.

+++++

Marge's sister
Roberta (Bert) Brass Garrettson: Sun Valley
(Interviewed at age 95)

Girl of the Golden West

In 1939 Roberta was **Miss Sun Valley, Idaho's first rodeo queen.** To promote Sun Valley as a year-round resort, Bert was sent around the U.S. outfitted in a spangled white outfit with a big, white Quarter Horse to ride. She rode in many parades; appeared at Madison Square Garden in New York; others included rodeos in Omaha, Nebraska and at a Union Pacific celebration at the Chicago Stockyards and several other celebrations in the eastern states. Back home when she wasn't riding she worked at Saks Fifth Avenue in the Sun Valley Lodge. This is why Bert always considered Sun Valley as her home roots.

We must respect the past remembering that once it was all that was humanly possible and that it is life without theory . . .

I remember many things about my friend Bert, and before I entered her daughter Marian's house in Twin Falls to get a horse story from her, I recalled that it was her pleasing voice I always looked forward to hearing. Bert was a good storyteller, and without me knowing it at the time, she was the heroine that a hero would have wanted to rescue. She spoke with great feeling and **a good heart.** Today I knew I would get the genre I wanted. Sometimes in the visits I would even get advice that made me smile—"Loosen the reins . . . be free spirited," she spoke this way.

In the little board walk town of Ketchum; Roberta and Richard Brass (twins) were born to Earnest and Gertrud Brass. They were children four and five of a ranching family that was raised during the depression days.

This is Roberta's story.

Never Really Alone

"These were hard times," Bert said. "Many ranchers survived raising their own food and hanging on to what they had until things got better—and they did. We lived in a small four room house sort of stacked up, but it was always neat, and we had plenty to eat." Bert remembers going out with her father on, Chub, the dependable horse that they rode out to irrigate the large range land they had along Trail Creek (Sun Valley area). This was the beginning of **Bert's love for horses.**

"After I was old enough to go ride on my own, I would climb up my favorite horse's tail, scoot up to the writhers and off we'd go; sometimes with my sister Marge. Oh, I also rode a lot at my grandparent's place in Jordon Valley, Oregon. We went to school in Boise in the winter months as my Hart grandparent's ranch was much closer to spend a lot of weekends there. Often we would take supply wagons to the Jarbidge area near Nevada, and except for these trips, I hated it away from the Ketchum ranch and I couldn't wait to get back."

Bert respected and loved horses and their companionship and riding was what made her happy in her younger years. Her sister said she had no fear, only **a spirit of adventure** and love of life. They explored the game trails near the ranch and often returned home after dark.

"When I was a teen, my dad bought a horse named Star. He was a big horse they used working the cattle. But I got to use him a lot, especially if I was helping out. I just loved **to ride**

out in the valley by myself, just my dog and I—oh, **not really alone**, you see I had my horse and dog. I loved the smell of fresh air, blue sky with white clouds and often gave thanks for this privilege. It's a good thing to do," she told me with a smile.

"Many times I would ride six miles up Trail Creek and never see another person. Sometimes later when we got more horses, Margie would often ride with me when she could get away from the house chores. We never ran our horses. Sometimes we would lope them, but dad would have been mad if we ran them. I remember riding up a canyon where there were silver mines. Sometimes the old miners would be sitting on tree stumps where **I would ride by and they would clap for us**—my dog and I.

My first horse was named Nix and Margie rode Doc. They were both black quarter horses and real pretty."

The picture of the sisters was taken in 1939 when Bert returned from representing Sun Valley as their 'Western Queen.' The Sun Valley Company sent her to ride in many promotion shows and parades as their ambassador they supplied her with a horse and outfits. She was spoken of as unpretentious and gracious. Although she was known **as the Girl of the Golden West**, she was also known as one of the Brass daughters.

"The ranch was lined with pole fences and often Margie and I would rent out some of the other horses, but we always went with them to keep the animals safe. Some of the boys would want to run them."

"I set up a target for **shooting from my horse** with a bow and arrows and then I would run the horse by it in the yard area where it was safe, but that was the entire fast riding we were allowed. I gave an exhibition of it once in the East when I traveled as Miss Sun Valley and I often rode strange, but well broke horses into arenas where **the horse would rare up** and I would lift my hat and wave at the audience. In Ketchum, Marge and I would dress up for the Rodeo Days and often people would take our pictures—one appeared on a western calendar."

"We were nearly out of college when Averill Harriman and his wife came to look at the ranch to buy it for the Union Pacific Railroad, which they did; it became Sun Valley where they built the inn and eventually the lodge. I remember meeting Mrs. Harriman when she came to look over the house. I wondered what she must have thought; we were just ranch people of that day taking care of cattle. We had a few sheep too, and my dad and I used to go up the mountain in the summer and take supplies to the Basque herders. But we were happy there. I continued to ride Nix for twenty years."

Bert married a handsome cowboy named Quill Garrettson and they had fifty great years together. They had two sons and daughters. Bert had other stories to tell, but we will combine some of these with Marian, her daughter's story in the following chapter.

When Quill and Roberta moved to Jerome, Bert met and became a very good friend of Frances Callen Sheneberger. They began to ride trails together in Magic Valley and up in the Wood River Valley. "We rode at least once a week during spring through fall and I sure did enjoy this Thursday riding group where I met good riding friends. I enjoyed my Arabian horse Ricky; he was a pretty sorrel and we were great friends. **When I ride I feel alive.** And every moment was such a pleasure," Bert concluded.

I remember many TSR rides with Bert and hearing her laughter you could tell she was a contented woman when she rode. She was very friendly to all the girls with an open gentle spirit just as her home had always been inviting others to join them in every aspect of their life. To each person she met they were, in her mind, 'good individuals'. To her every day was wonderful and full of lessons and happiness. She continued to ride well past her eighties and lived to be ninety-seven.

We will miss you Bert and our lives are much richer since we rode the trails with you.

+++++

Grab a Tail

Marian (Mi Mi) Garrison Wallace:
Daughter of Bert Garrison and a continuing story with Bert.

"When we lived in Montana my parents and I, in the fall months went Elk hunting. We needed to know the trail better and got off it once. When we came to a very steep spot we got off and led the horses up. I began to slip and realized I couldn't continue. Mom suggested I let my horse follow them and that **I grab on to my horses tail** and let him pull me up to the ridge. I had never done this before, but agreed to try. My mother looked back at me and had a very **big smile on her face** watching us arrive at the top. I learned a lot that day."

"Another thing I learned, the way of the west—at our camp we had made a canvas shelter for a bathroom that was three sided and only neck high. One day I was sitting on the potty chair when a couple of hunters came up the trail and walked right by me. We laughed a lot in all our events we had that day."

And laugh was what Mi Mi often did when out on the trails as she had a great sense of humor, often laughing when telling of events in her life.

Several years later, Marian was riding a very gentle horse named Ginger. She was a wedding present from Warren Garrison. They just reached the top of Iron Mountain in the Fairfield, Idaho area when she began to buck, and on the second jump Marian was thrown and landed on top of a sage brush.

"I never knew if it was a bee under the belly or what. **But I sure took a tumble**, but was **thankful for the scratchy brush** as there were a lot of rocks around that I could have landed on instead. It was a real surprise to me as the horse had never tried to buck before and never did since."

"I enjoy riding with the TSR women and value their friendship. I hope to do much more in the future, Lord willing," Marian concluded with her friendly smile.

Marian continued to care for her mother until Bert's passing. Thank you for these stories Mi Mi. You make us all smile.

Endurance Riders

Vicci Archer, Buhl Parade

Vicci

Valerie Pryor

To see a Fine Lady on a White Horse . . .

Not only is the Arabian one of the most beautiful horses to look at, but also they are one of the toughest and most enduring breeds. It is well known that they are famous for their stamina and endurance, have an incredible turn of speed, and make an excellent light, balanced riding horse.

Vicci Archer: Jerome
2009 Arabians

'To see a fine lady on a white horse' . . . This phrase may have come from a nursery rhyme but just as many words rhyme with each other, Vicci has been proficient in many horse projects that have worked together to achieve her accomplishments. **Her greatest triumph** was getting on her horse after months of battle with cancer. However, this thought is what kept her strong.

Ronald Reagan loved horses since his days in the U.S. Cavalry. He said, "There's nothing better for the inside of a man than the outside of a horse."

Life after Cancer

Last summer Vicci and her husband rode in the Buhl parade. They were dressed in the stylish Arabian costumes aboard their pretty, majestic Arabians. A white silk looking cloak with silver trimmings was draped over the back of the horses. They were a beautiful pair. After we talked and I saw the charm Vicci had, I wanted her story as I knew it was one that unites with a freshness of loving the equine—a love we all share.

In September 2007 Vicci became anxious to celebrate **five years of being cancer free** and wished to compete in the five day, 250 mile endurance ride near Oreana, in the Owyhee high desert.

"Besides a great family and spiritual support system, there is a lot of motivation to be on the back of a horse through the wilderness for keeping you going," Vicci said. Out of twenty contestants Vicci had her tough-as-nails, endurance horse, All Atonce (Ally), were one team of nine finalists who completed all five days on the same horse. You really have to know your horse and be aware of what they can handle. I felt so healthy and alive when I was out enduring and bonding with my horse for 250 miles; horse and I both finished with plenty of strength still left. **I want to be an inspiration to other women diagnosed with cancer that there can be life after cancer surgery and chemo."**

As she related this to me, I could tell she felt it was a key to a more abundant life—like take the opening door, between two worlds.

Vicci and her husband Jim love to ride. "Jim is my biggest fan when **I compete in the endurance races** that are offered close to home," Vicki said as her brown eyes flashed with pleasure. Vicci, an accomplished rider, is to this day taking dressage lessons to give her and her horse the experience of enduring many obstacles, plus she wanted something different—for at age fifty-four, endurance riding might not any longer be for her after having reached the **2000 mile endurance award** in competition miles.

Vicci attended many of the American Endurance ride conferences from the pacific to southwest Idaho. Her **longest endurance ride** that she qualified for **was for 24 hours**, beginning at 5:30 a.m. and going to 5:30 a.m. the next day.

"This night riding is real exciting. And I would do it all over if given the chance," Vicci said. "It is something I feel so strongly about. You learn to trust your horse out there on a quiet, peaceful, pitch-black night. The only guide is a glow stick off in the distance. Even though I couldn't see the ground below me, my horse never missed a turn in the trail and got us back to camp with no problem."

Vicci grew up with horses as her dad always had several good kids' horses that she remembers galloping down the road where often the neighbors would wave as she passed.

After she and Jim were married in 1974, her soul mate registered Arabian mare named, Roxi, was born. "She was pretty as a picture—an elegant grey and was chosen as background material by a well known photographer who often used animals in his photos. **Roxie was good mannered** and obliged to do a perfect pose. She also loved to show off in the parade of breeds at the Twin Falls County Fair as well as local parades," Vicci recalled with a tear in her eyes. "We have raised many beautiful horses and I have loved them all."

I learned this horse carried Vicci through hundreds of trail rides, was her first endurance horse, and took good care of many children and guest riders. I've known horses like this but as my grandpa used to say—'they are as scarce as hens teeth' to obtain.

God Bless you Vicci for your testimony and good luck in all you continue to accomplish with your know-how horse wisdom.

+++++

Valerie Pryor: Buhl
"If its horse related I'm always game"

Jane of all Trades/ and She Mastered Many

When I saw Valerie riding her grey thoroughbred mare named, Kitty, I began asking her about the horse and her events she had ridden this horse in. Her horse is a pretty long legged 16 hh equine that has smooth gaits. I learned this mare was bred for fox hunting but while she is maturing, Valerie uses her for trail riding.

This pretty blond with a special laugh and bright eyes continued to tell me the following stories. "I have participated in several organized trail rides such as the Chief Joseph one here in Idaho; Monument Valley, California; the Apache Land in New Mexico and the **Nevada Pony Express re-ride** to name a few. This would be about **500 miles** on this exciting young mare," Valerie said. "I am considering doing an endurance ride on her as soon as time with my kids let me. **I have always enjoyed a horse that likes to go.**"

"I was born in Texas but came to Nevada as a young adult, then moved to Buhl after I married. I've always had a horse, beginning as most of us did on a Shetland pony."

"Taffy and I were friends, she was never ornery. I did cart racing, show jumping and like most kids I would ride her backwards, upside down—hell bent for leather and just lay on her and watch the world go by."

I asked Valerie for a special story and she began by telling me she considered herself a 'jack of all trades' and master of none, when it comes to horse activities.

Her answer was, "I've participated in pony club and 4-H activities. I've done vaulting, 3-day eventing, gymkhanas, pony cart racing, endurance and trail riding. I've gathered cows out of the mountains, snuck up on wild horses in Nevada, run the surf of the Pacific Ocean, participated in Pony Express re-rides, **and jumped cross country in Ireland."**

"My horse story occurred in the summer of 1980 when I was twelve. I was riding a six year old Arabian/Quarter cross named Zesty. My Aunt gave her to me when the horse was just a colt. I was riding her by the time she was two and by this point she had passed me in maturity. She was a very 'motherly' mare and never put up with any guff. She demanded respect and had no problems with disciplining me if she felt it was necessary. **She always took good care of me."**

"Before this race my aunt had been very competitive in the world of endurance riding winning the Tevis Cup several times. When I rode with her I would just hang on for dear life as she never went anywhere at a sedate, calm and quite often controlled pace. Whining wasn't tolerated. I learned the valuable lessons of—**hang on, keep up and shut up.** She liked that my weight was light and had absolutely no sense of self preservation. We covered hundreds of miles together and had a wonderful time doing it. I don't remember much about the scenery but I will always remember with fondness the camaraderie I had."

"This was my **first ride**. It was **a 50 mile ride** through the foothills of northern California. I was a juvenile and unable to ride without an adult sponsor. Unfortunately just before the race, my aunt had injured herself and she knew the rules in and out that we needed an adult sponsor and had found one for me. Endurance rides generally start in the dark of early morning. My aunt was standing by my knee among the milling field of contestant horses saying that she couldn't find their sponsor in the crowd. So in the dark of early morning surrounded by fifty wound tight horses, I was on a horse that had never been in a field of this many horses as I took off in the mountains more or less **by myself**. Part of the challenge of an endurance race is being able to find the trail—in the dark. I've already mentioned that I lack the self preservation gene but **I do possess the competitive gene.** Zesty and I lead to the first check point and proceeded to wait for my sponsor to catch up. It almost killed me to wait and let most everyone pass. When she arrived we were both thrilled; for me because I could continue to race and because it would have been traumatic for her to lose a young person in the mountains. I could imagine the search teams of helicopters and television crews, let alone explaining to my parents. The rest of the ride went well. We kept on pace and the vet checks were a breeze. **We were moving so fast** that our crew couldn't catch us so we depended upon others at our rest and vet stops. People were very generous and supportive. We finished the race with a flourish—racing to the line. My sponsor and I finished in the race together. **I was first junior winner** and have a silver belt buckle to prove it. I competed in endurance rides up until I moved away from where my aunt lived. I've kept in touch with my sponsor and her. They still bring up the whole search party thing on a regular basis."

Valerie continued to tell me that she and Bret, ride as often as they can with their young children. Although I know her son and daughter like to ride nearly as much as she does and I know we will see them all, on our Idaho trails. Happy trails to you and your special family, Valerie.

+++++

Everything's been different
All the day long,
Lovely things have happened,
Nothing has gone wrong.

Pony Club

Julie Rietidorf & Jenna McCully

Jenna Adkins

Jenna Adkins

Jenna McCully

I questioned—what other Club activities can an inexperienced rider learn from besides 4-H? Then I learned that the Pony Club teaching was recommended.

The beginning of the Pony Club was in 1929 for those wishing to learn the many aspects of equipping, caring for, as well as riding a horse. Qualified teachers were given criteria to teach their students. Subjects ranged from giving the young rider information as well as suggesting entertaining literature about equine to the actual hands on experiences. There is no limit on age when a child can join Pony Club but the oldest age they can compete is twenty-one. At the completion of the students riding lessons tests are given that consists of hundreds of questions.

+++++

Elaine Dawkins: Jerome
Teacher, Rider and Mother
Julie Rietidorf: daughter

The Answer to My Dreams was Beautiful Melody

I read that it takes a special person to lend a helping hand when it's so easy to let someone else do it. I thought of this last summer when I renewed a friendship with Elaine at her home at Southwind Ranch. And this she did, lend a "helping hand" to many young boys and girls who were part of her Pony Club. They desired to learn not only how to ride a horse, but also the proper ways to make use of an animal that is going to be a part of their life.

Her home reflected the love for horses as I viewed beautiful pictures of world famous Arabians on the walls of Elaine's front room. There was a picture of Muzzy the first Polish import champion stallion that won many U.S. shows; as well as Nabor, a Polish bred stallion who sired many award winning colts. There was an impressive collection of old U.S. Calvary bits and some hand made ones.

The year when Elaine and Joe moved to Jerome, I had purchased a young, three year old gelding. He was a beautiful white Arabian and needed to be worked into a good trail horse for me. Someone told me about Joe's background of success at the Wrigley's Arabian Ranch at Santa Catalina Island, California, and I asked Joe to train my horse Macho. He agreed to work him for four weeks. A month later I pulled into the Dawkins yard to load up Macho to take him home. When I got Macho home, I was elated at what the now gentle horse could do. He obeyed all the cues and was easy to ride. I soon learned that this **horse knowledge** Joe had, was realized in all the Dawkins family, Elaine and her daughter, Julie alike.

Elaine is beginning her twenty-fifth year in her regional **leadership in Pony Club** although now, her daughter **Julie Rietidorf is coaching the Club** and also gives riding lessons to many others who come to Southwind Ranch.

This is Elaine's story: "In Pony Club instructing, I saw a whole **different approach for a new rider to understand their horse**, care for it and also become an accomplished rider if they so desired. Gayle Yakavac from Gooding helped me get started as a leader," Elaine said smiling in remembrance of a good friend.

And through all the years, **the ranch was home to hundreds of horse loving young people**. During the spring and summer, I had the privilege to watch Julie put several Pony Club members through their paces. I attended their Intermountain Region Tetrathlon rally there. This was hosted by the Ada Ridge Riders and McCall Pony Club. Karen Smith and Ana Egnew were the organizers. I watched the rally while four stewards, as well as many scorers and timers, kept the six teams moving in the competition of running, swimming, jumping and shooting. I learned that assisting with the judging were former students at Southwind in Jerome. As I observed the participants, I realized that even to the youngest they were totally on their own in four areas: getting to the line on time, tack room checks, saddling and getting into the arena to perform.

It is also my pleasure to announce that the Pony Club of Magic Valley was awarded several first places—congratulations to Julie and the teams.

Elaine tells of her life with horses, when she was young.

"I knew that someday I would have a horse and was fortunate, when my mother and I would walk around town that we often would go past a park or farm pasture where we could admire many equine in our neighborhood. I soon discovered that I was quite allergic to most animals and stayed away from them for a while. Then when I was fifteen I began going with my girlfriend and her horse to the fairgrounds and was associating regularly with many horses. I confessed this to my mother I reminded her I was still alive. I was allowed to visit there where I found a large pony that was boarded there. He 'needed to be ridden,' the owner said, however, he failed to tell me that this pony was only sort of broke, but I took the challenge. I had little experience and no saddle but with the help of my horse friend, I attempted to learn the art of riding in a somewhat primitive manner. The cinder track around the fairgrounds (in Illinois everybody burned coal) was where I attempted to communicate with the pony. Needless to say, I 'bit the dust' (or cinders) at frequent intervals. Did you know that this connection with cinders left black tattoos on my knees and did not fade for several years?" The pony and I actually got to be a good team and because of this success the man that owned the ponies asked me to gentle another for him and in return he would give me another horse to keep."

"I accepted the deal enthusiastically but I had to break the news at home that we were inheriting a pony. At that point, my aunt, who lived nearby said she was interested in having a horse and if I would ride her horse and teach her what I had learned she would pay for the boarding for them both. This was the answer to my dreams, and I eagerly agreed. It ended up that I traded my pony for a lovely Saddlebred mare named, Beautiful Melody, which I rode and shared with my three younger sisters. We all ended up being 'horse crazy from then on!"

Elaine said she went on to many horse related activities in Illinois and later California. She had successful experiences in harness race horses, showing English and Western, driving large Hackney horses and Holstein to name a few. During this time she worked for a horse veterinarian and still taught riding and driving.

With a sigh, Elaine continued, "Then I married Joe, the love of my life, a wonderful cowboy and well-known horse trainer. We bought this ranch in Jerome—Southwind. We started breeding and raising Arabian horses and trained our own young horses and a few for other people. I branched out in **instructing 4-H and Pony Club**. My daughter Julie was here learning from her stepfather Joe and before he died she helped us by showing our horses at the valley Arabian Horse Club shows, local state shows, 4-H and Pony Club."

I could tell by the gleam in Elaine's eye that she was proud of her daughter and it was exciting for me to learn that **Julie is continuing the tradition that her parents began**. Her achievements are that she helped start the Equestrian Team at Stanford University of which she was a member. Then after a few years in New York City, she returned to the ranch to help her widowed mother and is now busy teaching riding lessons and is the instructor of Pony Club members here in Magic Valley. She also coaches the Equestrian Team at the College of Southern Idaho. Like her mother said, "It is in her blood."

Glad to have, today, such a talented person as Julie available to help our horse enthusiasts. Happy Days.

> *The roofs are shining from the rain,*
> *The sparrows twitter as they fly,*
> *And with a windy April grace*
> *The little clouds go by.*
> *Yet the back yards are bare and brown*
> *With only one unchanging tree—*
> *I could not be so sure of Spring*
> *Save that it sings in me.—Sara Teasdale*

+++++

Jenna Adkins: Twin Falls
Young high school student and talented rider

A Ride of a Lifetime

"What have you done? This horse is way too young," her trainer exclaimed.

And yet, today Jenna saddles her beautiful, Thoroughbred/paint horse, Rocky, and together they walk down a small dirt road toward the jumping and dressage arenas. Yes, it was several years later, while after taking things slow and working with the young inexperienced gelding that **he became the fine riding animal** that Jenna knew he could be. It may be faith, but I feel it is a connection that women riders have with their equine.

The summer of 2009 I watched Jenna at a training session at a ranch near Bellevue. She rode her black horse named Black Magic, an experienced jumper. There she listened and repeated the instructions with her best ability. I could tell she was having a good time as her pretty smile told me all.

This work with the **Pony Club**, paid off and prepared Jenna for riding Rock-N-Road (Rocky) today, they are the best of friends. Jenna's story is an example to other young **girls who dream of owning and riding that perfect horse**—just for them.

She tells her own story.

"My interest in horses began a long time ago, but I started to ride and develop a real love for horses at age seven. At the time, my family lived in town and my parents knew nothing about horses but they agreed to get me a horse and we soon moved to three acres in the country. Little did they know it would be a ride of a lifetime and the adventure was just about to begin; for all of us?"

"My first horse was a gentle, older horse named Snoopy that taught me how to ride and get started. I rode him western in the pee-wee rodeos doing barrels and poles and also went on a number of trail rides. My next horse was named Cody and together we joined a local 4-H club and started riding both Western and English equestrian. Cody and I competed for several years in their shows and received many trophies and ribbons including Reserve Grand Champion Showmanship."

"Although I enjoyed riding western, what I wanted was to **improve my English riding skills** and learn how to jump, so I joined the Magic Valley Pony Club held at the Southwind Ranch."

"We purchased my current horse named Rock-N-Road (Rocky). I wanted him to ride English. It was April 1, his fifth birthday, I called to tell my trainer Julia our good news. She replied," What have you done? He is not old enough." She went on to explain that to get what you want to learn on, age wise, **you take the combined age of a horse and its rider and it should be minimum age of twenty for safety;** our combined age was only seventeen. We decided to keep working with Rocky and take things slow with lots of training."

"And that is why we bought Black Magic, an experienced jumper, so I could continue with my lessons at Pony Club. Magic was a 14 hh pony, solid black with a bald face. He definitely had that pony attitude. I learned how to jump and **I gained confidence** on riding cross country. We both improved after a year as I learned that the right horse can teach kids a lot."

"Now that I am older, **I am back to riding and training Rocky** full time. Magic is being used in the lesson program teaching other kids to ride and jump in Pony Club."

"In Pony Club we ride and train on a regular basis throughout the summer months. A few weekends a year, we travel to compete in different eventing rallies that include Show, Cross Country as well as Dressage."

"Working with a live animal is unlike any other sport I have done. There is a bond between horse and rider that's hard to explain. As the club teaches us, it's a sport built on discipline, knowledge, love and mutual respect. Riding horses has helped me focus on goals and move in the correct direction. As my trainers always say, 'don't look where you don't want to go.' It's funny how many of the **lessons on my horse transfer to life's lessons** in general."

"I am thankful for the time I share with my horse because I know there are many who would like to ride but never get the opportunity. As I find myself corralled in the equestrian playground, I look back on my years of riding and say "yes, I did it". And so it is . . . my life as a Pony Clubber continues into the future. Weekly I make the trip to Southwind Ranch for another lesson to improve my riding skills and enjoy the outdoors. I saddle up my horse Rocky and together we walk down a small dirt road to the jumping and dressage arenas. There I meet my trainer Julia, to begin the lesson. When I prepare to mount and ride, I toss the reins over Rocky's head as I gaze into his kind, loving eyes and think to myself—life is good."

Good luck to you Jana and I know you progressed even further at the Telethon held at the Magic Valley Pony club this year as the picture shows you with your 'blue' award. This event tested your ability to run, swim, shoot and jump and to do dressage work with this beautiful and extraordinary horse. You were awarded top points and we're all proud of you.

+++++

Jenna McCully: Jerome
Age 10: daughter of Tom and Windy McCully

During Spring Break

The March day was breezy with an overcast sky and a chance for rain, but this did not stop Jenna from keeping the appointment of her lesson at the Southwind ranch. Working as a team, Grandpa McCully and Jenna unloaded her horse Harry and tied him to the trailer. Harry at 13/3 hh was the right size for the small ten year old, Jenna, to be able to groom him, bridle, and saddle him by herself. She has been doing this for three years mostly by herself. Her first horse, Smokie, was a white Welch pony that is now twenty, and has been retired.

I watched Jenna put on her helmet and walk with reins in hand and lead Harry into the arena where her teacher Julie was waiting. Also joining her was another student whose name was also Jenna. Both the girls walked their horses around the obstacles there as it relaxed their equine before they got on. Julie checked the equipment before the students mounted up. In awe I saw Jenna put the reins over Harry's neck, held them with her left hand then, bring her leg up in the air to place her left foot in the stirrup and then swing herself up onto the flat-saddle. She settled in the seat, picked up the horse's reins and with both hands, placed them properly in her grip and turned Harry to the outside rail. She walked him confidently and kept the horse in a straight line. As Jenna walked by me **I saw a smile spread across her pretty face** with eyes shinning bright.

After the warm up session, Julie put the girls and their horses through new paces, teaching engagement and balance as the horses went over the poles—and moving across straight but bending on the corners. The horses were asked to go into a working trot using more speed over the higher poles. As they continued and did this over and over, the improvement they showed was so noticeable it was enjoyable to watch.

Julie instructed the riders to have 'no floppy rein,' telling them that this is a partnership of give and take with their horses. **It was beautiful—the sweet voice of Julie counting** "1-2 . . ." as the seat of the rider rose up with this gentle voice as Julie coached them. Julie continued her instruction for an hour even through a shower of gentle rain.

This is the story Jenna wrote.

To New Levels

"I have been riding ever since I can remember. Besides my parents, my grandmother, Margaret, let me ride with her a lot and I got a lot of encouragement from Grandma Jeanne. I have enjoyed riding Smokie as a preschooler, and then last year they found Harry for me to ride. I needed a Pony horse **so I could continue with the upper levels of schooling** and he is just right. I am proud to be rated a D2, but dressage and jumping will be more progressive with a larger horse. I love this training and live for it. Our big show and testing is in late June and it will be fun taking my new horse, Harry to new levels."

June 2009: Pony Club at the Southwind Ranch of Elaine Dawkins:

On this day new levels of higher goals were reached with many of the pony club members putting out more than just their best. It was a warm day in June at the Southwind ranch in Jerome. Elaine Dawkins and Julie, with the help of the host club, had the courses in great shape. A nice crowd represented the eight clubs from Idaho and one from Nevada. There were many people that helped keep time and get the next contestant ready.

At the beginning of the day, the younger contestants raced on foot through obstacles. They jumped with their horses over several poles in a designated pattern and answered the many questions given them.

Jenna came out smiling telling me, "I sure had fun today." And Jana did well in every event allowing her, **her goal to move to a new level**.

Oh, young people on bigger horses are not without accident. In the fall, her grandmother, Margaret, told me Janna broke her arm on a horse related accident but, "she's a real trooper and within several weeks wanted to get back on Harry," she said.

Thank you for your story, Jenna and go for it. We'll see you in the events many years ahead.

Ranch Women of the North

Ina's valentine:
"I'm sending you
this
message from a
friend of mine."
John 3:16

Ina Mae Krahn

Sketching by Heather

Heather Smith Thomas

The Lemhi County Museum in Salmon contains many interesting items from the early mining camps. Salmon was once called Trail City, and Salmon City grew out of the need for a supply base for the miners at Leesburg and other surrounding mining towns where much silver was found in the ore. In 1867 Salmon City was laid out by a Mr. Shoup who also saw the need for a racetrack as a reminder of the days when good horseflesh was admired and no celebration was complete without a race.

For good horseback riding here are many old roads and trails that go to the top of high ridges and the view at the top offers a panoramic view of Idaho's rugged Middle Fork Country. There, innumerable up thrust peaks traversed by deep, shadowy watercourses present the immensity of Idaho's mountains surrounding the valley known as the Lemhi range.

The life of a cowgirl always intrigued me. Whether they are in the arena, the corrals, or out in the pasture, they know what to do. And sometimes, because they are women, they have to do it three times better than any man there, to prove themselves and to be accepted.

God bless them, He knows their hearts, and may He keep them safe.

Heather Smith Thomas: Salmon

She is called; Wrangler of Cattle, Horses and Words.

Heather and her husband Lynn still operate the Sky Range Ranch four miles up the Lemhi River, near Salmon which her father bought when **she was a horse-crazy eight year old child**. Their main ranch was homesteaded in 1885. Heather has lived there except for a short while at college. This ranch lies in an incredibly beautiful valley just above the 45th parallel where Lewis and Clark passed nearby on their way to the Pacific Ocean in 1805. Also nearby is the trail of the Nez Pierce tribe's journey.

Horse and cattle were Heathers first love. However along with her horse riding adventures, she began writing as a young person—"just stories about horses," she told me with a smile. "I sold my first short story for ten dollars and when I found out I could get paid for something I enjoyed, I continued this through high school and in college." After graduation her first book was published. It was titled, A *Horse in your Life; A Guide for the New Owner.* She also wrote several children's books—most of which contain wisdom of practical knowledge about horses and cattle. Heather graduated from the University of Puget Sound, a Methodist College and planned to go on to Vet school, but it wasn't possible at the time. Her book titled *A Week in the Woods* was for the enjoyment of the younger age. In 1970 Heather began sharing some of her ranch experiences in self-help books—*Your Horse and You* was her first. She wrote for many top magazines including, *Western Horseman, Quarter-horse News, and The Arabian Horse Times* and *Thoroughbred Times.* Now over the past **45 year span she has published 20 books** and written many articles that appear in most of the ranch magazines and on the book stands. In 2005 she published, *Stable Smarts; Sensible Advice, Quick Fixes and Time tested Wisdom from an Idaho Horsewoman,* Her latest books are, *The Essential Guide to Calving and the Cattle Health Handbook.*

Now for Heather's "horse times":

In the 1970's Heather and Lynn began breeding and **raising their own part Arabians and Anglo-Arabians.** They were tough and agile with Heather, and daughter, Andrea, often **riding them in endurance rides.** Together, they got them ready for this, by riding them to check the cattle as well as roundups—over treacherous mountains and steep canyons. First they did fifteen mile schooling rides, then up to thirty. Heather has been shoeing her own horses since 1958, starting when she was fourteen years old. She calls her experiences with her horses as 'homegrown.'

Heather continues her story in her words.

"In the late spring, for many years, my daughter Andrea and my son Michael and I would herd the cows up the higher BLM pasture, and then in the fall move the cattle back to the Whithington Creek pastures near the ranch house. Most of the time Lynn and Michael were busy cutting hay, mending fences, doing the many things a ranch demands done in order to survive."

"Today our son Michael, his wife, Carolyn and his family live just down the road at the next ranch and we enjoy having the grandkids close. Granddaughter, Heather, still trains young colts in the summer months and next semester at Carroll College in Helena, Montana she will be demonstrating horse-training methods in her Human Animal Bond Classes. Our daughter Andrea lives near Salmon with her sweet young family of four." (I met them fishing along the Salmon River one spring, and I am not surprised to learn that she is interested in working with others who has suffered burn injuries as she has.)

Andrea is a burn victim survivor. At the time of the accident she was helping a friend build a fire breaker to try to stop a range fire when the wind changed and blew the fire over them and she jumped off the tractor into the blaze. Her clothes caught fire and gave her serious burns over fifty percent of her body. Heather wrote a **book about the incident that would help any burn victim**. It's called *Beyond the Flames; a Family Touched by Fire*. You can get it from her.

"We thought we were going to lose her," Heather sadly related, "She was at the Salt Lake Intermountain Burn Center for more than a month; we are blessed to have her back although she still receives doctor's care for the after affects of the incident."

Heather stated that every day they experience the glory and power of nature at their home. They see coyotes and cougars which threaten, but in contrast enjoy seeing a few bighorn sheep, mountain goats, lots of antelope, deer and elk that she feels they must live in coexistence.

"To change this, something precious would be lost. My love affair with this land, the animals and the mountains began when I was ten, and it grew to become one of the abiding passions of my existence."

Today, they raise mostly Angus cross cattle which they raise on their land and also on the range that's leased from the BLM. I learned that she has taken care of expectant cows in temperatures as low as—42 degrees, taking them to the barn to dry them off and getting that calf its mother's warm milk.

"For many years we calved early and we're often up all night," Heather said, "but we survive. The rest of the year I am up at 4 a.m. when I write the stories and articles, but **my life revolves around the animals,** the mountains and the elements. This gives you a sense of purpose; you know you were appreciated at least once when you fed the critters," she said, "I zeroed in on making this small place of the world the best I could and becoming totally familiar with it and totally in love with it."

"One of my favorite quotes is a saying my Father always told us whenever we worried too much—"Do your best, and leave the rest.""

Heather told me **she still rides when the cattle go out**, and when they need to be checked on the rangeland. "What a privilege it is," she stated with a smile. She and her husband are helping Michael and his family with their ranching needs as the herds grow so does the need for more rangeland.

And what a privilege it is to know Heather. Her hospitality at her beautiful ranch surpassed my search for a lovely ranch woman to write about. Thank you, Heather, for sharing your story with us. (For more info go to http://insidestorey:blogspot.com)

+++++

The wife of a Camas County rancher, Ina Mae Krahn was affectionately called the "mother of the prairie." Early in their marriage, she drove teams of horses in the hay harvest in the absence of her husband as well as attending to all the household chores and decorating cakes.

Ina Mae Krahn: Fairfield
1911-2011

Pioneer Woman

The Fairfield Prairie is one of the last, best places to find solitude in the quiet places whether it be the green, lower valley or the high Sawtooth Mountains, which is often painted in yellow light. Its sparse population allows this peace to the visitor and the ones who live on its ranches.

Ina had the privilege to be born in this beautiful valley. Born Ina Mae Reagan whose grandparents had come to the prairie in the late eighteen hundreds.

My first impression when I met Ina was—what a friendly woman. Her hospitality made me feel very welcome. At ninety-seven years old, as far as I know, she is the oldest person still living that was born on the prairie; a person of clear memories and a vivid personality. **Ina has survived droughts, the Great Depression and several personal tragedies.** We could have talked for hours and almost did. But I was not surprised as I have known her son Don and his wife Carol for about ten years, and they have always treated Bill, and I, as old friends. However, it is this same with most of our friends in the Fairfield area, people we have known for more than thirty years. People like Bob and Clara Frostenson. Clara and Ina were honored as **Queens** of the events by **Camas County** the year of 2008.

Ina's stories are as follows.

"I was born and raised on a farm in Fairfield and I could ride or drive horses at a very young age. It was our way of getting around, going to school, visiting our friends, going to town, church and so forth. Our favorite mare was named Kate and she provided most of us Reagan kids' transportation. **One day riding the horse double, two miles to school**, we had to carry our supplies which included a gunny sack full of hay and grain for Kate to eat while at the school yard. We were riding near a waterway when the horse shied and shifted all the weight—the saddle started to slip. **I fell off** (with the sack) **into the water**, and got to school soaking wet, but it was summer as school was held in the summer because of our hard winters. Our horse, Kate was older, probably twenty, with lots of gentle training and things like this did not happen very often that was her fault," Ina recalled with a smile. "We could hook her up to a buggy-cart so more of us could go."

I learned later that Ina was an honor student and hardly ever had to take final exams. She graduated with twenty-four others in 1930. Getting a good education was always a subject she talked about to young people when she **served on the local school board** for several terms.

Ina continues with her story, "There were times of the year that we were needed to go out and chase cattle out of the hay fields with our horses; so my neighbor friend and I often played nearby as there were not very many fences to keep them out of the hay and grain."

"One spring we had several feet of snow, and the sheep were herded up to the mountains to feed. In order to get them moved, we hooked up a large tree trunk to the horses and made a path for the sheep to follow in single file to an open road."

"As my brother, Lonzo and I were older; we spelled our dad **driving a three horse team** that pulled a plow. I liked it better than driving a small tractor that we bought several years later. When you did the tractor work, you had to get off and trip the plow at the end of each row, turn the tractor around, then get off again and trip the plow to go into the ground. We did a lot of chores with the animals, and helped mother even put up hay when the men were away with the cattle, but we had a lot of time to ourselves too. Sometimes **we would ride to the fishing place**; we imagined there were fish in the ponds. As a family outing we often camped at Camas creek to fish and swim. When we went to Magic Dam we could keep all the fish we caught."

"My brother and I attended country schools, and often had to go to summer school when winters were hard. Sometimes we went to Sunny Slope School north of Shoshone where we stayed in the area with families there. When they finally built the new high school in Fairfield, I started as a freshman. My friend Clara and I are the only 'survivors' of the first class to go the first four years there in 1930."

I was tickled to learn that during Ina's older teen-age years, she worked at Tingwalls Department Store in Gooding. (It was one of my favorite places to shop when I was young.)

I could see that a lot of history had passed Ina's way. She had met Indian tribes that camped just down the mile from their place where they rode out to greet them.

Ina recalls one event, "I remember an Indian woman that wanted some milk. One time when mother filled her pail with milk and handed it to her, she still wouldn't leave. She kept pointing to the pail. Mother told her that is all the milk she could get in it. But the woman persisted. Finally, with a lot of hand motions, we figured out she needed the pail lid. Sometime, we would find an Indian man sitting on our front step. He stated he was, 'a Blackfoot man named William Penn, and was guarding their house and that he was honest and would never steal.' We gave him some food and he left."

Ina met Eddie Krahn at a dance at a small town that was called, Crighton; later they married. "We had two sons and one daughter and returned to Fairfield to build a nice house at the family farm, and began to farm and ranch."

"Our Daughter, Diana, loved to ride a small horse named Trixie. She and a neighbor girlfriend would **plan on having a rodeo**. They made their arena with straw bales and would get a small crowd to come watch them do **trick rides** that they had practiced. She liked horses and being the youngest of our children, she had more time to ride and she became a good rider. We lost Diana to cancer when she was only thirty. Her beautiful daughter, my granddaughter, often comes to visit me."

Ina still lives on the same farm at the age of ninety-eight. Her home tells the story of her successful life. There are pictures of her beautiful family in the home. Ina is a real flower, caring for others and enjoying the grandchildren when she can. Her son, Cliff, lives next door and sees to her daily and social needs like taking her to the Community Church on Sundays. She is a joyful, Christian woman showing Christ-like love. One of Ina's life-long traits was **"to always do your best at whatever you work at."** Her beautiful, decorated cakes, satin Valentines and lovely flower garden that she is known for, prove **her ability to create lovely things**. But she told me that her love for her God and all the children she taught in Sunday school has been her most recent passion.

"I miss my horse riding days and if I could go back I would have ridden more," Ina said.

There is so much history of her early life to learn about and Ina could relate it for us. It has been my privilege to have her horse related stories in this book. God Bless you, Ina.

March 1, 2011, Ina went to be with her Lord, just missing her 100 year birthday by about three weeks. At ninety-nine years she said, "I don't feel old." She had just worked on her beautiful valentines before she went to the hospital—you see one she made on this chapter page.

Raising Horses

Cheryl Hymas

Carol Pugh

Chris Dickard

Bonny Detwiler

Jan Bartlett

Virginia Spafford

Eva Ellis

Over the centuries, as different breeds of horse have evolved, they have each become highly adapted to their particular environment. To a greater extent, nowadays they are used primarily to recreational pursuits.

Eva Ellis: Salmon & Jerome

"Patterns become apparent after many years,"

Eva spoke these words gently while looking at her new colt. "He looks just like I thought he would. I am really happy." A smile spread across her tanned face and Eva's eyes sparkled. She was a short, bright and talkative horsewoman. She never knew envy and liked everyone. I ask her **how many of these colts she had raised.** She had told me she couldn't even come close to an accurate number. Then thinking about this, she replied. "**Perhaps hundreds**, with the ones my nephew and his wife have also raised." After I learned of this family that was close to Eva, I wanted to meet them.

Several years after Eva's death, I had the opportunity to meet her nephew. Glenn and Carolyn Bradley now live west of Shoshone. As I drove into the circular drive, the first thing I saw was, Crescendo, Eva's last riding horse grazing in a beautiful green pasture. This scene caused memories to come flooding back . . .

I thought about Eva riding and ride Eva did, often times with friends on weekends as well as the Thursday Sage Riders. Eva had ridden more than eighty years and nearly forty years with the TSR group before her death. Her good riding friends were: Virginia, Frances and Adria.

On the last ride Eva rode with this group I had the privilege that morning to pick her up at her place and load, Crescendo, in my trailer. She was ready early and I could see the excitement in her face. Off to the South hills we went, talking about our horses all the way there. She was cheerful as we saddled up to ride Third Fork about six miles to the top. There we ate lunch under the tall pines on the ridge with ten other riders. It was a memorable time. After lunch we took the trail for home. We crossed the ridge and came back down Trail Creek then joining Third Fork, which in two hours would take us back to the trailers (a 15 mile circle.) With every beat of her Arabians horse's steps and with a smile, Eva, at eighty, **rode our buns off that day**. However, we had no sooner hit the road in the pickup till Eva was fast asleep in her seat. What a gal!! Years later when I visited her in the hospital just before she died I asked Eva if she remembered that day, she said yes, and she thanked me. I told her it was a privilege to have her with me.

When she moved off of her acreage to the apartment in town, she still went to the Bradley's farm and rode Crescendo there in the pasture or down to the foothills to the north. She did this for many years up to her ninetieth year.

She described her summer rides in Salmon when she was young, as often being lost among the thousand hills that rose like waves of the sea, one after another for here, Eva found herself captivated by sights and sounds and that is why she often went out alone.

She gave me an idea of what a true western spirit was when I asked her for an early story of where she grew up in Salmon.

This is her story.

"When Elmer Smith and I married, we lived on **our own ranch** near Salmon. My husband liked horses as much as I did, but in order **to raise horses** in the early days we needed more income so we had cattle to pay for our expenses. Among these were fifteen milking cows that I took on eight of my own because no one else could milk them but me. We continued to raise a nice herd of strong Arabians that would do anything any ranch horse could."

"My memorable times there were riding with the Women's Posse called the Salmonetts. We performed for many rodeos all over Southern Idaho. I so enjoyed this time," Eva said with a smile.

I learned that in those early days, Eva would ride the horse from their place four miles to the fairgrounds for practicing drill with the Riding Salmonetts twice a week, and do the same with a youth riding club which she also sponsored and directed, called the Rancho kids, then she would ride the four miles back. She was with this group for twenty years. You could ask anyone in Salmon and they knew who Eva was.

Eva continued her story, "Several years after Elmer died; I met and married Owen Ellis, who worked for the Fish and Wildlife Service. He was an officer of the predator control division. **We often rode into the Sawtooth Mountain range to camp** alongside bands of sheep where Owen would shoot or trap most any wildlife that would attack the band of sheep. It was very enjoyable to camp and ride in those early days. Owen and I moved to Jerome to retire on a small farm and it was appropriate for me to continue to raise my Arabians where I gentled most of the young colts. I went to some seminars and watched experts work with yearlings. After this my training was quieter, but firm with them. And it must have paid off—some of them became good riding horses."

And I agreed with her for I watched her ride four great saddle horses that she had trained herself, in the thirty years I knew her plus she sold many to satisfied customers.

The year that Eva was widowed she still rode on New Years Day, when the weather allowed, then she would wish most of her neighbors a Happy New Year. I'm sure it was her very Happy Birthday also.

Glenn and Carolyn, often rode with Eva. He told me that even when his Aunt Eva had a horse accident that **broke her pelvis, she still rode as soon as she was well enough.** Glenn was there to help her climb aboard her favorite Crescendo (each of her Arabians had musical names as they were decedents of Melody her first mare.) And he said her comment was**, "It sure feels good to be back on."** He also confirmed that Eva rode at their place when she was eighty-six years young. The Bradley's were accomplished horse riders as well as horse breeders. Eva leased Melody to them so they could begin their herd. The agreement was that she would get every other colt. Glenn and Carolyn and their families have ridden these fine horses for forty years. They have Eva's last horse, Crescendo and at 25 he serves as a very exceptional mount for all of their grandkids and guests today.

In my tribute to a friend like Eva, I gave her a sprig of lilac—for a lilac blooms first.

And she was first in my memories of **a great horsewoman**. Thank you, Eva, for giving me a part of your story so I could learn how delicately and intricately your life was ever woven together with your beautiful Arabian horses.

+++++

Cheryl Heiss Hymas: Hailey
For fresh do the morning,
Thus would I chant a song for you—In paths untrodden . . . . Walt Whitman

The paths untrodden are where Cheryl loves to go.

Trails in the wilderness area are what she and her husband, Forest, have worked to keep open by their early involvement in the Idaho Horse Council where Forest serves as Executive Director. They also have manned a booth at the Horse Expo every spring to promote the horse industry in Idaho. I applaud them for this labor; thank you, friends.

Let's Go Ride!

When I asked Cheryl what horse she was riding this summer, she replied, "I ride one of six. I keep the horses for Michelle and still have four I raised including the yearling."

I asked, "Are you still breaking colts?"

"Yes, I ride three to six days a week and I guess that gives me time to train a new one," Cheryl answered with a smile. She is a woman that speaks her mind, especially when it comes to working with a horse. The years of horsemanship gives Cheryl a confident air. She is a contented horsewoman who is able to cross barriers. She spoke with great feeling about doing this training herself. Coming from a skilled equestrian family Cheryl has ridden earlier than she can remember. She has not been without accidents on horses, but when she remembered these times we concluded that '**failures help us to grow and learn.**'

"For more years than I can count, horses have been my passion," she told me one day in early May when we were at their cabin at Smilie Creek. The trails had just opened up and it was no surprise to see this avid rider put on a warm coat and hat and saddle up for one of our first ride of the year. We would be riding in the lower elevations of the Sawtooth Mountains. I have had the privilege of being her guest at their cabin many times. We went on rides in this area on her beautiful horses. How grand it was to **visit the quiet solitude of an old mill** at a place called Vienna. Other times we would ride to Sawtooth City and **see the remains of the old mining camp** with the logs crumbling which someday will be only a few words in a page in Idaho history.

Cheryl became interested in **raising Peruvian Passo horses** after her return trip from Peru almost thirty years ago. She loved the soft, distinct gait as well as the eager disposition of the horses. After Cheryl studied the many breed lines she bought some mares to breed as well as a registered stallion. At her ranch she produced some of the finest looking and smooth gaited horses. Cheryl also became a judge at many of the shows.

I remember going to see her mare, Angel, she had just bought from Stuart Hamblin's ranch in California. Today her beautiful and dependable horses are praised; Chatar, Angel and Shaski to name a few of her loved ones that she has kept for more than twenty years.

The year **Cheryl raised seven colts**—all born within a month; I spent some time at her place that was in Jerome. From the day they were born she also taught them many things, to be halter broke, to creep-feed and load in a trailer.

"I gave up my social life when those colts were born, but it was worth it. Today they are in good places and are being enjoyed as fantastic riding horses. Some of the mares I kept and ride them today. They have such incredible heart that they will not complain or tell you when they are tired and I caution others who ride a Passo to make them rest when they are not in shape."

I met Cheryl when she was a young teen. She was an accomplished rider then. Cheryl joined the TSR group when her two daughters, Shelly and Nicki, were in school in Jerome. Being raised with horses, the daughters are accomplished riders today. Cheryl and Forest did not move to Hailey until the daughters were out of high school.

This is Cheryl's horse story.

"In the summer when I was young, we took our horses up to Ketchum. Often my family and I would ride up Trail Creek, ride over the top across a ridge, and come down into the East Fork, north of Hailey, where someone would pick us up. We fed the tired horses in a corral and left them there overnight only to return the next day to ride them back. We never bought a horse trailer until 1968."

Cheryl told me they spent hours on horseback not just in her youth but when she married Forrest and moved to Jerome. She bought and raised several horses for their daughters to ride. One of these horses was an Arabian named Brooke that was a pistol. The girls spent many hours gentling the right horse for their competition, getting all the teaching ability from their mother. The other horse was a horse Virginia raised named, Ben, a three quarter Arabian that Cheryl had been using herself for trail rides. **Shelly and Nicki** both won blue ribbons on these horses. The girls were each **Rodeo Queens** and very pretty ones too.

More than twenty years ago Cheryl raised several dozen more at their place and trained them on mountain trails often beginning with letting the colt just follow along. Their eighth stallion, Avatar, is being ridden not only on the trails, but in parades also. This year Cheryl rode her last, young colt on a ride we took around Redfish Lake and he was a perfect gentleman. I asked Cheryl if she would do this again. She replied, "**A lifetime of dedication has been rewarding**. Yes, I would."

Cheryl rides three to six days a week from spring though late fall. "October 20 to November 11 is usually the beginning storms in the Sawtooth Mountains," she said. "I ride with a variety of friends, many who borrow horses from me."

We often call on Cheryl to take us on overnight rides to the Sawtooth Mountains, for going there is as familiar to her as a walk in her horse pasture. I have been places we might never have gone if it wasn't for Cheryl's pioneering spirit. Together Cheryl, Lonna, Marlene and I and several other riding friends in the area have found old trails, some one hundred years old.

This is a story of one of those rides with Cheryl, Carol, Lonna and I.

It was a warm summer evening when we arrived at the edge of the **Frank Church Wilderness** area north west of Stanley. We camped at Beaver Creek where that night we spent some time in front of the campfire before retiring. We were excided about our early morning ride. This was the first time for most of us here and we were depending on Cheryl to guide us down the trails to several lakes and make a circle back to camp before dark.

The Sawtooth Mountains loomed around us that morning as we rode up a canyon and crossed many streams that fed the Middle Fork of the Salmon River. An eagle soared high over the bluffs showing their tiny splash of black against the summer, blue sky. After riding just over two hours we saw the first lake shinning below us. It was aptly named with an island being the outstanding sight to see—Island Lake was beautiful.

We continued on because we were planning on having lunch near the pass of Ruffneck Lookout. All went well until, ahead in the trail, was a sign telling us **our northern route trail was closed**. The alternative trail would take us in the wrong direction from where our camp was located.

"Maybe we should go back," one rider suggested.

"No, I think we can go down another way. Yes, let's go by Kinger Lake and come back down Falls Creek and end up back here," Our adventuring, Cheryl stated looking at the map.

"But how long would that take us as it's already afternoon," I asked, skeptical of staying out late.

"We'll have more than six hours before dark," Carol argued not wanting to go back yet.

"But we're not sure of the trail," Lonna said, agreeing with me.

"It's marked here on the map," Cheryl replied. "Let's try it for a while at least."

Not wanting to be a wet blanket on the day's ride I agreed.

The trail took us down to a creek that we followed for an hour then up to a high ridge. We found most of it was passable except several times we were not sure we could get through the fallen burned logs from a fire, five years earlier. The blackened mountain dwarfed everything with many fallen trees on the trail, but time after time we searched and found a way around. More than once we got off the horses to move black, charred trees so we could continue on. By late afternoon, we came upon the large lake designated on the map. It was a glowing, shimmering body of blue and we watered the horses there and rested for a while. When we started back, the trail was not distinct. We didn't know if we should continue on or go back the same way. The **shale trail** above the lake that went back across the mountain looked like it had not been used in a long time.

"You may wish to get off and walk with your horse if you feel more comfortable, but in order to get back while it's still daylight, we need to go on," Cheryl said as she urged her horse across the soft sand of the lake, then onto the narrow shale slide area that took us high up above the lake. Several riders did get off feeling uneasy about the unstable flat rocks. Without a word about what might happen, we walked slowly as we climbed about two hundred feet, but I breathed a sigh of relief when we got to the far side and found a better trail heading out. We returned to camp by eight, and had supper by the light of the warm campfire. This concluded the great day's ride with special, gutsy friends on a new trail. What an adventure!

Cheryl and I agree that being in the mountains has a dreamy way of folding up a noisy day and giving us peace in our soul. Thanks, Cheryl!

+++++

Chris Dickard: Kimberly
Fox Trotters

A Tribute to Trooper

*"Life should **not** be a journey to the grave with the intention of arriving safely in a pretty and well-preserved body, but rather to skid in broadside, thoroughly used up, totally worn out and loudly proclaiming; Wow! What a ride!"*

"Ranch women are as sharp as nails and just as hard."

Among the women I have interviewed for their memoirs, Chris too said if she could go back she would ride more. But how a busy career woman like Chris could have found more time with raising a family and teaching school I wouldn't know. Chris and her husband began raising Fox Trotters for their exciting gait, their beauty, quick learning, and loyalty to those who became their friend. One of these horses named Senator, is a horse Chris's three year old disabled granddaughter rides for therapy. This 'horse riding' therapy is the Rising Star Disabled group.

Chris's daughter heads it up and Chris helps with the planned events. The smiles and enjoyment the children and adults receive from these rides is priceless. They have fund raising events to keep this group going. These events are usually in August. They need volunteers to come with a good horse and spend the day with the less fortunate. Volunteer if you can as Chris and her friends Karen and Shirley find it very rewarding.

Chris has a Fox Trotter named Gypsy which she likes to ride as her favorite horse.

"Oh, I ride Dusty when I think I'm in a good mood," Chris said with a laugh. "Yes, this horse has tried everything with me; if I had it to do over I would have had a firm trainer start him as I love the horse. He was our first Fox Trotter foal, but **has been real challenging**."

"When I came home from work, I often saddled up a young one and put miles on it working for a first class trail horse that my husband Jerry had started. I would go out to the pasture or as they progressed, ride the trails of the South Hills. We love to ride our new horses in the Sawtooth Mountains in the summer. And in recent years have **taken them to Arizona with us to ride** in the winter months."

Although Chris has ridden on and off since she was nine, the last nine years has been especially fun to her, for riding younger horses is now possible since retiring.

The following is Chris's tribute to a horse named Trooper, who she said came to them with the name Phantoms Pleasure. "When we first saw Trooper he was a skinny four year old who looked like all he needed was a good meal or two. He was a classic bay, Tennessee Walking Horse with a nice long walk and a calm disposition. We decided a bit of grain wouldn't hurt and we found it boosted his weight and also his energy as he was capable of a pretty decent crow hop—just to prove how good he felt on a cool morning. It was just such a morning that Trooper earned his name. About two weeks into his joining our family my husband and I were trail riding in the Sawtooth Mountains above Stanley. Trooper and I spied what we thought was a lush green meadow and I decided to take a short cut through it. About ten steps in, Trooper sank to his belly, as **the meadow was a bog**. I stepped off on a more solid area. My feet were already on the ground and I made for a higher ground. I know now I should have kept the reins in my hands, though I was panic stricken when it happened. Trooper looked at me with his huge, soft eyes and it passed through my mind that a helicopter would never arrive in time. I pleaded and pulled and he lunged and struggled one front leg at a time to where I was. He hauled himself out, shook, and was ready for the day's ride. What a trooper!"

"As time passed he was the horse that was ridden only when teaching our grandchildren to ride. He seemed to be spending more time in the pasture than on the trail. When **we began raising Fox Trotters,** we found he was standing in the pasture instead of going to the mountains so we found him a good home. A Montana couple owns him and they travel the Big Horn Mountains. Every year or so I receive an email telling me of how he saved the day on a trip down a hill too steep for the other horses or a river too swift to swim. It seems that Trooper continues to troop through life watching out for his humans who sometimes lack the sense to watch out for him."

I wish a most deserving Chris, good luck as she is still 'teaching, coaching, and mentoring' others today, that is if they have a good horse under them. It has been my pleasure to have a new friend like Chris and watching her work a new horse has taught me that patience requires a lot of waiting—a good practice I'm sure she has learned and taught in her school room.

+++++

Carol Pugh-1942-2007: Shoshone
Quarter Horse and Appaloosa

From Raising Top Quarter Horse to Miniature Teams

She finished in the top ten at the Nationals just two years before cancer took her life.

"If you can't excel with talent, triumph with effort"

"I have thought of my life with horses as an adventure," Carol said with a sparkle in her blue eyes. And as she began to tell me of her love for the equine she was associated with, I believe she met with a force that was larger and stronger than the logic she had in the beginning. I am talking about the **Quarter Horse breed** she held in her mind after she saw Joker Asorkie Pat on a ranch in Montana.

As I continued the interview, Carol said, "Sometimes the dream of having a large horse ranch turned women into fools but common sense fought to remain in charge. Then after several months, **my love for this breed of horse was so strong**, I was ready to go to war to have this alien, compassing force triumph."

So, over the protests of her companion, in **the late 1960's she started a horse ranch** on her place outside of Richfield. This occurred right after she purchased Indian Joker RH. With her expertise of training, this horse was a **champion cutting horse.** He as well as some of his offspring, was **third in nation** and went on to win many cutting events. He was also an ION **champion stallion** several years in a row. This is an Appaloosa club that covers Idaho, Oregon and Nevada.

Carol's daughter Kim entered state high school rodeo events with Joker and did real well. Although Carol later sold him, she had many mares that were from this champion horse. She would buy registered mares, breed them and show them and their offspring. **She trained and rode them herself** often winning first and even **placing third in the nation in a cow cutting class.** Carol sold as many as she could as this was a chance to grab what she always wanted.

Carol said to me, "it wasn't only what I wanted to do; **it's what I had to do** so I wouldn't regret it later. And I don't."

Carol also enjoyed the years she spent as a 4-H leader in horse projects in her community. She was a sticker for each of her students wearing appropriate riding attire and helped them in acquiring their outfits.

This work was not without some down time. One winter when Wood River was iced across, Carol **lost three nice horses that fell through the ice.** "I felt that if you can't excel with talent, triumph with effort," Carol told me when she recalled her early days at her horse ranch.

I met this lovely, intelligent, horse woman when I was looking for a gentle, experienced horse for my young daughter Sara to use in 4-H; as well as to ride in rodeo club in her teen years. Carol sold me exactly what I wanted; a part thoroughbred quarter horse. Our new horse Bourbon was enjoyed by our family for more than fifteen years. Carol's 'effort' was a triumph for people like me who was a receiver of her real talent in training, and raising horses. I had Carol as my friend for many years.

Carol also introduced the Shoshone area to Silver Creek Chariots racing that is still enjoyed by many members.

Carol especially enjoyed her mini horses when she could no longer mount up on the full sized equines as cancer began to take over her body. She was introduced to these darling miniatures by her granddaughter and instantly fell in love and had to get some of her own.

I saw Carol at a horse show in Twin Falls, "Win," she said to me, "I have found joy in showing or riding in a cart pulled by my favorite mini team. I can't tell you how much it means to me. **The Minis give me a chance to take advantage of the time I have left to enjoy horses.**" I later found that Carol trained her minis to drive, chariot race and do tricks. Carol belonged to the Snake River Miniature Horse Club that promoted the miniature equine. She won many blue ribbons showing and driving the pretty miniatures. **She finished in the top ten in the National contest** just two years before she died.

Her twin sister Claudia told me that in Carol's last days, she was smiling brightly as **she held a new born miniature horse in her arms.** Claudia is also a lover of the equine. This special twin sister took care of Carol in her last years. It seems to me both these women are champions.

In being human there are only beginnings, and the good beginnings I've enjoyed finding friends and good neighbors. It is the unique ability which we can delight in.

+++++

Bonnie Detwiler: Jerome
American Saddlebreds
And Peruvian Passo cross

From Pettit Lake to Redfish

Bonnie has lived up to the command of "Love one Another," as she shows to others a love that lasts. Bonnie grew up at a family homestead several miles from Seward, Alaska.

"It was a beautiful scenic place I have gone back to many times to visit," Bonnie said.

And she is right. Bill and I drove right by the house where she grew up on our way to Exit Glacier. It is a very scenic valley in the summer months, with sparkling, white, glacier covered mountains against a blue sky. In her younger days Bonnie and her sister were able to keep a pretty black and white Shetland pony that they often rode up this road to the neighbors.

This is Bonnie's story.

"I always wanted to have my own horse, and perhaps raise them. When Elmer and I were married and moved to Nampa, we had a chance to fulfill this **dream of mine**. Some of our best friends owned **American Saddlebreds**, and through this association, we bought two registered mares that we bred to their stallion. Our first Saddlebred was named Cindy and the other was Lady. Our first filly out of Dolly, we called Ginger, and she was the horse Elmer rode for many years."

"I would never submit to the hard jarring that many mustang type horses gave out in their ride, as I had tried that on a lengthy mountain ride. My legs were battered black and blue and after much abuse on the horse, I became convinced there was a distinct difference between gaited and most non-gated horses. Elmer and I then began to ride in the great Idaho wilderness with the Valley Riders from Nampa. We also rode in several city parades. I had a neighbor friend who sometimes teased me about my practice of wearing a split skirt while riding. It was a spiritual decision however, that I have continued to do."

"Being sold on the **Saddlebred** horse, we **purchased a stallion and twenty more mares** that foaled lots of great colts. Our Dolly mare was from Cindy and our young stallion; she was a delightful and easy riding horse with a quiet disposition and a willingness to please. This allowed Elmer and our three sons to help train the foals. We also rode the older ones on the trails. It was a great feeling to ride an animal we raised, knowing their personality and abilities as they matured into real quality horses. Cindy was the mare I rode when **I joined the Thursday Sage Riders** after we moved to Jerome in 1973. I kept Dolly for 32 years. I now ride her granddaughter we named Princess a part Peruvian Passo. I treasure the friendships I received from this women's association and the great rides with such horse loving women."

I remember Bonnie's mare, Dolly, more than twenty years ago I rode this horse into the Pioneer Mountains one snowy weekend with the Detwilers and Linda Hine. By the end of the day, **I too was sold on the idea of riding a gaited horse.** Bonnie often lets others ride one of her Saddlebred/Passo cross horses today. This year I enjoyed an early spring desert ride with her and her friends, Joni, Lisa and Melissa as we went out to the Hunt area near Eden and explored the Wilson Cave. What a great ride we had.

Here is Bonnie's story of a ride she took several years ago.

"One of the memorable rides that I had an exciting incident on was in the Sawtooth National forest when Twig Schutte and I were staying at the Jack and Marlene Sears cabin near Smilie Creek. Twig and I began the early morning ride from Pettit Lake trailhead, rode to Edna Lake and instead of going to Imogene, we planned on making a long circle in this pristine wilderness area. It was a bright clear day and with the early morning start, we felt we could make the **thirty mile trip** if we moved out at a good pace. Dolly was in good condition, and so was Twig's horse and that is what it took in this rugged mountain setting, as the trail led us over several steep passes. After an hour climb up to a narrow shale pass, we were beginning wonder if we had made the right decisions on some turns on the trail. However, we decided it was not wise to go back as we were over half way and it would be dark before we got back. Thanks to the ability of such great steeds we were making good time when Twig, who was in the lead, said, "You are not going to believe what's coming down the trail on the next rise."

"What is it?" I questioned.

"It's **a mother bear and her two cubs.**" she replied, stopping her horse. I looked around us. We couldn't get off this narrow trail and an immediate conference was needed.

"Yes, we must stop and wait to see what direction the sow will go when she sees us or hears us. Let's begin to make a lot of noise." I suggested.

The sow bear did not seem to pay any attention to us so we dismounted in case the horses acted up or tried to throw us from being frightened. We walked forward still making a lot of noise. The mother bear must have instructed the cubs to climb a tree to 'safety' and safe they were in that big tree right beside the trail. We looked up at them and for a while we watched. The sow bear stayed on the opposite side of the trail, but moving a little closer to a large tree stump. She put her front paws up on it, looked at us as if to say, *Just come closer and . . .* We began making so much noise she finally joined them near their tree. We mounted up and hurried by them making a sashay as far from them as possible and as fast as we could."

"Whew!" we both sighed with relief. "And some people say God doesn't watch over us?" I joyfully exclaimed.

"It was a memorable day. We continued down the dimming path to the Redfish Lake inlet when all of a sudden the horses stopped right in the middle of the trail. *No!* We both thought expecting more bears. But looking where they were looking we saw a lone deer that had come up from the stream. She was standing still just watching for our next move to go on by."

"The last rays of sun were sinking over the tree covered mountains as we rode by the large lake. What a beautiful sight, but we still had at least five miles to get to the lodge before dark, so we did not linger there. We put our horses into a fast pace and managed to get to the lighted lodge at deep twilight. We called our friends to come pick us up. They were glad to hear from us, but thought we were crazy to make that ride in one day. As Twig and I waited for them to arrive, we had time to thank God for our safe trip. But we well have special long-lasting memories in our minds and hearts forever from this trail ride."

Thank you Bonnie for sharing with us your good times with many great horses you raised. And thank you for sharing another story of one of your mountain rides.

+++++

On May Morning
Hail bounteous May!
That does inspire Mirth, and warm desire
Woods and groves are of their dressing,
Hill and dale doth boast thy blessings
Thus we salute thee with our early song,
And welcome thee, and wish thee long.—John Milton

When we entered the Grandjean Creek area we could view the majesty of Grandjean peak to the east. I was looking forward to a corral for my horse and for me a warm shower before we ate the steak dinner we had ordered in advance. The twenty-seven mile ride was tiring for all of us, both horse and rider were anxious to get to their destination of Grandjean Lodge. I learned that it was an establishment that had been opened in 1927 by the children of Emil Grandjean who came to the Boise National Forest in the early days of the 20th century. The original structures were remnants of a Forest Service station. The four rustic cabins will soon be occupied by our group. At a fast trot we wove around the tall pines through the lodge's trailer park and in a few minutes brought our fast moving horses to a stop at the tie up poles in front of the big barn.

I never fail to think of those eight friends who shared this wonderful adventure with me but I smile at the **memory of Virginia Spafford** as one special friend who helped make this time even more enjoyable just because she was there.

Virginia Spafford: Kimberly
Arabians

It's Hard to Let Go of a Friend

Virginia was Born Virginia Strope and grew up on the Lost River Ranch in Howe. She went to school in Pocatello where she met James Spafford. They moved to Twin in 1972 where Dr. Jim practiced medicine and they raised their three sons. They moved to a small acreage south of Kimberly where Virginia raised many Arabian horses for the next twenty years. Virginia was known in the Arabian clubs throughout Idaho as **raising the best moving Arabian horses**.

She was a respected horsewoman and promoted the sport she loved with exceptional skills. She belonged to the Magic Valley Arabian Horse Club.

"They were long gaited and not short trotters on the trail, unless you let them," Virginia said about her Arabians. She will also be known by her friends for showing and mountain riding her Arabians. Two Arabian horses I know about in our TSR group that Virginia sold were a three year old gelding named Ben that was purchased by Cheryl Hymas. The other horse was one I bought, named Bingo Majurs. For twenty years I rode Bingo in the south hills and Sawtooth Mountains. I retired him as my trail horse but, all the grandkids including my four year old, great granddaughter Alexis often rode him. He took good care of them while they learned to stay on board. This was the kind of horses Virginia raised. Horses that made others happy and in return Virginia was happy.

"It's hard to let go of a friend," Virginia stated with a tremble in her voice over her ill horse Jalure. "Yes, he was suffering, and I have had to do this before, but it never gets easier. However, I need to do what must be done and give my time to the other horses. I remember the last ride Jalure and I had together. It was a blue-sky, spring morning; we had unloaded at one of the canyons in the south hills—my favorite place to ride. I brushed him good before I put his saddle on and then I put his own bridle on his beautiful face. Jalure pricked his ears as he strained to hear my voice telling him what a great day we will have. After I mounted him I could feel how strong he was beneath me as I settled in the saddle. I will never forget that day, we did have a beautiful time together." Virginia continued. "It was unlike the day when Jalure, at an early age dumped me in south Soldier Creek. But that is another story," Virginia laughed as she recalled this event.

"I still own a horse named Ozie, which I retired at twenty-eight. He still gets oats and carrots every day. He had been showing his age for years and deserved to be turned out to the soft pasture. Ozie has served me with silent and irrevocable loyalty. This gelding was trained by Oakley Bernard. He and his wife became our good friends often riding with Jim and me on weekends."

Another horse she raised she named, Dodger. He was the horse I remembered Virginia riding a lot when I first met her in the late 1970's. Virginia was a good rider and I admired her for this ability also. Bill and I became good friends with and her and her husband Jim. We had many rides together in the White Cloud and wilderness areas of Idaho often camping out and spending several days there.

There were few women who raised horses who has as much integrity, grit and determination as Virginia Spafford. **It is hard to let go of such a friend** and it has been a privilege to know her.

+++++

Jan Bartlett: Burley
Fox Trotter

Guide of My Favorite Ride

There are several fun rides in the south-central Sawtooth Mountain range that is called Cache Peak. The cowgirl we often call on to lead us on these trails is Jan Bartlett, as Jan grew up in Mini-Cassia area and is now living on a nice country home where she keeps her eight Fox

Trotter horses. The day that her pretty horses were turned out in their pastures I had the pleasure of visiting that day and getting to pet the friendly horses. Jan often takes her young Fox Trotter horses into the Albion mountain range for them **to gain good trail experience.** Jan is shown in the picture on one of her first, grey geldings that she named Blue.

On this day, when I took the picture of her, we had ridden across the Pomerelle ski area near the top of Mt. Harrison, then down a beautiful canyon to a nice abandoned house. Jan told us the story of this picturesque place as it is part of the history of the area. We had a great day riding in an area where we don't often travel.

I have known Jan and her sister Carolyn for more than two decades. Back then we all enjoyed riding our Arabian horses at some Arabian shows.

Jan told me she rode Shala with the TSR group when I first met her. She was invited to come on our Thursday ride by Iris Bowers a neighbor and long time rider of Arabian horses. During those years, she often rode side saddle in a parade on a pretty Arabian mare named Tuxanna.

Jan tells her story.

"I grew up on a farm near Heyburn and often rode one of two riding horses called Skipper and Flash that was from a mare we had. We also raised a colt we called Charro, as he was very pretty. Back then there was ample room to ride along canals and dirt roads. The first horse I bought was a bay that was part thoroughbred, she loved to run. Her name was Sugar, and she was a lot of horse. One day she reared with me, causing us to go over backwards and I was lucky to get away with only a broken leg."

"Then about 18 years ago I went to riding Fox Trotters. My first horse was Blue and he had a lot easier ride than those I was used to. For many years, I rode a Fox Trotter I called Chance, with the **Thursday Sage Riders** activities."

"My horse raising days were not without accidents; I should have known better than to ride a colt up a highway. He had a lot of energy; he spooked and started to buck. When I went off he broke my leg. I call it a learning lesson, as I know now that he needed more arena work or I should have warmed him up there."

Jan raises several horses a year, and always has a young one coming up to train.

"In 2010 I'm training a blue roan named Tonman. One of her newest colts was recently **featured on the front page of the Fox Trotter Journal**. His color is unique described as a Palomino Tobiano. He is called Wind Waker." Jan said, "It's a joy to work with the young horses and get so much satisfaction watching their progress. I would do it all again,"

"I like to say—if you don't do things right, don't expect a perfect ending."

Thank you for your friendship all these years, Jan and may we have many more good times as we ride the trails together.

The following is one of the rides that Jan was our guide. My favorite ride in this southern range is on Cache Peak near Oakley, as it has a great place to camp at Stimpson campground. It is the trail-head to the Independence Lakes Trail. The other reason I love this ride is that the journey around the top of this 10,000 foot mountain is an all-day event. If I drive more than two hours to get there I want the ride to be worthwhile. An hour out of camp we came into the Independence Lake area, where we let the horses drink from the clear cold water. In another hour we began to see the famous City of Rocks National Reserve below us. As we turned into the south side of this trail, the huge rock formations are below us. After lunch we continue our ride around the mountain and soon heard a lot of dog barking. Curious, we entered into a sheep camp where two young barking dogs were tied to a wagon. They were barking at a large coyote that had invaded their domain. Or should I say they were in danger because they had placed themselves into the coyote's country. We frightened the aggressor away and went to find the herder to tell him of the problem. Upon hearing the familiar bah-bah of the sheep, we rode into the band that was blocking the trail only to be stopped by two large white Siberian Sheep dogs. When we yelled at them, they let us by, but we got the attention of the herder; a young dark haired man who came loping his horse up the hill toward us. He asked the dogs to be quiet and commanded them to stay, as he wanted to accompany us along the trail back up to the top. His name was Herb, and we learned he was a student at a college in Arizona and took this summer job because he loved the outdoors. Herb's heritage was from an Indian tribe in that area. When he had gone with us as far as he dared to leave the flock, he headed back, but not until we gave him all the candy bars we had in our saddle bags. We smiled and bid him goodbye.

But it's the view at the top looking down on the old towns of Elba and Almo below us that you feel you were **on top of the world**. Traveling on, along the western side of the mountain, we began to view Magic Valley a hundred miles west, and north. It was late afternoon before we got back to camp and I thank Jan for being our guide for a day of beauty and companionship on horseback.

+++++

Whatever your choice, make sure you check the weather forecast as this high mountain seems to attract storms making it the best snow for skiing or snowmobiling that you could ask for, unless you are on horseback.

Ranch Women

Marilyn Aggeler

Verla Ruby

Verla Ruby

Ranch Women

Stacie Harvey

Lola Blossoms

Carla Liesen

The history of women in the west and women who worked on cattle ranches in particular, is not as well documented as that of men. However, institutions such as the national Cowgirl Museum and Hall of Fame have gathered documents and state contributions of women who worked on cattle drives of the Old West. There were times women did ranch work due to wars, illness, death or many ranches just could not afford to hire outside laborers. These women worked side by side with men and thus needed to ride horses to be able to perform related tasks. When we look at the history of women's rights in the United States, it can be noted that **the western states could claim the beginnings of giving the women the right to vote.** Women such as Annie Oakley became household names and it was women like her who helped "Cowgirls" come into their own.

In this chapter, I didn't just write about chores that these western women did—but of ranch women who train colts, write for newspapers, one who does horse hair hitching, one who holds competitive trail challenges, of being outfitters, some who give themselves to helping others, and many other admiring talents such as painting artistic pictures. And yes, **I have missed acknowledging thousands of Idaho, ranch women who have helped make the ranching livelihood a success.** There are women such as Katie Breckenridge, of the Picabo area (who is a descendent of one of Idaho's first ranch owners). She promotes new and changing ideas for the beef and lamb industry at her B-Bar-B Ranch as well as wanting to get rid of the perceived notion that ranchers abuse the land and abuse the livestock. I know that Katie's desire is to let others see that at her ranch, there is a good ranching lifestyle. I salute you, Katie, and ranch women like you.

The following memoirs are from the women who have crossed my path in the last two years.

Carla Liesen: Three Creek
2009

"Young Lady, you don't belong here . . ."

This is what Carla was told several years ago when she asked for work on a desert ranch south of the Idaho border.

Today, women in ranching are as well known as their male counterparts. Working hard to keep their home they go out in freezing storms as well as summer heat to help with the stock. Carla told me many stories of her times in The Three Creek area, south of Twin Falls. She loved it there; she loved the open spaces and did not like crowds of people to contend with. Carla Liesen now lives south of **Kimberly** with her teenage daughter, Carol Ann and son, Nathan, where they raise cattle and horses. Carla works to make several young colts into good riding horses; she is strong, tireless, dependable and talented. She is a very busy single mom attending to the demands of her high school offspring.

She has spent most of her young adult life on ranches from Bishop, California to Tuscarora, Nevada and then to Three Creek at the 7 Diamond Cattle Company, where the family has spent most of their lives.

When riding near Three Creek, Carla loved to ride the vast expanses of unseen terrain and there were many times she and her horse entered a canyon untouched by any other.

Carla's story follows.

"Oh, I worked for ranchers in other states that I did not admire their way of ranching, and yet, some were the best stewards in the care of the animals and land."

In Carla's early years there were other ranches she worked at driving, branding cattle, and general ranch work including some cooking. She has been misplaced in snow storms, and had **nearly frozen** when the weather was fifty degrees below zero. She desperately worked to save newly weaned calves. During calving season, she toiled many nights without sleep. The more I learn about Carla, the more I agree with what her neighborhood friend, Lola, stated, *"I feel she is a lady of courage and values and a friend I enjoy being around."* Lola and Carla have been friends for twenty years.

Carla continued her story.

"Some of the ranch owners I meet when I was younger did not accept me as an equal cowhand. I got less pay for the same hours the men put in and at one place I was told I did not belong on a horse all day. But I loved to ride and hear the sound of the squeaky saddle as the horse takes off at a fast trot to find some cow to boss ahead of him. There's a lot of skill in getting a herd to move as a unit without a lot of fuss. I liked it; no two days were ever the same. **A normal day on the range lasts eleven or twelve hours** depending on what happens and what needs to be done. I guess you would say 'it's the cowboy way'." The cowgirl spoke with a faraway look in her blue eyes.

"I miss the wide open spaces of Three Creek very much! We all do," replied Carla speaking also for her teenage children Nathan and Carol Ann. "Oh, they're doing all right at school, but it **was home for us in Three Creek** and I home schooled a lot. The old house is now history but a community church holds Sunday services there now. The kids and I could ride out from the ranch house on a new horse where we would find a new canyon to go up, one with naturally challenging terrain of the backcountry. We had many close friends we could visit such as Lola Blossom who I still visit a lot today. It was a good place to raise kids or to start a young horse," she said with a smile. "There we seemed to have the whole prairie to get acquainted with each other. A new horse like the gelding I just worked with **excites me and invites me into his young untamed world**. I feel some of his free spirit. Oh, I don't get on just any horse these days, but if we've done the ground work and I know the horse, it is different—I might, but not like I used to."

And there are several young unbroken horses to work with at Carla's place as she is often given problem colts to gentle. Carol Ann and Nathan are good with this task too. I know this because I watched them ride a new, green-broke gelding at the fair grounds. The family finds time to ride out into the south hills, breathing the fresh air of open places that they still seek.

A Cowboy's Thanksgiving Prayer—author unknown;

Dear Lord,

> **This last year was rough on us cowboys—With calf prices bein' low.**
> **And the drought and the snow last winter—Didn't leave a lot to show**
> **For a lot of really hard workin'—where were times, I confess,**
> **That I lie awake nights and wondered: Lord, how do I get out of this mess.**
> **But I turned it all over to you, Lord, Put my trust in your capable hands**
> **And I thank you that you let us keep on—Makin' a living off of your lands.**
> **I thank you for every morning—When the sun rose out of the east,**
> **And spread light over the meadows,—And thanks for that cool summer breeze**

That cooled sweatin' backs in the hay fields. And thanks for new friends I made,
For the joy of seein' baby calves curled up, asleep in the shade.
Thanks for these good friends and neighbors—And the love and the help that they
give.

+++++

Carla introduced me to Lola Blossoms. She resided on a ranch near Three Creek until retirement.

Lola Blossoms: Three Creek

Trust Your Neighbors, but Brand Your Calves

Lola Blossoms was born on one of the oldest ranches in the Three Creek area called House Creek Ranch. It is located sixteen miles from the Three Creek store at the post office, up a desert road. It is settled in a valley that is green till late summer. The creek is supplied by the high Elk Mountain snow melt.

When I met Lola with her bright blue eyes, thick grey hair and a big smile, I could tell at ninety that she still gets a kick out of life.

The family of Lola Blossoms lived in Three Creek more than one hundred years ago when Lola's grandparents came to Idaho from Illinois just before the turn of the twentieth century.

Her grandparents were surprised at the primitive, open country, but began their ranching in the Flat Creek area.

Lola's story: "In 1933 we moved to our Cherry Creek ranch and lived the first summer in tents. My youngest brother was only six weeks old when we moved; the wind flapping the tents would scare him and make him cry. A scary incident happened when a rattlesnake crawled into our kitchen tent. That fall Dad got a log cabin moved in. The house was small but comfortable for the large family of eight. I was the oldest and much was expected of me as far as helping with the smaller children."

"In 1946 when my brother, Cliff got back from World War II, he and my brother, Walt, along with Dad, built a nice home of logs that they hauled from Shoshone Basin. A year later, Harvey and I decided we wanted more space of our own, and we added on to both ends of the house. Later, after working on a ranch in Nevada, in 1953 we moved back to my parent's ranch on Cherry Creek and remained in that area until retirement."

"Horses have been in my life ever since a fifteen year old girl rode her pregnant mare several miles through deep snow drifts to get a mid-wife to help my mom when I was born. However when I was five years old I remembered riding an old Sabrina roan horse called Bolley. I had an awful time getting on him and I remember falling off a few times. One time I got dumped in a thorny wild rose bush. Up till I was about ten I had a chance to go out and ride some, but riding was in my blood and I did this every chance I got."

"I finally did get what I wanted—my own horse," Lola continued with a far away look. "He was probably a mustang off the range as he was only a two year old bay gelding. I named him Dandy, and he was dandy good. He was broke in a fashion, as I recall he tried to buck me off and succeeded many times. He took a lot of control, but by then I was at least twelve and strong enough to hold him. **He was my pal** and I rode him many miles trying to help my folks get a little herd of cattle built up."

After Lola married Harvey Blossom, they left the area and worked on the Horseshoe Ranch near Beowawe in Nevada for eight years. While her husband did ranch work, Lola often cooked for large crews and **worked from daylight to dawn.** Moving back to Idaho in the Cherry Creek area, they begun raising cattle, a small band of sheep, chickens and a big garden with the necessities it took **to keep a family going when you live in rural Idaho.**

"As the years passed and the herd progressed, we were able to go into town, (Twin Falls) once a month. When four horses were gone from the lower pasture, we went looking. We never found them, but several weeks later the young ones came trotting down the road. I feel the older ones were shot for coyote bate, as at that time, the coyote skins brought more than good meat did."

"On our ranch at Three Creek we remodeled the house of my parents and eventually ran up to two hundred head of mixed breed cattle. It was a small ranch for the area in later years. We've had a lot of cowboy help, some were real characters, but many that were good to know. In the 1950's we watched the coyotes increase and cause a lot of trouble and then the helicopters came in with marksman and slowed that problem."

"Some years later, I wrote for the <u>Owyhee Avalanche</u>, where I met many friends in the Bruneau area. This newspaper originated in Silver City in 1874: moved to Murphy and is one of the oldest newspapers in Idaho."

"I also became a riding friend of Frances and Shenny. The Shenebergers often came out to ride the canyons of Three Creek. Sometimes they spent the night at our house along with Marge Heiss, a friend of theirs. There was also Dr. Landwiler's family who liked to hunt and camp near our place. I like to say we had lots of friends—**Doctors, lawyers, and Indian Chiefs visited us at Three Creek."** Lola laughed a joyous laugh that was all her.

"Those middle years at the ranch, I rode a bay horse named Johnny that kept me paying attention guessing what he was going to shy about. **He could swap ends pretty fast.** However, my favorite, I guess, was a pretty palomino cow horse named PoGo. My brother, Ray Colyer and his wife, Bonnie brought him for me. I rode him till he was retired, I was seventy-two at the time. One day I had just tied him up to an evergreen tree when a big robin flew out of her nest and hit me in the head, bounced off me onto the neck of the horse and got mixed up in his mane. It frightened PoGo nearly out of his wits."

"One of my most frightening experiences on a horse was being out in some of our spring **lightening storms.** For miles there was **no place to go.** This one day Harvey and I decided to get off the horse, tie them in brush a ways away from us, while we went to lie down in a lower ravine. While the storm was raging, and lightening cracking all around and rain pouring down, I looked up into the eyes of my horse, Johnny. It seems he did not want to be left alone."

"There was another time we were pushing cattle toward home when a streak of lightening came down between us and the cattle. My horse spun around and the sound made our cattle run like crazy. We had animals running in all directions. **It took a day to collect them.** Things like this and a little cattle rustling, made life interesting."

Carla asked Lola to tell me about one of their many honors they were awarded.

She replied, "In 1994 we were inducted into the **Southern Idaho Livestock Hall of Fame.** It was a real nice award. And the following year, were made <u>Life Time Honorary Members</u> of the 71 Livestock Association. We came a long way after the **criticism I got for marrying a Native American man,"** Lola chuckled at the memory of those early days saying, "it was not "popular" to do this, but I never regretted it, Harvey was a very kind, hardworking man."

Lola lost Harvey just five years ago which is why she moved to Filer. She told me she misses Harvey and living in the range country.

"But a person does what they have to do and I feel good at ninety and just had a great birthday party with many friends here, my brother and nephews to name a few." Lola giggled over the fact that she had received five cakes. She offered me a piece from one. We had a good time getting acquainted. I found out she was an avid reader of local history. (One more thing we had in common.)

Looking around her front room I see many chronicles of Lola and Harvey's life together including the **Idaho Cattlemen of the year document**. Hanging on the walls are pictures of the two of them on nice ranch horses. There were the hand braded rawhide ropes and bridles they had made with a pretty bit that was showing it had a lot of use. I saw their many branding irons hanging on the wall and a beaten, western, felt hat hanging over a doorway. All this was mingled with many books, mostly of western history. There were pictures of their friend's children who she keeps in touch with today.

Lola and Harvey's story is of a successful ranching couple. Lola said, "I give credit to **hard work from daylight to dawn**—it was a good life and I enjoyed every minute of it." Lola smiled as she handed me another piece of her birthday cake. She continued, "But as I often say, **Trust your neighbors, but brand your calves.**"

+++++

Diane Sawyer Meeks: Jerome

From an Outfitters Family to a Ranch in Jerome

"Filling my lungs with horse sweat is best for my soul!" This quote from Diane where she resides at Sugar Loaf ranch near Jerome may not be completely understood unless you read about her upbringing. It is a story of Diane and her families' early lives when they lived in a remote area . . . enjoy.

"Horses have nearly always been a part of my life. My parents Dick and Lareal Sawyer are from Magic Valley but moved to Northern Nevada to find work. In 1958 when I was five, we moved to Virginia Lakes Pack Station where as **outfitters** we built many camps for the visitors that we took into the area. Nestled at an elevation of 9600 feet on the backside of Yosemite National Park, we spent June through September there. The two room cabin we lived in didn't have any electricity and the only cold water was at a hand pump in the kitchen sink. Our baths were taken in an aluminum tin tub when we heated the water for mother with our help, cooked on a woodstove for the five of us and the four wranglers we hired to help with the horses and pack mules. Both sets of our grandparents and my dad's brothers and their families, often helped with all the chores and taming the many mustangs Dad had acquired a few years earlier. Our herd consisted of around eighty horses and forty mules we used to pack other families into the high country near Dunderberg Mountain. It was a beautiful area that sheltered us, our corrals, tack shed and bunkhouse. As our horses and mules grazed in the evenings we put cowbells on the lead horses and mules for Dad and the wranglers to be able to retrieve them for the next days work. Many times we would set the guests up with their own camp and leave them into the back country for several weeks before we brought them back. This would include some Boy Scout troops with all their gear."

"The lakes we went by were exquisite in beauty and isolation. However some of the trails were called 'The Steppes' which ran along a very narrow rocky ledge. This required us to lead the pack mules down two at a time. There were many yards of low hanging pines, dark lichen covered rocks and at the end an ever upward trail. One of our treasured mares, Ebony miss-stepped and went over the ledge. It was a sad day when we had to put her down. I had to get used to this setback from the lives of our animals."

"Sometimes when Mom, my sister and I did not go out with the pack team one of my fondest memories was watching for a little mule named Jenny to come home to the meadow near the cabin. This told us that my dad and brother, Dennis and the crew would be coming home within an hour. Jenny always beat them home and Mother and I would put her in the corral. At these times, my sister and I would wade in the creek near the cabin where we caught tadpoles. It was a great place to grow up."

"When school started Mom would move us kids back to Hawthorne but we looked forward to the weekends when we could join their fall camps back in the mountains. I still think of our evenings at the pack station with the bon-fire as we roasted hot dogs and marshmallows. There would be competitive rounds of horseshoes with some of the area Park Rangers, guests and family. My little sister Lanea and I had crushes on two of our favorite teenage wranglers who were from the Piute Indian tribe. This time in my life was just a good time to grow up in."

"Today, here in Jerome when we have lightening storms, they don't frighten me like they did when living in that small cabin with the tin roof. The ping, ping noise of the rain and hail along with the crack of the thunder at that elevation, seemed to us kids that we were in the heavens where it originated."

"When our family was able to move back to Idaho where we purchased a home and attended high school in Jerome. I enjoyed meeting new friends, but as I think of the summer days of my youth and a chance to grow up around horses, I realize today why I am always happy on my horse Grasshopper here at our ranch. I ride when we move our cattle from pasture to pasture and as often as I can. Where Jim and I like to go is to ride in our Idaho Sawtooth Wilderness—its home to me as it reminds me of the days of my youth."

I knew Diane and her sister from their high school days in Jerome and was very glad to renew a friendship to such nice people. I learned Diane took Jim to the Dunderberg Mountain range one summer to show him the "old outfitters place". Thank you, Diane, for your story and happy trails.

+++++

Marilyn Aggelar: Twin Falls
Painter-White Horse along the Snake River

I met Marilyn when I went to see her art work at a showing in Twin Falls. I knew when I viewed her beautiful art work that she had been a part of the landscape. Her heart was in her work. I asked her to paint me a picture for the book I was writing. She said she would try to find the time. When she called me with the **'White Horse along the River' painting**, I was elated. I asked her for her horse related memoirs.

This is Marilyn's horse story.

Crossing the Owyhee River

"Last year I went back to see the old place, it was there, but many of the old roads were not. We were not able to see much of the canyons, creeks, and places where we had lived and worked. I felt bad as the activity of trucks and saws at the old site excited me, but there wasn't any of this. It was that I had reached out to recapture the past and felt empty when we left."

"When I was two, **I lived on a cattle ranch in Leadore** and was there through my late teens. It was there where I experienced my first real relationship with horses. Dad dreamed of having a cattle ranch and of course he knew that we needed horses for this. One of these horses was an older mare; she was a pretty buckskin named Fawney. We had a bay pony too that the four kids of our family called Babe. Bareback riding became a natural pastime as it was mostly 'mane-reined' for us."

"In the winter months, either horse could be harnessed to the sled and the buggy when weather permitted. I learned to respect and care for both horses and they were never mistreated. We loved them like we did all our other pets. We grew up that way, with not a lot, but we raised most of our own food and had plenty of love."

"I was married, to a rancher when I was in my late teens. We lived in Jordon Valley where I rode on long rides. I was often the only woman on many cattle drives and I also fixed breakfasts and supper for all the crew. We drove cattle into spring, summer and fall pastures. One trail I remember was a drive **across the Owyhee River** to a place called **The Hole in the Wall.** There were no roads, so we had to drive the herd to where the trucks were parked near the holding pens. We stayed at the line shack which was called the "Pink Lady" as we rounded up cattle over hundreds of acres of BLM land. I rode with my little terrier dog, Missy. She was perched on the front of my saddle."

"I was scared to death on the first adventure of crossing the main river. I think it helped that I hung on tight to my dog until we were across. I fully loved and respected my horse for she never faltered or shied from my novice riding. Many times the spring run-off was high and I thought my little mare would slip. I had my knees pulled up to the saddle horn to keep from having water soaked boots. But that mare never failed and kept me safe."

"My husband decided to end the cattle operation and we spent the next two years at Orofino after our two sons were born. My in-laws leased land for a logging operation. I became cook and helper, fixing lunches early morning for the loggers, kept the wood stove stoked all day for baking bread, cakes and main meals. There was no running water, electricity. The tar-paper shack was insufferable hot with dust everywhere from the huge logging trucks rolling by the camp. It was quite an adventure for a very young woman with such young sons."

"When we moved on a cattle ranch, horses were more than an asset. Of all the horses we had one that seemed the most promising for herding and cutting ended up being my horse. The mare was only partly broke with a nasty disposition and though I worked with her she bucked me off many times. Eventually we came to terms. She began to trust me, but I never did her."

"After many years, I moved back to Idaho leaving my love of an active horsewoman behind. I knew my later years would not include the enjoyment of owning another beautiful horse. Hopefully, Joey, my granddaughter will be able to pass our mutual love for horses to her own little girls, Evelyn and Emery"

Thank you, Marilyn, for your art work, for your friendship and especially your memoir.

+++++

Karolee (Lee) Blackwell: Glenns Ferry

"My Desire to go back to Idaho was Strong"

*Talented at **horse hair hitching** as well as working with young horses . . .*

Lee quoted an old Arab poem, "A Horse quote: Uphill—hurry me not, downhill—flurry me not."

When asked about rewards with horses, she replied, "One with horse, One with God.

It's a feeling you can't attain with anything else."

Lee journeyed back to the ranch country when she was twelve years old. She had stayed with her mother in California for several years, but her desire to be back on her dad's ranch near Glenns Ferry was so great that she tried to travel by herself, but her dad came and got her. Now I understand why Lee feels as she does about life at her home.

Lee and her husband Sam, now reside on a ranch stead that is located about eight miles north-east of Mountain Home down Bennett Mountain Road marked also as the Oregon Trail Road. At Cold Springs Creek , where **their winter ranch** is located, their land was homesteaded by Sam's father, it boarders BLM ground. A covey of Hungarian partridges flew up in front of us as we drove onto the lane to their ranch home.

When I met Lee I learned that she had just acquired a grant to learn more about <u>Horse Hair Hitching</u> in a class at Boise. Before that class she was self taught, her learning was from books that she had studied and applied. During the Intermountain Horse Associations yearly meeting in Jerome, she was selling some of her beautiful, hair hitching work, where I also was selling my <u>Journey Series</u> novels of western romance. Since that time our friendship grew and we have shared tables to sell our wares. I enjoy seeing her beautiful work of items she has created. Today she mostly does consignments of belts, headstalls, and reigns as well as smaller related items. People see her work and ask, "Will you make one for me?"

Today when Lee goes out to check cattle, she rides a Paint/Quarter horse named, Nifty. This **open range country has beautiful views from this high plateau**. They raise cows, calves and a few horses where they winter them all at the Glenns Ferry homestead ranch.

The summer place is a third generation cattle ranch.

"I enjoy working with the young colts, and we begin to train them while we move the cattle so they can be **sold as working cow-horses**."

"There was a story of Alex the Great that had watched one of his horses act wild, and he asked why a beautiful horse such as this horse couldn't be ridden. I often asked this question of the problem horses that were on my dad's ranch. We raised mixed blood mares with a Anglo Arab stallion and found their feet tough and were good 'rock' horses. One of the first ones was a great running horse named Flame. My sister and I often rode her in **competition in the barrels**. I remember a mare named Julie that didn't always want to go into the arena. She was a good horse to queen on, show in 4-H and do gymkhana competition on. **My favorite event** to compete in **was pole bending** as I enjoyed teaching my horse the rhythms of the run. It was a lot of fun and a good place to meet others who liked horses."

"My mature, growing up days left me 'out of territory' or yearning for a horse. Then fifteen years ago I got that chance when I married Sam. Since then I have enjoyed that 'one with horse' feeling and there is no other like it. **I love this relaxed life**. No neighbors, very few trips to town, (one a month); yes, it's **an independent feeling out here**."

++++

Stacie Harvey: Thistle Creek Ranch, Wilder
Horses are in My Blood

Mountain Trail Challenge

"Seeing people have fun and the quality of families that participate is very satisfying," Stacy said as we talked about why she began the format of the long anticipated ranch she now has. "This ranch has **permanent Mountain Trail Challenges** that have been developed on two of the ranch's fifteen acres. This obstacle course of fallen branches, bridges, ditches, shallow pieces of loose stone and other items for a horse to cross teaches them to do well on most mountain and desert trails. And I teach it is a test of both the rider and the horse, the rider controls the horse and the horse must have confidence in the rider. I have learned that most of the time, **the quality of the bond between them makes their success.**"

Stacy had competed in a Mountain Trail Challenge in Oregon and had enjoyed it so much that four years ago she began to build their Thistle Creek Ranch into what it is today.

"I went with 'The Challenge', because it is more relaxed than other horse related events. We have older riders who love to ride and come here just to enjoy the horse again. From all over the Northwest there are many 4-H groups and families that come to compete. We also provide some clinics for the owner to better understand how to control the horse. To see other people's happiness when succeeding in The Trail Challenge is very rewarding to me."

"I am rewarded the most when I have a good relationship with my horse. This is what makes riding so much fun—to be a team. With such busy lifestyles, it's wonderful to get on a horse to enjoy the great outdoors and see what God has created. I believe we should take the time and enjoy life."

I learned that **Stacie is a recovering cancer patient.** After her recovery Stacie wanted to start showing horses again. When she bought Rudy, this tall grey was perfect for English showing.

"This new eventing has been unbelievably fun, but a lot of work," Stacie said with a smile.

We are Women and We are Strong

This is Stacie's story.

"I was born in Arco to Trudy Gibson of Jerome. Mom later met and fell in love with, Joe Terherst, of Green Forest, Arkansas. Joe had two daughters from a previous marriage, Willmetta Terherst and Jonetta Terherst. They combined their families and made their home in Arkansas.

I remember my love for horses started with a little Shetland Pony named Lady when we lived in Arkansas. My dad's parents Glenford & Nellie Terherst had a huge farm with a few horses. One of them was Lady. She was just the right size for my sisters and me. We rode her as much as she would let us ride her. When she was tired, she headed for the cloths line to have us **dismount her way.** We called it being "cloths lined". I don't think we ever got off her the normal way. Grandpa and Grandma Terherst had several other horses but I remember looking at the biggest horse I had ever seen. Her name was Star and I wanted to ride her. Sometimes I would get lucky enough to have one of my aunts take me for a ride on her. The Terherst farm holds some very dear memories for me."

"We later moved back to Jerome where my mother's side of the family resided. My father was a hunter—a bear hunter. I was raised going bear and coon hunting, fishing, and all other activities that a farm kid did. I learned to shoot, track, and train dogs, pull porky pine needles out of dogs, bait a fishing hook and even clean that dang old fish. I loved the thrill of a hunt with coon hounds. I still do as I get that natural rush or high. Dad's friend named, Willie, had a black horse that I would go and stare at. She was the most beautiful horse I had seen, except Star in Arkansas. One day Willie came over and asked me if I wanted to buy her. 'Well of course,' was my answer as a seven year old. He asked how much money I had and I only had around seven pennies. Well you know how this is going to end up, I ended up with a beautiful black mustang off the Nevada Range that I named Cocoa and she was all mine. I did everything on that horse, my sisters and I made a homemade saddle with a gunny sack and rope. We fell off quite a bit as double riders. I was usually lucky because I landed on my sister when she hit the ground. Probably because of that reason my dad decided that we needed another horse, which is where Mustard came into the picture. My sisters and I rode many miles on those horses. Those horses put us through fences, under trees, dumped us in stickers, stepped on us, ran from us, yes we got hurt, but that was the life of having our **baby sitters be horses**. We played cowboys and Indians; we were in parades and even joined a 4-H group called Leather 'N' Lace, led by Freddie Hopkins Stacy, in Jerome. Using those two horses taught me so much about life, myself, my friends. They were my best friends at times when I could just put my head on their neck and cry. It's **the soothing feel of a horse** that can take so many worries away. They taught me patience and anger. They were my vehicles, my friends and I would just take off on the horses in the morning and be back at dusk. We sometimes rode to the Snake River Canyon, to the desert, and other times we would just follow the railroad track into town. Oh but those railroad tracks into town can be bad if you take a wrong turn. I did one time and somehow we ended up on a railroad track that went over water. What to do? Who would have thought that Mustard would then end up with all four legs between the railroad tracks dangling in the air? How the heck were we going to get out of this mess? We started walking back to the house and to this day I have no idea how that horse got himself out and came running over to me. Another lesson taught, never give up. Some years later we lost Mustard. Life lesson . . . death. These animals that we spend so much time with and **know your deepest secret,** how could they leave us all alone? But with owning and loving animals comes learning to let go."

"In my high school years I decided that I was going to take after my mother and rodeo and enter queen contests. Well, I couldn't do it on overweight Cocoa. We looked and I ended up with two wonderful horses that were lent to us. Their names were Bobbie and Emmers and they had speed for high school rodeo and I enjoyed the contests on them. Being a rodeo queen could be like being a Miss America but with boots, spurs and well, a hat. Ok, at that time it *was* all Polyester outfits too. Oh so much attention! I learned how to walk, talk, stand, ride, interview, chew my food and answer impromptu questions. I learned to Vaseline my teeth, poke hair pins in my head or should I say my hair. I learned to drive a horse trailer and find my way home after being lost. We were beauty queens and were expected to act like a lady of rodeo. Three women were inspirations to me in this time of my life: **Karen Lavens James (Miss Rodeo Idaho then Miss Rodeo America) her daughter Joni James Smith (Miss Rodeo Idaho then Miss Rodeo America.** Karen knew me, as Joni and I grew up together, and went to school together. My mother was another inspiration. Her love for horses was passed down to me. She schooled me, groomed me, and showed me how to get back on when my two legs went on one side of the horse and she was there when I won and lost. She had great words of wisdom and she had a nice big stick. Thank you, mom for giving me life."

"I was holding the crown of Filer, Wranglerette Queen, and next I was supposed to run for Nampa Stampede Queen, if I could capture that it I was on my way to Miss Rodeo Idaho. Well, God and life had other ideas for me. I was at college and met the most gorgeous man in Sacramento, Ca. and I decided to work for him. We were married in June and horses and competing were done for that stage of my life. It was time to grow up and be a wife for my husband Dennis and mother for my beautiful boy, Bryan. At twenty-three, two years later, came Rebecca. The horses and farm life may be gone, but they were never out of my heart. Like the sign says **you can take the girl from the farm but you can't take the farm out of the girl.** We bought into the American Dream when we found two great horses, Woodrow and Lacy."

"After ten years, these two horses moved with us to Caldwell, Idaho. **I started a 4-H group** in Canyon County called Leather N Lace, that group is still going today after thirteen years. My son showed Woodrow in 4-H for several years as well as my nephew, Daniel. We have had many long hours on that horse in the hills. Rebecca took Lacy in 4-H her first year, she did so well. We were getting Lacy ready for a class and had her tied up to the stall front, when she spooked, pulled back then came down on the sharp point of the stall door. She had ran that into her chest and cut her radial nerve which made her front leg non-working. We put Lacy down a few months later. At nine, Rebecca started learning quick about being attached to horses and losing them. Two other horses came into her life for show season, Brownie and Brick Ridge. She did well in showmanship those two horses winning round robin three times. Rebecca also learned to ride English. (Hmmm that is a very interesting thing for me, this English). I didn't even know how to put on an English saddle, much less the bridle. The last year Rebecca was in 4-H she did a speech telling her story about **not giving up.** Here was a little girl that lost her first horse at a fair and went on competing. About Becca—she had to have four years of speech therapy because she couldn't pronounce her words correctly. The title of her speech was, "I think I can, I think I can with 4-H I know I can" She talked about overcoming and conquering. She had the audience in tears as well as her mom and dad. Her story was of heart ache of losing her horse and being made fun of because of her speech problem. I am one very proud mom.

In 2005 at age thirty-seven, **I was diagnosed with Kidney Cancer**. Boy, can that news take you down a bit, but I new God would take care of me. I didn't have any usual symptoms of kidney cancer, except being tired and wanting to sleep 24 hours a day. It all went pretty fast, the surgery; then the healing had to begin. I new that God was with me in the surgery room, as my doctor was a Christian man and my nurse too. We prayed before I went into surgery, all was good. HE was with me."

"I was not prepared for what followed. I could barely get out of bed for a week. While I was in the hospital recovering, we sold our house and all emotions came out then. I came home from the hospital to finish recovering with strict instruction not to lift anything over ten pounds. Well dang it, my cat weighs over ten pounds. How was I going to pack and move into a new house when I couldn't pick anything up? FRIENDS, FAMILY, they packed for me, they painted, they unpacked my boxes. They showed LOVE. During the recovery time, I have never had that helpless feeling before. Dennis bought me a swing to sit and look at the unbelievable views from the other home. You could see the Snake River **and the Owyhee rolling hills from my front yard.** I did a lot of thinking and praying during this healing time of my life."

"One thing that I wanted to do was learn to **ride English.** I worked it all out down to the type of horse that I wanted, a big gray one. A trainer just happened to have a big gray gelding that I saw and fell in love. Ted, a great trainer, worked with this two year old. Then came the time for me to ride him; with the palms sweating, and **my nerves jumping, I got on**. Oh, it felt just right, me even at the walk, since I was too dang scared to trot or lope. Will I screw him up, what if I cue him wrong, **what if I fall off?** I practiced and learned. I also found muscles where I didn't know I had them. I had to two point and other crazy things that you never had to do in a western saddle. This was a hard transition, but **was the most rewarding thing I had done.** I was hooked and had *new* goals to strive for on a horse. Even Rebecca and I showed a few times together. We did very well. I am still learning things every day. My trainer, his wife and Kelsey and Katie have been such a great support system on the horse show circuit for me."

"How we began Thistle Creek Ranch is as follows. One of my best friends, Terri, told me about this new horse sport going on in Eugene, Oregon and that she wanted to go down and try it. I asked if I could go, she said YES! We took the big trailer and truck and headed out to try this new type of trail competition. Eight hours later, we scouted the place out. It was amazing; the owner had taken an outdoor trail course and put it in the arena. We were in awe. Terri did very well at the end and we had a great time—so great that all the way home we had a plan for Wilder, Idaho. Terri and I came up with a business; Terri's dad had the equipment. I wondered where we would get the contestants and how we were going to go about doing it. The one thing we didn't figure out was talking with our husbands that we wanted to start a business together. But what would go wrong? **We were women and we could do it.** So in Wilder, **Thistle Creek Ranch LLC was born.** It all starts with a dream and we were dreamers Terri and I."

"Thistle Creek Ranch LLC, began as, Terri, office manager and I was the grounds person. My husband, Dennis, and Terri's husband, Tom, built the tall bridge together. We love that bridge. Horses hated it. The course has logs, and rocks—we had bruises, blisters, and stickers in all kinds of places on our bodies. We had help from Terri's kids. I have pictures of them in the mud bog all covered with mud. There is this slab of concrete that we put a canopy on and later reconstructed an old barn for our reception area. Our first challenge event was in May of 2007. **It is a test of both the rider and their horse.** The majority of our riders are above the age of thirty-five. We have several riders that are in their sixties to seventies. They don't have to have the glitz and glimmer on the outfits you wear at shows, but wear just what you would in the hills. A come as you are with a family atmosphere. We have bon-fires where everyone just sits around as if they were in the hills. We have had a young boy play his fiddle at some of the gathering and Dennis pulls out his guitar occasionally. I love that everyone cheers everyone one on. If there is someone on the course having trouble, but that person gets through it, there are claps and whistles from the onlookers."

"In the year of 2010, Dennis and I, with the economy like it is, had to cut back, but we still own the fifteen acres where Thistle Creek Ranch sits. There have been changes in our life, but **we have our family, health and friends**. We will continue with the Mountain Trail Challenge. Those things we lost this year were just that—things. We still have the most important and that is US! You continue, and you dream, you love, and sometimes you loose. We learn to be strong and continue with life. **We are women and we are strong**. We pick up pieces and bind our families together."

"There have been some special people in my life to thank—my mother Trudy, my Aunt Marilyn, my handsome son, my beautiful daughter and my husband, who I love so much you are the best blessings that God has given me. I thank God for **everyone in my life** and everything that I have gone though. They have made me the person that I am today."

+++++

Diana Lynn Shobe Adams: Moore

"You have not fulfilled your life if you have never owned a good horse."

One other branch of this Snake River system is Lost River. It is called that because it literally loses itself in the lava which underlies much of Butte County, then comes out again one hundred and fifty miles further down through the porous cliffs of the famous Thousand Springs. In running its lonely course it joins the lost things in the silent expanse of sagebrush, jackrabbits, grazing cattle and coyotes, while in the midst of the highest mountain range in Idaho.

To ride amid such grandeur one should find it impossible to ever forget what we saw in these opalescent lands and feel their force. Descriptions can never convey adequately the extravagant lavender and cobalt blues of the sunset, or the quintessentially lovely beauty of the untouched land. We could never convey how a haunted river remains just as it was amid a forgotten branch of the Oregon Trail as it wound along its crooked banks. The always fresh air at over six thousand feet did often pick up the scent of the grey sage that lined the valley floor. It was a vastness without echo, stretching between mountains that are usually snow-capped and often lost in the white, puffy clouds of summertime.

This Lost River Range is where I met Diana Adams, although she grew up with her parents on a farm near Jerome. Diana was in the upper grades when they moved to the McCammon area that she loved. At that time she wished that someday she might make her home near mountains like they had there. Her wish came true as she and her husband now have their home at Moore. They raise a large herd of horses there and view the high mountains of the Lost River Range.

This is how I met her.

"Behold the light is coming down the mountains! Ed-da-how," one of our trail riders exclaimed on our early morning ride near Antelope Creek. From a high ridge we viewed the Pioneer Mountains about twenty miles away. This Lost River Range held a magic we all felt with the view of the Pioneer range to the west, and the Copper Basin Mountains looming up in the North. Our Thursday Sage Riders leaders on this ride were **Melissa Bench** (who has a place along the creek) and **Terry Pritchett**, who now lives in Mackay. It was not long before we heard the barking of dogs and then a sharp whistle followed by the stomping and mooing of cattle. We stopped in awe to watch a lone cowgirl riding a pretty paint horse as she gave instructions to six cow-dogs and quick cues to the horse as they helped her move a small herd of cattle out of a watershed. The job was done in a few minutes and the cowgirl and her dogs pushed the cattle upon the ridge. She smiled and waved at us before disappearing over the top.

Late in the afternoon on our way back down a narrow track these same dogs came out from under a small trailer that was parked off the track. The dog's happy yaps brought out Diane Adams, the cowgirl that owned them. She greeted us with a friendliness that was enjoyed by all. In the short talk we had, I knew I wanted her to write her horse story for this book.

This is Diana's story,

"I feel that horses were part of me when I was born, as my mother rode a lot when she was pregnant with me. Maybe this is why I feel a natural ability with animals, especially horses. When I was little I would have my dad give me rides until I was old enough to ride on my own. A scar I still have on my face was given to me by a colt, but it did not detour me from horses. Dad would let my brother and I ride double on an older, well broke mare. Once while riding

83

in some trees, my brother ducked down, leaving me exposed to the head high tree branch and I was knocked off. Oh, I have been drug in the dirt by a horse I roped when I missed to dally the rope and I continued to hang on to it. My old mare just stood there looking down at me as if to say, 'well dummy, are you going to get back on'? And I did. The sad thing was that when I let go, I had to retrieve my rope. All these incidents did not discourage me from being around horses and I never got seriously hurt. Oh, I have been bucked off, kicked, bitten, stepped on, but never broke a bone (that I know of)."

"I rode a sorrel gelding named Copper at the ranch and in youth gymkhana events. He was very cowy but I would often ride him bareback. Dad said I would get dumped, but I never did. Copper was a great horse for High School rodeo. In the fall of my senior year, we were doing real well at the poles and often in the winnings, when turning around a last pole a camera man snapped a photo. The flash made Copper come to an abrupt stop and I went off and hit the dirt. I still have the photo of me landing on my butt."

"I was about nine when my dad encouraged me to train my first colt; he was a four year old appaloosa gelding that turned out great, and since then, I have been doing this for our horses and for other ranchers horses. My first horse Driftwood, that my dad sold me, was a J.B. King Skipper stallion. Then I traded a Hereford heifer for a bay and a white paint mare. This was the beginning of many horses for me and I have raised and enjoyed riding each one."

"We as a family had several years in 4-H when our three sons each had a horse project. They did not continue with horse association at that time. If I could go back I would have participated more in rodeo and attended more horse shows as I loved the challenge."

"Working with horses is my sanity. It relieves stress for me when, for the last fourteen years, I ride the range for the cattle associations during in the summer months. It is a good place to start my own colts and I have received many compliments when I have ridden others horses out on the range. This does not surprise me as I've been told I have a natural ability with horses that seem to trust me. Oh, I have to be careful with some horses for they become what I call one man horses. I was raised with the philosophy that if a horse was not a good one there was no reason to own it. You take a chance on getting hurt and so far it has proven to be true. My main horse is a palomino mare I call Goldie (Sharee Command). She has been a four time champion mare that I use today **to rope, and cut on, team pen, team sort as well as ride her on the trails.**

I show my gold mare and others at horse shows and have won top awards with them. One of my saddest stories happened six years ago at a horse show in Mackay. Our big stallion, Prides Big Zipper hemorrhaged and died of an aneurysm. I felt very helpless to help the big guy. He had the best disposition of any stallions I have owned. He sure was missed. Oh, I have had some good stallions. Five years ago I took a three year old stallion to show at halter in a horse show at Mackay. A girl friend of mine talked me into **riding the colt in the junior western pleasure class.** I had never loped the colt before that day so I had to take him to the warm up arena and hurry and get him to lope so he would know what to expect. **The colt took grand champion** that day. I was so proud of him. A friend was upset with me after we won as we beat her sister on her horse, and they had been ridding in preparation for the show all year."

"We have enjoyed belonging to the American Quarter Horse Association and the American Paint Horse Association for more than fifteen years."

"I ride every chance I get with friends and enjoy the five months I ride in the summer for the Association Ranchers. I just pray this riding does not change and the ranchers do not loose the right to turn their cattle out on the ranges to graze on the tall grasses that is so important for their growth as well as the shorter grass would help **prevent the hot and dangerous fires** in these forests."

"Recently, I became a part of the **AQHA's horseback riding program.** I log the hours I ride and after several years I received a Montana Silversmiths buckle when **I reached 5000 hours**. I am working towards a second buckle."

Diana told me that there has not been a time when horses have not been an important part of her life. She said she would not change this. And once you have lived as Diana, amid such grandeur in these Lost River hills and mountains you would find it impossible to live as unadorned as others live.

+++++

Verla Mink Ruby: Hill City/Gooding

Seven to Seventy Seven

2009: She spoke with great feeling of her early days riding at the homestead that had been in the Mink family for three generations. This area called East Demsey was named after a man that was killed by the warring Indians and then buried there. This was where an Indian war uprising had begun and it is where at the age of six, Verla Faye **nearly lost her leg and maybe even threatened her life.** No, she didn't get involved with this war, she's not that old, but it was a battle to save her leg as they were miles from a doctor.

This is Verla's story of the accident and her adventures with horses.

"The morning had started out bad. I was unable to catch Nifty my horse that I usually rode so I settled with a big horse not real well trained named Prince. There is a lot of old **barbed wire** in most areas of the old homesteads and big Prince got tangled in it and **threw me.** He was real scared, but not as much as I and after the second buck I went off. Then he **stepped on my leg**, and I yelled which frightened him more than him fighting that wiry mess. **The horse drug the wire a ways before I got free of him.** My leg was bleeding a lot and I was crying a lot, I guess from the pain and fear of seeing that much blood. My wound was from the knee to my ankle and the cutting of the wire had chewed up the flesh. I still **carry the scars.** I was weeks recovering and wore a bandage that had to be changed several times a day. I remember how much that hurt me. Mom said I screamed when the treatments were administered. When I did recover enough to get around on a pair of homemade crutches, the first thing I did was go get on a good ole' horse bareback and the spanking I got for doing this was a different kind of war," Verla said with a smile. "You see, at seventy-seven, I'm still passionate to get on a horse and I don't care if I die on a horse (what a way to go). Horses are my life."

The family moved down to **Hills City on to a four generation homestead**. One summer when Verla was a teen she and a neighborhood girlfriend Carolyn Pahl packed their horses into **Chimney Creek where they camped for several days.** When up in that area, Carolyn and Verla found an old wrecked buggy wagon that they drug off the hill and with some fixin' up they used it a lot during their teen years. Most of her saddle horses today will pull a cart, as Verla always drove them when the horse was very young as it was part of their training.

This love for horseback riding continued for years for Verla, even through the raising of her children. She and her husband Lowell and their kids would saddle up the horses and **drive the**

cattle from Wendell to the summer range of Hills City, just as in the 'old days,' Verla would say. This drive would often take several days but they loved doing it and ranching was their life.

I looked around Verla's home and saw a life filled with love, hope and pictures of horses. There was her first pair of spurs hanging on the wall; trophies of the days she spent competing as **a member of the Gooding Sheriff's posse.** There were colorful quilts with horse's pictured in them that she placed across chairs; as well as pictures of her daughter Sandra and grandson on horses.

Verla and Sandra still ride together as often as they can as Verla has been a widow now for seventeen years. When they can, **they go up to the old ranch in Hills City to ride.**

My husband and I have been to this out of the way ranch and found it a beautiful place with good trails to enjoy. We rode up one of the highest hills that overlooked the valley of Hill City. At the top was a sublime and wonderful scene. It was on Memorial weekend that the Mink-Ruby families celebrate their heritage with a three day camp out, barbeques and hearty breakfasts, and of course all enjoyed horseback riding. We met brother, grandkids, cousins, nieces, in laws and former neighbors—too many to name as well as Verla's daughter, Sandra, and her two sons Bret and Terry. We enjoyed a day with this Ruby family where we renewed old friendships from our times we had skiing together at nearby Soldier Mountain. We were privileged to be invited to this family's annual heritage get-together, they are a special family.

Today at her acreage in Gooding, Verla harnesses her horse, Cruiser up to a cart and she and her daughter ride in most of the Gooding parades. Verla was often seen on her Tennessee Walking Horse, Crescent, until she lost this horse from an illness. Verla still rides several times a week when weather and health permits, as **horses are still her passion** just as they were seventy years ago.

+++++

Liz Allen: King Hill

"A Way with Horses"

This year I became acquainted with a fourth generation horse lover that lives in King Hill. She is Liz Allen, and I learned she is able to be a big part of their ranch business working there now full time. This makes her happy because she has more time to give to her family and the horses.

She said, "Spending time doing things you love is really a great way of life."

Of course this gives Liz, as the mother of their fourteen year old daughter, Marisha, time to ride together more, especially in the summer months.

Liz and Jim have been married sixteen years and have dealt in horse related products, **supplying the needs of any who call and desire to have a well kept horse.** This is important to each of us that have equine. A good shoeing is essential to a good riding horse, and Jim can supply that—if you call Liz and make the appointment. The next need may be a good saddle and the Allen's can supply a 'hand-made one.' And when there is time they will ride a young horse to give it experience as this is also included in their talents. Where they find time for all this, I do not know. Except Liz's husband, Jim **credits this to Liz as being a big part of this business,** making appointments, answering the phone, keeping the books and doing general chores.

It's good to meet a man who **proudly says such great things about his wife,** as far as helping with their livelihood, like Jim does about Liz.

Good riding Liz, and enjoy life as it should be. I am glad we have found new friends like you both.

Pleasure Riders

Salmon

Cecelia Regnani

Little 8-Mile Creek, Leadore

Homestead near Continental Divide

Cecelia Regnani

We see in the new trail, and register every breathtaking vista in our minds, and a few pictures we snapped. Each color vied with the others; the bluffs from chalk white to coal abaca and weird sculptures of and ancient visitor added to the magic. In all directions—all around us, our adventure had begun.

Take an Adventure to the Continental Crossing

A great scientist who was also a brilliant geopolitical man was responsible for sending the Lewis and Clark expedition to open the door, at least a crack, for U.S. expansion into the West. President Thomas Jefferson asked congress for an intelligent officer and a dozen men to go up the Missouri River to explore the whole line, even to the Western Ocean. He had heard of the **continental crossing** and wished for a trail to be blazed across it. This foothold for the United States was made necessary after the Louisiana Purchase. It transformed what would have been a semielandestine reconnaissance of foreign territory into a bold survey of American-owned land.

Cecelia Regnani: Salmon Idaho

Pleasure Rider on the Salmon River Range

When I first met Cecelia she told me about her **love for horses** and how she could not wait to get back to being a horse owner—at first, I did not know whether to put her in the chapter under those who when younger, loved to ride their horses along the beaches or a woman who loves to ride in the North Country. But it didn't take me long to decide when I met her at her home in Salmon, as the first thing we did was to go out to the pasture to see their horses.

"This is Jasmine," Cecelia proudly said as she introduced me to her big blaze-faced sorrel. I stepped up and petted the gentle mare. She loves her quiet times in the pasture and it is not uncommon for her to eat away from the other horses. She loves to be groomed and does not spook easily but is very curious about everything. She is very gentle with small children as well as non-experienced riders. Yet she loves moving cattle as Gary and **I often help our friends near town to bring their herds down from the high mountains.** She is a good packer as we use her to help us during the hunting seasons."

Later, as we pulled into the Regnani acreage, I saw a nice home that was very attractive and I complimented Cecelia on it. "One of my hobbies is gardening along with sewing, painting, and photography—I just love working with my hands," she replied.

I learned she was also very talented with acrylic painting, and many crafts. Also her husband, Gary, who had a career with the California Highway Patrol until retirement, had authored two mystery novels.

Cecelia's story is as follows.

"We had never heard of Salmon, Idaho before a friend told my husband about it, so we flew out here to check it out. As soon as we flew over the mountains and had this gorgeous valley in site, it was like **God said this is where I want the two of you to live.** Our feet had hardly touched the ground, when we found a nice home to purchase."

"I enjoy going back to the California coast to visit our adult children, but I do not miss it although I had a great childhood there. As a child we lived near the ocean. My friends and I rode our horses along the beaches, sand dunes and wooded areas of Northern California. **I loved riding on the beaches** seeing the ocean waves breaking on the shores, smelling the salt air, watching the birds and all of nature's sounds. It was so refreshing and free feeling. We loved racing our horses along the beaches with the wind in our faces. On warm days we would ride our horses out in the water and they loved it. Often we would ride bareback. It didn't matter, rain or shine, we would just ride."

"I was involved in the Mendocino Coast Riding Club. At fourteen, I competed with my horse, Rowdy, in the gymkhanas doing barrel racing, relay races, key hole, and poles and jumping. Often we placed first and won many second and third ribbons as I had a great horse and loved what I was doing."

"Now I ride with my husband, family and friends here in the valley. We average over one hundred hours a year even though the riding season here is shorter than we would like. We do ride in the winter depending on the temperature."

"We enjoy trail riding and ride mostly in the Salmon surrounding areas, but try to go to a new place every time we ride. We enjoy horn hunting; it is so much fun and is like looking for Easter eggs. There is so much public access all around us where we see wildlife abundantly and beautiful sceneries. Jasmine and I like to ride in the rear so we can take our time often talking to the Lord, just enjoying 'smelling the roses' and take a ton of pictures of God's creation. I enjoy the sounds of nature like the waterfalls and creeks that make peaceful sounds to me."

"One of my favorite rides is up Freeman Creek, beautiful along the creek with green foliage. Up there we pass an old log cabin and an old sawmill near the ridge. At the top we can see most of the mountains in the area with jagged rock formations. I often wonder how the people that lived in those cabins faired the winters up so high. It makes me think how blessed we are to have all of the luxuries in life. But I think it would have been very nice to live back then. On the warmer summer days **we ride toward the Continental Divide** as that elevation cools the horses down. I enjoy the outdoors and the riding that it now afforded me."

"We are so blessed to live in Idaho. God's hand was in the move we made here eight years ago; this is where He wants us to live."

Welcome to our beautiful state Cecelia and I am glad you enjoy it here and I am looking forward to riding together in the coming year.

+++++

The Rides We Took: In the next three days there was time for visiting as we rode our horses together. The first day we went up Freeman creek out of Carmen, to view all the old buildings and several mines. This valley was beautiful, as the spring had been wet leaving flowers everywhere and the view at the top of the ridge overlooked the Salmon River valley below. We rode into rolling grass of a large meadow and went by log structures—homes and sheds, that still stood; we talked of the lifestyles of the early families that had lived here. This journey to the other side of the mountain was living connections of America's past carrying forward the traditional skills of the pioneers.

The next day at Little 8 Mile Creek (in the picture) we had a good climb as the trail up took us into a canyon where we came to a beautiful lake. In the early afternoon there were reflections in the glassy lake of the mountains that lay beyond. The granite mountain sides, with a maze of tan color, seemed the sort of place where outlaws would 'hole up'. As it narrowed, walls of rock rise up on both sides of the trail. Beyond this rugged landscape the streamside habitat along the 8 Mile Creek looked nearly undisturbed except for an occasional animal trail leading to the cool, clear stream. This is a place I can become enchanted by. As we rode up to the pass I felt like I was a part of the early expeditions that came this way in the early eighteen hundreds. According to the map, very near here, is the continental divide pass and it is marked as the way Lewis and Clark journeyed.

If you get a chance to flee the city, load a good trail horse and disappear into the wilderness of the covered wagon days, I do recommend this area. I believe it made us feel even more civilized with this opportunity to see another part of Idaho's vast wilderness.

+++++

The small settlement of Rogerson has been on the Idaho map for more than one hundred years. Today the residents there and the ranches surrounding it depend on the friendly, helpful people who have for generations run Helen's Convenient Store along highway 93. As you come into the community from the north, you see a nice arena and often there are people riding and working horses. Nearby there are pastured several pretty Quarter Horses. I often wondered who they belonged to and who uses the arena, so I stopped at Helen's place to ask some questions of Helen's daughter, Anita. Anita Robinson gave me some answers and as we visited I asked her for her journey with horses and about this year's **class she was taking with horses.** She consented to write for me because she hoped to **"give something back"** when she completed it.

While there having a good cup of coffee, I met Logan, Anita's daughter, who loves animals and has ridden. She is now a student at CSI taking classes that will help her when she gets into a veterinarian school, as her goals direct her. She is success oriented, so look for her when she hangs up her shingle.

And good luck to Randi, Anita's youngest daughter. She is a young lady who loves riding her horse and competing in rodeo events this year.

Mom, daughter, and granddaughters—all horse enthusiasts, what a fine family!

I received this story of the memoir of the **Brass Horse,** written by Anita Robinson—enjoy.

Anita Robinson: Rogerson

To Give Something Back

When I was little my brother got one of those saddled-up **brass horses**. It even had the detailed headstall with the free-swinging chain for reins. My plastic horses were much prettier and had removable saddles and came in all sorts of colors as well. Yet there was something about the sturdiness of the brass horse. Funny how one simple moment in a day can change or rectify the direction of you path in life."

"Forty some years later as I was dusting it, my heart was swept back to a time when **horses were almost everything to me.**"

"Flashes of my fifth birthday, me with a new saddle, just my size atop, Tinker, my Mom's mare. And us packing a lunch with her and riding up Harold's Canyon pretending to be a barrel racer, a jockey, a cowgirl, all the while trying to learn to ride better. Just Tinker and me, she was my best friend."

"Flashes of when I was eight my Dad got sick with cancer. Tinker listened as she took me far away into the sunset. She was an angel."

"Flashes of the day my Mom said we did not have enough money any more to feed her and her buddies, Brandy, my Dad's gelding, and Tuana, her foal. It was because of all the hospital bills. I cried. **I buried my tears** in her beautiful, soft brown neck until the trailer came to take them away".

"Flashes of my wonderful 4-H steers who helped me buy Beggar when I was a junior in high school. He was big, black and so fast, and he loved to goat tie. I did not know how to teach him to come to a sliding stop, so some say we started the run by. Wow! What a send off he would give me. We made quite a team until I had to sell him. At least he went to a good home."

"Flashes of Logan and Randi with Dixie, an old mare given to them, and her newborn foal. We called her Snow's Dancing Ghost or Snow Princess for short. She was Logan's best friend."

"Flashes of the much joy she brought us. She was loaded with talent and ability, not to mention personality plus! Snow was amazing. She was a gift and when she was five she died a terrible death and it changed us. It changed my Logan."

"Flashes of our other horses lined up at the fence nickering as we lowered Snow Princess into her grave. It changed everything."

"Flashes of my Amigo, truly everyone's friend. I paid $300 for him to a family that was moving when young "grade" colts were only bringing $50, but they needed the money. There is something to be said about the "eight cow wife" or the "$300 colt". He lived up to his price. Because of their lack of understanding they were a little abusive to him. But he trusted us and would do anything for us. He died just a few months after Snow. He was just three. Thankfully we got a foal out of him before he died. She's so much like him."

"Flashes of memories, some of the happiest and saddest times of my life came to me as I held the **brass horse** in my hands. I questioned myself. With horses such a part of my early years where were they now? Why did I change direction without them? Yes, we still have horses and I ride a little, but I knew it was not enough. My path with them is somehow one. We are meant to be one. I do not know what that means. I hope to someday. As I put the sturdy, **brass horse** back on its shelf, a number came to me from a memory twenty-five years previous, 733-9554. It was the number to the College of Southern Idaho. I dialed and asked about the **equine massage class**, and if they still have it and were there any openings left. I was told "one", and it was mine and I knew it."

"They teach me. They talk to me. They listen to me. **They are sturdy to me like the brass horse.** I love horses. It's time to continue our journey together, and on our way to **give some thing back** to them as they continue to teach me and help me on my path. Thank you for a great class and lots of healing."

This class is called the Equine Massage Therapy class located at CSI. It is led by Melissa Bench who has been the instructor for eight years. I have talked to others who have enjoyed this class and each replies that when you give to your course group, the equine will respond to you in return. The other great gifts you get when mother and daughter is in this class together, the therapy in oneness abounds. It is a special way to bond—people or horse. And Melissa just asked that you enjoy it.

Mules Riders

Karen Majerus

Abby & Karen

Myra Beck

Karen Majerus

Kathy Kerley

Kathy Kerley

Kathy Kerley

A Mule is the offspring of a cross between a male Donkey and a female horse. As a general rule, a mule has the front end of a donkey and the back end of horse—they have a donkey head, with long ears, an upright mane, strong legs; and horse-like hindquarters with a long tail. Mules are more popular and are more commonly seen today. They are exceptionally strong and have good stamina and usually, a good, quiet temperament. They are enjoying a revival in America where they are used for pleasure riding and even jumping competitions.

We all have our own kind of life to pursue;
Our own kind of dreams to be weaving
And we all have the power to make wishes come true:
As long as we keep on believing.

+++++

Myra Beck: Burley

Woman of Many Talents

650 Miles Riding a Mule—One Summer Ride

I first met Myra at the Jerome History Days celebration last year as she was sitting on the tongue of their covered camp wagon with her husband, Glen and grandson, Derringer. The Beck's had just completed the planned historical trek along the Old Kelton Road, which for two days as a horseback outrider, I also accompanied the five wagons as they rode into my county. Getting to meet Myra was a real plus to me as the drivers of the other wagons informed me that **she had ridden as their outrider the first three days**. On those early June days, it **rained, snowed and hailed**, but **she never quit** until, for two days, the mud restricted the ride for all of them.

I learned that **Myra's dream** of riding across Nevada (where she lived in her younger days) on a horse was fulfilled. Several years ago **she rode a mule as the outrider of the wagon group** that traveled to Bishop, California where the Mule Days Celebration is held each year. The mules she rode were 1450 pound mules and up to 16hh. Many of them **she had raised herself.** Myra's husband told me she works with their equine consistently and is responsible for the quiet manner in which their mules perform.

Myra and her husband, Glen, are members of the local Mule Skinner's Club. In April of 2002, they left Burley bound for Bishop, California with three other mule drawn wagons and an outrider. Each wagon was pulled by a four-abreast hitch of mules. They expected to arrive at their destination by the last weekend in May. The 650 mile journey takes about **six weeks averaging twenty miles a day** by mule train.

Myra has taken shorter rides aboard a saddled mule but never one this long. She told me she enjoyed looking at the ranches stretching across Nevada remembering as a child she was inspired to cross the state in a saddle.

Their newly made (sheep camp type) wagon was equipped with food that was partly refrigerated by propane refrigerators and also has a comfortable sleeping bed. The wagon wheels were equipped with disc brakes and a new front axel supported the front half.

Myra said she enjoyed leading the wagon train, saddle mounted on a different "Beck Mule" every day.

"**I am the trainer** and this way I get a chance to school the beloved mules. Some of my favorites are Debbie, Dinah, Daisy and Sampson, to name a few," Myra said.

Upon arrival to the Celebration of Mule Days, the Idaho group planned to participate in various races. I greatly admire Myra for her skills with these mules and it was my pleasure to meet her and talk about her adventures and the courage she has to tackle the unpredictability of what may come with trusting a team and riding one of them, with so much ease. She had brought **a taste of the past** with every mile they traveled. You will also read about Myra in the Drill Teams Chapter as she is a woman of many talents.

+++++

Kathy Kerley: Jerome

I met Kathy three decades ago when we rode together on the trails with the **Thursday Sage Riders.** She is a good friend and I admire her giving heart as well as her fun personality.

"Stay on the Trail"

A year ago, Kathy Kerley introduced me to the **High Desert Back Country Horse Club** here in Magic Valley and gave me the following information. The suggested rules put out by the Back Country Horsemen of Idaho are very good.

1. Don't cut switchbacks.
2. Try to keep stock in single file on the trail.
3. Loose stock can stray off trail and cause trail damage.
4. Repair and clear trail if needed to avoid detours.
5. Don't run horses for safety reasons.
6. When meeting other stock users, whoever can get off the trail easiest should do so. a. when you meet hikers be courteous and take time to talk with them. b. explain the advantage if they stand on the downhill side.
7. When stopping for lunch, tie all stock well off the trail and hobble if necessary.
8. Watch wildlife from a distance—keep quiet and keep moving.

I thought of an old poem I remembered reading by Rudyard Kipling that went something like this . . . "*They shut the road through the woods seventy years ago. But when you enter the woods, you will hear the beat of the horse's feet steadily cantering through the old lost road through the woods.*" I know it is not quoted completely or correctly, but I thought of it as I think of the Back Country Horse Clubs, as they clean many trails.

The BCH club philosophy is *to disguise the sight and sound of your passage, leaving no sign that you were ever there.*

These are the words I read in a newsletter written by Kathy Kerley. She has been the secretary of this Magic Valley club for many years. Many Saturdays she rides with the other members **cleaning many of the trails** that we all use. Even a serious **accident** and two bouts with **cancer** did not keep Kathy from riding.

Truly Charmed by a Horse

"You can be a rider of both horses and mules—if you change your mindset," Kathy said. And this is her story.

"The mountains have been my passion for years—such peace! I can get on my horse or mule and go to the great outdoors and ride for most of the day and I forget my troubles, fears and doubts. Do you think most people can hide themselves in something they so enjoy that it **may change their life?**" Kathy asks me.

I agree as I look at my longtime friend and see Kathy as I remembered her when our teenage children were in school together. In those days, Kathy was slim (still is), she had pretty shoulder length blond hair and still does. Her smile was sweet and often followed by a slight laugh and even that has not changed. I smiled remembering **the dozens of trail rides** we had together.

Kathy, now a single woman, has for the last thirty years, lived in a nice home on acreage near Jerome where she keeps her horse and mule. I see Kathy as an independent woman—a woman who worked, took care of her grandson for several years and **even her two serious bouts with cancer did not change her** as far as keeping her focus toward her dreams.

"These challenges might have stopped me," Kathy said. "But, it's been in me to still have that determination I have that **I'm going to ride.** The other day my friend Bonnie and I went to ride the canyon. **I saddled my gelding Tiger who is twenty-six now,** blind in one eye and has arthritic joints. I don't ride Tiger on long rides as it is probably time to retire him, but the aged Appie still loves to go. I thought heaven only knows when it's going to dry up this spring and we can go to ride in my favorite places. Down in the Snake River Canyon is good for those early rides and that is where we went with him. It was good to finally get out."

Kathy's country roots began in Nebraska when on her parent's farm, at age five she was given the reigns to drive the wagon to haul the hand picked, corn to the storage crib. At least she thought she was driving the team, but now knows that the horses were responding to her daddy's voice commands.

"From then on, I was hooked and have loved horses since. My cousin, who lived nearby, had a black Shetland that was given little attention. My dad asked Uncle Jack if Blacky, could stay at our house for a while. When he said yes, **I was very excited and rode him a lot.** However, when we moved to Idaho he was returned to my cousins. Until I was seventeen, I begged and borrowed a horse from anyone I could."

"It wasn't until I graduated and got a job did I manage to buy **Chris, my first horse**. Then when I got married and within a couple of years, we had two boys, my sister Peggy would come by and baby sit for me so I could ride. Peggy liked to ride also, so eventually we gave her a horse for helping me."

"Chris was a Palomino filly and ever so pretty! One of the events **I rode her in** was a group called **the Jerome Square Dancers**. My horse learned fast, and seemed to enjoy **performing at local rodeos**. One day, Anna, a friend of mine was riding the routine just ahead of me when it appeared that her mare would turn a corner too fast. It's like she would hear the whistle and would 'gee' when Anna thought they should have gone 'haw'. One time at a fast lope Anne tumbled to the ground at this sudden turn. I went over where she lay in the arena dirt and looked down. My flag we each carried was flying over her. I asked, 'Are you all right?' She finally got her face out of the dirt and replied, *Heck no, do I look okay?* But she was okay and we laughed over the incident. Even though performing made me nervous, **it was challenging** and fun and I would do it again."

Kathy and her pretty palomino preformed with precision and flair. Such things I will never forget as I love to watch most horse events. (I would like to add that I watched most of the Square Dancers events one summer as my daughter, Janell, rode with them, her story in Family chapter 21)

Kathy has owned several nice pleasure horses through the years. They took her on many rides through the Sawtooth Wilderness. She rode with her friends of the Thursday Sage Riders often going with Carol Sobotka and Lona Smith. She has been a member for nearly forty years. In this group of women she has established many lifetime friends.

One summer when she was looking for a horse to ride, as her horse had a growth removed, her neighbor and friend Bonnie Stacy **loaned her a mule to ride.** "They were fun and I learned that you have to change your mind set as the mule think and react differently. I had a lot of fun learning this challenge and when I did, **I bought one. His name is Dillon.** He has been with me for six years now. I think he is a beauty. We take good care of each other in the fresh air and sunshine riding the plains and hills of Idaho."

"My most serious accident on him was when he was young. It occurred while riding in the Sellway Wilderness a long way from the trailhead. We were a train of twelve horses and mules traveling on a narrow mountain side. Dillon spied a backpacker that with the tall dark pack moving above his head looked like something he had never seen. **I spoke to the hiker, but got no answer.** Dillon had stopped in his tracks and the closer the man got to us, the more Dillon backed up. When he bumped into the pack mule behind us he was knocked off the trail. We began stumbling down the steep hillside trying hard to keep upright. What stopped us were some sapling trees, but Dillon got tangled in them and dumped me off when he nearly fell. I went sliding below him landing on my back and side. It took a while for me to recover from the bruising, and **cracked rib,** but Dillon just went back up to the trail and joined the rest of the pack. After some recovery, I was helped up to where Dillon was and mounted up so we could continue to camp and I could rest there. We stayed for four days and then headed back to the trailers. I was not riding very soon after that accident **as it took several weeks for recovery.** I was just thankful Dillon stayed upright on the way down that mountain."

"I joined the Back Country Horse Club because I liked their philosophy and enjoyed the friendships. Our group, **the High Desert Club,** has summer work rides as well as informative meetings in the winter and I agreed with the need to repair and clean the trails. **This group has been responsible for keeping many trails open.**"

In their program Kathy appreciates telling others to leave the area 'without a trace' after you have camped there. "It is very important to leave it for the next generation better than you found it," Kathy continued with a gleam in her eyes. "To have a part in that is to give back what the outback country has done for me and others like me."

And being a giving person is what Kathy is all about. I would like to be more like her.

+++++

Karen Adams Majerus: Buhl

Knee High to a Grasshopper

Meeting a new friend is always an exciting time for me, especially when we feel the same thrill about riding our horses in the back country. Karen has been fun to ride with and a good rider and horse person she is, as you will learn.

This is Karen's story.

"I was born and raised on a ranch in an area that you could ride in any direction as far as you wanted and not see another person after you got out of town. This took all of three minutes. The town is Malta; at that time, just two hundred people living there. When asked "How long have you been riding horses?" My response is, "**I have been riding since I was knee high to a grasshopper.**" There is not a time that I don't remember riding. When I was too young to bridle my own horse, I was riding a saddle on a rack with a bridle that hung on a nail. I chased many an Indian and outlaws for hours that way."

"I do not remember being taught how to ride. It was just a matter of getting on and turning right to go right and turning left to go left and pulling back to stop. Dad must have had some pretty good horses although they did teach us how to ride or how to hang on. I wasn't allowed to ride with a saddle until I was a teenager because my grandfather was dragged for a short distance before he got lose from the stirrup."

"When I was eight, Dad woke me at five every morning and told me to go get my horse and go get the cows in to be milked. I was so eager to ride that he only had to tell me once.

"My dad used to say 'If you get bucked off or fall, you get right back on or you'll never ride again'. I was so afraid that my dad would never let me ride horses again, that I even got back on no matter how much it hurt. At the age of thirteen, I was riding bareback on a small mare named Pepsi. Well, she didn't like me laying back on her and off I went. I landed square on my behind. I thought I had broken my tail bone it hurt so bad but all I could hear were my dad's words; so I swung back on and held my bottom off her back by putting my hands on her withers and lifting till we got home. It wasn't till later in life that I figured out what he meant by 'never riding again.

"I grew up with great horses such as Dynamite, Pansy, Flicka, Fury, Old Red, Old Tommy, to name a few. But the one that was born when I was eight and I had till I was thirty-eight was Kocamo. She went through my growing up years, my marriage, my divorce, my college year, **I barrel raced, roped, and goat tied off from her.** Neither one of us knew what we doing but we had fun. She was my salvation when the world was falling in on me and we went for a ride in the mountains. There, we would discuss things with God and come home, ready to conquer the world. **Some people go to a psychiatrist: I go for a horseback ride.**"

"I had horses, even when I had to rent pastures for them. I raised a few colts and broke them myself for about fifteen years. In telling people how to get along with the colts and showing them how I rode, people just didn't care, all they wanted to do is be able to get on and go. Thirty days does not break a horse, it makes them rideable but they are still learning. I felt sorry for the colt, now I help horses that have people problems, like needing help with loading, standing still, touchy ears, etc.

"When my son was in horse 4-H, I helped where I was needed. I also was involved in the Helping Hands Freedom trails program with Chester and our beloved Ruby. I say beloved (now this is a mule I'm talking about) because when she was a four year old, I was getting one of the horses haltered so kids could ride, when out of the corner of my eye, I see my niece's four year old daughter, crawl under the fence and run behind Ruby. I drop what I'm doing to catch her. By the time I got to her, she had both arms wrapped around Ruby's hind legs with her head between them. I was so grateful for Ruby, who just stood there and didn't move a muscle that I promised her then she had a home for the rest of her life. That was twenty-one years ago and she is still with us, Chester will be remembered by a lot of kids that rode him. He was the most gentle, kindest animal you would ever want to be around. **He put a smile on many a faces and took care of many a kids.** The grandkids still talk about missing him."

"Now that I've broke the ice on mules. Let me tell you how we came to have one. My husband Dave (no matter how much I love him) had the hardest hands on a horse. This drove me crazy so I decided to get him a mule and Ruby was perfect. With mules, you do it right or you don't do it at all. It took awhile but she finally taught him. There was a lot of frustration on his part before he'd give.

I have started a breeding program for mules. I bought a nice two year Fox Trotter mare named Mickey, and she has thrown some nice colts. They are, Jed and Buckwheat that I ride today."

"One my most favorite things, is going camping in Stanley Basin for two weeks with the horses and mules. I've been doing this now since 1992. I started by taking my niece with me when she was still in school. She went for five years until she graduated from high school and got a job. When my grand daughter was old enough to go, (four years old) I took her along. She is now eleven and we will ride all day and the closest she ever came to complaining was when she asked me, "Grandma, can I get off and walk? My butt hurts.""

"We pack the horses, as I ride the mules. We ride trails on the Sawtooth side and on the White Clouds side. We have seen every thing from goats, bear, elk, deer and Llamas. We have been in snow, rain and tremendous thunder storms on our travels. But my grand daughter, Abbigail, still wants to do it again next year. Yes!"

"You don't go that many years without sometime, running into trouble. Several years ago, I was riding with my niece, Katie from the Petit Lake area up over the Snow Slide Pass before they widened the trail. It was mid July and I didn't check to see if the pass was open. I knew sometimes it had to be dynamited to open it. When we got there it was a solid snow pack with ice from one side to the other. We couldn't turn around as the side of the trail was too steep up and straight down on the other. I could see that I could get a horse though once we got to the other side, (about twenty-five yards). The plan I made was to go over shale that had at least a 500 foot drop chute. This is where horse and rider come together in trust with no hesitation, even a fraction of a second in doing what I ask; or I would have lost them down the chute. After getting Katie's horse through and over to the other side I climbed over the ice to get another horse. When I looked down I realized how dangerous this really was, but like I said **my animals trusted me.** We got through and continued on our journey. Having good reliable animals makes all the difference in the world. That is why I like to train my own.

"My husband and I hunt together and we also pack a tent and stay in the back country most of the week. When we get an elk, we have to know that we're not going to have trouble loading meat or horns by getting hurt by some idiot horse or mule. We were in the back country sleeping in our two man tent when about one a.m. Dave pokes me and said "Karen, do your hear that?" about that time an **elk bugled** out in the meadow **and another one bugled** in unison right after that behind us. My horses and mules were getting scared and going back and forth around the trees. So I grab pants and boots and out to them I go. As long as I had a hand on them—one on the horses rear and one on the mules neck, they would stand still. The elk came off the mountain and stood within forty yards of us then he went around us in the trees, he sounded like a buffalo herd. Point is, my animals trusted that I wouldn't let anything happen to them."

"I teach my mules to lie down to get on, just in case it is needed in the back country if something happens to Dave or me. I can't say mules are my favorite, because I enjoy riding a good horse now and then. But **they are fun, smart, and seem to be quite loyal**. My mules enjoy going as much I do. All I have to do is open the trailer door and holler, "Lets go" and they load themselves, especially Ruby, as she is the first to get in."

"I was fortunate enough to be sponsored by my friend, Win, into the **Thursday Sage Riders** club. We ride most every Thursday come rain or shine. I see more ladies riding in the mountains today, than I did twenty years ago."

"It's a great way to see the beauty that God has created for our joy. I am proud to have been born in Idaho, where the skies are still blue, the air is clear, and the trails are long."

"God forbid that I should go to any heaven where there are no horses, or in my case Mules!"

+++++

Jennifer Clarkson: Oakley

Straight to the Heart of the Horse and Mule Life . . .

"I was born in Gooding Idaho and throughout my life I have been around horses. My father worked the Double Diamond Ranch in Bellevue when I was a little girl. I can recall him always breaking the colts, shoeing his string or hitching up the sled to feed hay in the winter. Horses always brought something good to my life that you could not get from the seat of a truck, four-wheeler or dirt bike. I find that even when I hike I see less of the beautiful country due to having to watch my step."

"I can remember going with my father to Bear Valley, North/West of Stanley. He would pack up; load all the horses so we could go on Elk hunts in the winter. He loved the time that he spent with his family in the mountains. I can recall him putting the saddles on and pulling me up with one hand so I could ride on the back of the horse with him."

"When I was ten, my parents **bought me my first horse;** an older Shetland pony that my parents were not afraid to let me ride on my own. His name was Chuggy and he was slow but gentle."

"My husband was raised in a family that farmed in Jerome, and his paternal grandfather farmed with horses. His maternal grandfather grew up on the Ranches of Grouse Creek, Utah, so horses have played a role in his childhood, too."

"When we first met and married we did not have the money to have horses at that time. Once when we were on our feet and had roots planted, my husband injured his back. While recovering, he constantly stewed over the thought of what to do about his passion for hunting, especially elk hunting. The answer was simple—horses. We soon found that gaited horses were the direction we needed to go to ease his back. Then he started riding with a mule man from Jerome and once he got on that **Peruvian-cross mule** everything just came together. The country he could cover **and the intelligence of the animal** attracted us to that breed. Soon we convinced the owner of the mule to sell to us. Well, we were off and running **straight to the heart of the horse and mule life**."

"On our tenth wedding anniversary I got a new horse trailer (this is where we met the Mobley's) and we would go riding as often as we could. We rode a lot down in the canyon; a quick spot for an evening ride. Sometimes we would head for the south hills looping up third fork and back around making a nice day of it."

"But if we were going to head for the hills we mainly rode around Carey, Triumph Mine, and Fairfield. Oh the beautiful places you can reach and see with our horses. As the kids grew we started to teach them how to ride horses though Chris does not let hardly anyone touch his mule or my Tennessee Walking horse. We had a hard time finding a kid safe horse, it was not a fun task. We were sold a horse that was drugged up out of Twin falls and once the drug wore off, all I can say is WOW. The guy would not give our money back so we ended up running her through the sale, luckily we came out even. Finally we found **an old white mule** out of Fairfield and when I say old she was thirty-six. The kids had a blast on her although she was not as fast as the others; she fit in our family well."

"We would saddle the horses and mules on a nice spring day and work with the kids in the pasture. Hailey our oldest was riding Hawk our large 'Walker' gelding, Clayton was still too small for a saddle so Chris just lead him around on his mule and we put our daughter Cassidy on Snow Flake the new old mule. Everything was going good until Snow Flake stepped on a stray cat, well she crow hopped once and this scared Cassidy into a wild panic. Snow Flake did not know what to do Cassidy had dropped her reins and jumped off. Truth be told, I think Cassidy scared poor old Snow Flake more than the little bobble in her step scared Cassidy. We all had a good laugh and Cassidy was back riding a few days later."

"Family riding was usually in places close to home as we never found enough horses that suited us so that we all had one to ride. We tried everything, we even found a nice kid safe ground pounding quarter horse but it just could not keep up with our walking horses/mules. So we would pick spots where we **could build a camp fire** and make s'mores while either Chris or I took a few kids down the trail for a while then switched off. Finally in 2008 we gave up on finding the perfect horses and let the kids ride ours. Eventually we bought a few green broke brood mares so we could **raise a gaited mule string.** That way we could finally take the whole family on trail rides but Chris and I would pull out the brood mares and ride them while the kids were on our good horse. I do not think we enjoyed the ride on these mares as much as on the mules, but we knew the kids were well mounted with our horses. We would laugh and say all of our horses are good horses some are just more of a Cadillac and the others are an old Buick. I guess I should mention that by this time we wore out old Snow Flake. She served us well for five years and we sold her to a grandmother to lead her grand kids around on. **She was forty-one** and the last we heard she was enjoying the warm barn and pasture at her new home."

"We have lived in the Oakley area for the past four years now and have taken our kids almost all over this area. Looking to the east of our place, most would not believe the south hills has a lot to offer as compared to places like Stanley; but if you get out there and find **those place that you can only reach with your horses** and visit them in different times of the year you see a lot of new beauty. A person would truly be amazed at the wild flowers and wild life that's there. Just seeing the difference, in a water fall from high water and later with low water is special. It has taken us four years of trail riding to the east that we are finally ready to take to the west and up to Independence Lakes and Cache Peak next year though we have sold off a few horses due to the recession and harder times. We will still have fun as a family as **horses and mules have brought so much to our family** that we can't see ourselves without them. Our kids would rather be out exploring than inside glued to a TV or video game. Without the horses and the ability to show them what is out there I think our kids would have been like so many others that spend their time indoors. For this alone we are **proud to be a simple country horse/mule riding family in this day and age."**

"I think I have used the term *Horse* too much in here. I bet my husband would have preferred if **I replace**d **horse with Mule."**

In this new friendship we have with Jennifer and her husband I am looking forward to the summer rides we have planned with them in *their* country. So look for us on Cache Peak.

Team Drivers

Penny Hodges

Helen Park Ruby

JoAnn Lee

105

Putting the Horse Before the Cart

The sport of driving seems to be growing in popularity in Idaho, even among the traditional western breeds. There is much to learn from the fitting of the harness, the vehicle and the right horse, or horses, up to learning how to driving one. I learned that the horse does not pull the cart; he actually pushes it with his chest and shoulders—unless you ask someone who has actually put the collar and hames on and they will say the horse pulls from the shoulder . . . so much to know.

Helen Parke Ruby: Wendell

*"If you too have **a secret wish** to get away and go back to where the passion is, come escape to the excitement of what the ranch life offers you."*

When I drove into the Ruby Ranch that spring day, I was anxious to hear Helen's story of:

Her Secret Wish

"My second chance in life at having horses around me, came in 2000 as I got re-acquainted with driving a team. Oh, as a young teen, I often drove the horse, as I walked behind a young colt training it so it would obey the bit. I remember a time my dad and I had a young runaway team we were working. The only way we could stop them was with a lasso that we hitched to a passing post. Yes, I had some negative times with a team, but this is different here. These are big teams of Percheron, Shires and Spotted Draft horses—harnessed to large wagons, carriages, and carts. They are well trained before they are hooked up as they would be very hard to stop and would tear up the wagon. It is very exciting and relaxing to drive them."

"The club activities of the Southern Idaho Draft Horse and Mule Association are enjoyable for us to participate in. As members we give free rides at local events where people can participate and help others learn how to drive a team. The club often has wagon train trips to the hills for campouts."

"Most every day, I get a chance to horseback ride with grandkids or to work cows here at the ranch," Helen told me. Then she showed me a pretty paint quaterhorse she is working with. I ask her if working with the young horses are like pouring your last jug of water down a well to prime the pump so plenty of good water will come out.

"Yes, lots of time and patience, and I enjoy all the horses and the amenities here at the ranch it had been **a dream come true** when Harold and I were married."

"I was born Helen Parke in Malta and soon our family moved to Burley. I don't remember a time when I didn't have a horse or know how to ride. My first horse, named Miss Idaho, was a grade grey mare that my dad competed with and won on at the cow cutting contest at the Cow Palace. My dad was a pioneer cutting horse trainer and therefore at five, I began competing in horse shows and continued into high school rodeos. Even as a young adult I roped with mother where we were a family team, when time and money allowed.

"In August of 2007, Harold and I took nine work horses to Boise for the Western Idaho Fair. We competed in performance driving, cart classes, ladies driving, mare teams and gelding teams, 4-up, 6-up and farm and implement classes. We were **awarded many first places.** It was a lot of fun as well as a lot of work."

I have seen the teams Helen drives around the Magic Valley; they are beautifully groomed often having braided tail and mane, wearing their black, leather harnesses decorated in chrome with the hames shinning around the horse's neck. I learned the difference with a four-wheel vehicle and a two is how the weight is distributed so it is important that the harness should be fitted properly. A horse can pull twice its own weight if the weight is balanced. The most beautiful wagon I saw was a shining dark green buggy with white trimmings. Helen told me they often do wedding receptions and showed me the white buggy with burgundy silk finishing. It too, was beautiful and I wanted to ride in it. Then there were the Fore Cart, a **Unicorn carriage** and a single horse cart. There is also a sleigh that is used in the winter at Sun Valley where one of their draft teams pull tourists up to Trail Creek for dinners at that lodge. "Harold's son lives there and he is in charge of this team," Helen recalled.

As I listened safety was emphasized often. Driving offers an opportunity for anyone to learn more about horsemanship. And best of all as far as Helen is concerned, driving is fun.

I asked Helen what her favorite team was and she replied with a smile, "That would be Duke and Dan; they are an older Shire team that can go forward on their own and are not a lot of work like some of the 18 hh teams are."

But Helen is not afraid of hard work, she sews for hours turning out **beautiful western outfits** that are worn by competitors at the rodeos and horse shows. She is a maker of quilts, and she also likes to cook for the driving school they sponsor. The list is endless for a woman who is from hard working Idaho stock. The picture shows Helen with a Haflinger team pulling a load of hay to feed their stock. You can tell she enjoys this type of chores, plus she is giving this team a training lesson for Penny Hodges, who asks for her help with this new team. I would like to give a tribute to Helen that I feel fits her at this time in her life.

Just as the winter turns to spring, our lives have changing seasons too.
So when a gloomy forecast comes, remember—God has plans for you.

Whatever the season of life, attitude makes all the difference

+++++

Belgian horses are popular in America for their more refined and stylish gait. They are one of the heaviest draft horses and combine their incredible strength with an extremely willing and generous temperament, making them an ideal heavy work horse. Typically, they have a small head on a thick and muscular neck, huge powerful shoulders and quarters, short legs with feathering around the fetlock. They have a good walk with free movement. They can be measured up to 17hh.

JoAnn Lee: Twin Falls
Erica Lee: Her daughter,

Lesson of Trust

"The only two things a horse needs are, something to do (with you) and something to eat."

I was impressed when I saw a young lady driving a team of Belgian horses in the Buhl Parade. On their wagon was the name *Lee farms of Idaho*. I was even more impressed when I learned this team pulled their wagon in the **Pasadena Rose Bowl Parade** the year before, and that not every entrée gets accepted.

This was the day I met JoAnn Lee and I was in awe as I questioned her about keeping this giant team under control. We made a date to talk again and when the Twin Falls County fair came around, I went to the arena on Friday morning to watch the competition of many teams pulling a wagon.

While Jo Ann competed in the farm class, I watched as the pretty, slight built driver put Jim and Jack, the well behaved Belgian team, through the course. They worked well together and responded to her commands at each obstacle placing them high in the class. Erica, Jo Ann's daughter, sat beside me and told me what the judge was looking for. (Erica said she enjoyed the teams, but has competed in rodeo events with her quarter horse. And that is her forte. Her friendly smile and eagerness to help me understand the event gave me the welcome I really appreciated.)

The Lee's bought their first Belgian Draft horses ten years ago. Their first team was purchased from an Amish blacksmith in Ohio.

The Lee's belong to the Southern Idaho Draft Horse and Mule Association where they were elected President this year (2009). The Association has over seventy members. Besides the business meetings the **group has fun days, play days, sleigh rides,** etc. and whatever promotes the connection to our past when wagons and teams were so necessary.

This is Joann's story.

"We also compete with our horses and wagons in the Twin Falls County Fair and have been to the fair in Boise, and The North Idaho Classic in Sandpoint. We compete in about ten parades and a couple of shows during the year. Another parade was the Salt Lake City Days of 47. They are all a lot of fun along with a lot of work."

"I wouldn't do much different—I have a wonderful family that has shared many years of memories with our horses. We have lived our lives the way we want filled with **many blessings that we enjoy daily."** Besides enjoying these bonding times together the Lee's have won many trophies, ribbons and plaques.

"I would call this a lesson in trust," JoAnn said as she continued with her narrative.

"A friend of ours had passed away and we were asked to transport his casket to the cemetery in Shoshone. We hooked up Charlie and Eli to our turn of the century Ice Wagon to transport the casket. When we delivered the casket we headed back to the horse trailer and made a turn onto highway 93 to cross the **three mainline railroad tracks**. All of a sudden the tongue on the wagon broke. We brought the team to a stop and their front feet were on the first set of the rails. Eric handed me the lines and jumped off to unhook the team and back them off the tracks. All of a sudden, lights flashed and bells whistled and **the barrier arm came down between the wagon and the horses. We couldn't move!!** We looked down the track and saw a streamliner coming at about 45 mph in the middle track and maybe there would be about ten feet between the oncoming train and the horse's heads. Eric yelled for me to get back as he went to the front of Charlie and Eli. He stood between them and held on to their bridles talking to them as the train barreled by shaking them violently. **Man and horses stood their ground** with great trust in each other during this tense situation. Then the signal arm came up and we looked around to move the horses and what we saw was a crowd that had gathered including our friends George Silvers and Cotton Riley. They both had tears in their eyes and exclaimed they had never seen a team and horseman have so much **trust in each other**. They said we were the luckiest people on earth and we felt we were to have such a trusting team. We will never sell Charlie and Elli for any price after the trust they showed in us."

"I wouldn't want to be in this situation again but it was very heartwarming to know we had a team like this. Oh, there have been other times we were proud to be owners of an equine team, but none as hair-rising as this lesson of trust."

Yes, I know from the rewards they have won that Joann was proud of their teams; however she wanted to share this story to let others know; if **you work as hard as they do with their teams, horses can respond well to you at a time when an emergency arrives.**

Congratulations, JoAnn, for a sport well done. We'll see you in the coming celebrations and parades.

+++++

I met Penny the summer of 2009 when we went on a historic wagon train ride together as the outriders. She enjoys riding her horse on the trails and in the desert, as well as, now driving her team of horses. She is a fun person to be with.

Penny Hodges: Buhl

A Life Time with Horses

"Where to begin . . . may be at the beginning. I am the first child of Bob & Betty Studebaker born in Salmon. In the "olden days" (according to grandkids) Salmon's main industry was ranching of which my parents were a part before the big war. With dad's parents they raised sheep, cattle, and pinto horses."

"I can put my life in chronological order just from Mom's pictures. Mom has pictures of me sitting on a horse in front of Dad before I could sit by myself and then on the horse by myself. There is a gap in the pictures while Dad was in the navy during World War II."

"The spring before my sixth birthday Dad went to work for the forest service and we spent that summer on Redrock Lookout in the Salmon National Forrest. The next five years we spent the summers at the Yellowjacket Ranger Station. Horses once again became a big part of my life. My brothers and I rode in a designated area around the station; it was the folk's rules. But we got to go with Dad once-in-awhile when he visited the lookouts. He also took us into the Big Horn Crags for a "vacation" one year."

"There were a couple of riding 'lessons', one I remember well. The barns and corrals at the Yellowjacket were on one side of the creek and the houses and office on the other. A nice bridge crossed the creek and as a rule the horses crossed with no problem. But horses are like kids when you think they know the rules they try to change them. I was on a horse named, Lady and about the middle of the bridge she starts crow hopping, she reared-up then drop. It didn't' matter what I did to her she would not go on across. Dad hollered "what's going on?" I told him she was bucking and would not go crossed the bridge. When my hero came to rescue me, I got a surprise. Dad pulled me off Lady gave me a good swat on the backside and put me back on the horse and told me to **make her go across**. I swear that **horse giggled as she very proudly went to the other side** and wherever I wanted to go the rest of the day".

"We had a horse named Tarzan that I was *not* to ride without Dad along. Well, I did as told *most* of the time. It was after school, I was in the fifth grade, no one was home and I wanted to ride. Tarzan was easy to catch and by standing on the hay manger I got the bridle on him and off to the lower end of the pasture we went. All was going well until we turned to head back. He was very hard mouthed and I could not hold him back as the barn came into view. I was sticking with him until he jumped the ditch. My landing must have been something for my mother to watch as she drove into the yard; I hit my head against a fence post. That was in April and I remember still being in bed on the 4th of July. One of the highlights of the July parade every year was the air force jets flying over, Dad carried me outside and laid me on a blanket so I could see them. The family tells me I screamed when they went over because I could not stand the noise. The **damage to my eyes, ear and brain** took months to heal but I was ready for school that fall. My youngest brother remembers me after I came home from the hospital. He said my skull mended, but my eyes were crossing and when I could walk again he described me as a skinny cross-eyed wild-haired girl, a strange-looking big sister—odd, with thick corrective glasses."

"Anyone with any sense at all would have stayed off horses after this but not me. Dad sold Tarzan and Lady grew too old for my kind of riding (I wanted to look good) but lots of people had horses they didn't ride and were willing for me to ride them."

"I had a long spell when there were no horses in my life with marriage, children, and all that goes into raising a family. Then came the divorce and I returned to Salmon. My brother had a ranch east of Salmon and was willing for me to stay in the "old house." I bought dairy springers and helped out where I could. Once again my love of horses had a chance to surface. For four summers I checked the beef cows that were out on BLM ground. I was like a puffed up blow fish when I was able to cut out a cow and her calf and bring them back to the ranch by myself. There is a kind of excitement, even the horses felt it, hard to explain when the cows are taken out in the spring and rounded up in the fall."

"Fred and I married in 1990 and once again horses were put on the back burner, until my son William came to live with us. He bought some horses and all the stuff one needs to care for and enjoy horses. It wasn't long though until he had to move on and I inherited the horses and stuff. About that time I realized I didn't know squat about riding and training *young* horses, until I met Karen Majerus. With Karen's guidance, much of the time doing it for me, I now have a couple really nice riding horses. But it hurts to ride most days. Hence, **the next stage of my life with horses I thought would be driving them.**"

"Fred enjoys auctions and at times I'll go with him. There were horse pulled carts at several of the auctions and we bought one. Okay, I've got a horse and I now have a cart; how do they go together? Karen showed me how to ground drive them and I did well, got some exercise, but the cart was still in the shed. Once again Karen came to the rescue. She told me about her cousin's husband who drives and trains draft horses. I called and made a date to take me, horse and cart to their place."

"I found Harold and Helen Ruby, are good and knowledgeable teachers. He hooked Bear up with one of his horses who are big enough to take Bear wherever Harold asks them to go. Then he taught *this greenhorn* basic driving before sending us home. I drove Bear for several months before doing something stupid that ended his driving career."

"During all this Fred found a Studebaker buggy that was advertised. He wants to give his special model Studebaker (my maiden name) a Studebaker buggy. We made a trip to Oregon and brought it home. It needs a lot of work which Fred wants to do himself."

"Do you see where I am? Carts, buggies, and no horse! During 2008 I borrowed one of Amy Christianson's horses so I could be in Buhl's light parade. In 2009, I borrowed Tiny from the Rubys so I could be in Buhl's 4th of July parade, won a first place in the wagon & drays category. Then, for Sun Valley's Wagon Days Parade, I borrowed Tiny again and took second place in restored buggies."

"Let's back up here a minute. I am not an easy one to get along with when I want to do something, have the tools, but it just isn't coming together. I told Fred I was tired of looking and was going to go buy whatever I could find that pulled. He tried his best to discourage me but I was determined, and he had to let the cat out of the bag. Harold Ruby had found a Haflinger filly and told Fred about her but wanted to wait until he was sure she was right for me. Well that took care of the waiting. We brought, Cindy home and I worked some with her then took her back to Harold's to be trained to pull. Cindy and I finished off 2009 by entering several parades including Twin Falls and Buhl light parades."

"The story does not end there nor did we get this far with nothing but smiles and giggles. Because both Cindy and I were new to this exciting sport, mistakes were made, **we tipped over a couple times**, broke up a cart in the mountains and both have had scrapes and bruises. As you may know by now I don't quit because of a bruise or two and Cindy is a sweet heart so we just get up, brush ourselves off and tried again."

"In October Fred found some Haflingers' for sale in Ontario, Oregon. We went to see what they were and came home with Anne. By the first of August she joined Cindy and they became a team. It was fun to see how well they bonded and their relationship to each other when we are driving. Cindy often bites at Anne when I get after them like she thinks it's Anne's fault. Fred has built me a wagon so I can take more than one person at a time for a ride. This summer we participated in giving rides at the Idaho Farm Museum, at the Art Show on Ritter Island, church functions, and a family get-together."

"Cindy & I were busy during the summer of 2010 with many parades. At the Draft and Mule Competition in Gooding **we won a 1ˢᵗ & 3ʳᵈ place,** and the Sun Valley Wagon Days Parade where **we received a first in restored buggies**. Anne's first time in a parade for the team was a first for the wagon. All did well!"

"I still ride as often as I can and go to the mountains with Karen for a week in the summer. We have packed into some beautiful country that I would never have seen had I not rode horses."

"Often I am told the journey is more fun than the destination. I am not sure what, when, or where my destination will be, but **I am having a ball now**."

Thursday Sage Riders

Francis, Eva & Bert

Twig Schutte & Ruth Staley

Donna Baird

Adria Blair

Helen Marshall

Thursday Sage Riders

Carol Sobotka

Canyon Ride

Blanch Lanier

Lois Petersen

Thursday Sage Riders

Carol's Cook Out

Connie, Darleen, Bonnie

Lisa Callen & Valerie Pryor

Karen & Shirley, End of the Trail.

"Nature gives to every time and season some beauties of its own"
-Charles Dickens

This is a tribute to a ladies riding club called, the Thursday Sage Riders, that began **forty six years ago**.

This women's riding club was initiated by several women in South Central Idaho who enjoyed riding their horses not only in the desert lands, but also the mountains to the south and north. They quickly realized you don't learn safety rules by accident and outside of safety had little need for other requirements. Frances Callen Sheneberger the club's first trail boss, often said, "If you have a **good** trail horse, and ride it wisely, you do not need anything else."

She and Pearl Cross led the group for more than twenty-five years as the group grew to thirty members. This chapter is a tribute to many of these women, who together enjoyed many trails with longtime friends as well as sharing their love for horses. However, in some of the other chapters of this writing are many other Thursday Sage Riders members—look for them.

(Often in this chapter, I have used TSR as an abbreviation for the Club.)

Women I Have Known

Besides stories of horsewomen who were acquaintances, I have written about close friends of mine, many who are members of this woman's horse club. I have had the privilege to be **a member of this group for thirty-nine years.**

This group of women has a unique way of enjoying their friendships. The two regular meetings they have a year, gives them a chance to renew that comraderie with others who may no longer be riding at this time, because of illness, loss of a horse, or having a weekly job; people like Donna Baird, Betty Slifer, Marti Ambrose, Margaret Gray, Jerrine Laudert and Stevia Webb and many others I have had the privilege to visit with. I have also included some of the TSR members in other chapters that are associated to their horse skills.

The friendships you develop you can dream with through riding. Most of the women of this club have unique lives with varied interests. It gives us an opportunity to share with other members. It's about life and living. It's about what you can uniquely contribute. I believe we promote healthy lifestyles, a kindness we can share as we ride together. These are the people I laugh with the most. It's a special ingredient that makes time with them joyful.

The air was thick with the scent of the wild roses along the stream. Oft times we speak of nothing and everything, but never negative—we just ride along inhaling the fresh air and the sweet scents of spring. All is right with the world. Win Mobley

Frances Callen Sheneberger: Jerome/Twin Falls
1913-2004

To Dream is to Realize Your Purpose

Have you been through the silver valley? Many of us of the Thursday Sage Riders have. Why do I describe it as this? It is because Frances always looked for the silver lining in life. She shared with us her clear mind and gentle spirit. This was apparent on Thursdays when we rode along the trail together, each moment was a joyful, simple experience. When I think of a great lady like

Frances, I think of the woman described in Proverbs 31, *"She is clothed with strength and dignity; she can laugh at the days to come, she speaks with wisdom, and faithful instruction is on her tongue."* And instruct us she did to her best ability. What most of us now know about trail riding, we learned from Frances.

Frances Callen Shenberger began the Thursday Sage Riders in 1965. She and a friend were riding horses in the desert when they discussed inviting additional **women to ride with them**.

Frances said, "We were planning on limiting our group to twelve, but within two weeks we had more than that. And within five years we claimed about twenty-five riders. Although most of the time there were about twelve active ones," Frances explained. "We called our group the Thursday Sage Riders as we often rode in the desert and always, as weather permitted, on Thursdays."

Frances was one of the trail bosses that set the rides and explained what was expected of each rider, which was; when they rode three times in a row on their *good,* trail horse; they got a pin signifying membership.

"We didn't know everyone when the group grew to over **fifty members**. I don't know of a time when there were more than twenty riding on a single day though. Many of these women became good friends of mine. I often went to visit many of them in their homes. Sometimes we original seven members would go to a member's cabin and have an overnight event, riding for several days."

"We began having an early breakfast ride in the springtime where we discussed any changes the gals might wish to instigate. There we also planned the two summer overnight rides we had each year. On this ride members only could invite one guest, but was responsible for them. This was a delightful group I enjoyed very much, but I never dreamed it would be continued for this many years. I think **the cooperation, leadership, and comrade of our love for horses, their safety (and ours) was the main factor that made it successful,"** Frances said with the wide smile she often showed as she remembered the good times.

But I believe it was the leadership of this woman of Proverbs, for the clubs long running success. I miss her very much and especially her poems she recited at our luncheon get-togethers during the winter months.

This is part of her early horse story. Born in the early 1900's, Frances said that it was natural for a farmer's daughter to often ride a horse. "It was our way of getting around. When we moved from Hansen we put our belongings in a wagon, loaded two cows, **several riding horses on a flat boat** and **ferried them across the Snake River** just above Shoshone Falls. We lived in Shoshone during my school years where I enjoyed many friends, and if you want a taste of heaven ride down the trail when the sun goes down, as we often did this."

"We moved to Jerome and it was there in 1931 that I met and married Paul Callen during the beginning of the depression years. We had a boy and a girl who enjoyed riding horses. That is how I lost my young daughter—in a horse racing accident."

"I loved the ranch life, and with one son I often was out on a horse helping move the cows and horses to graze in the adjoining desert."

It was there twenty years later that she lost her husband in an accident. She married Schmall Shenberger several years later. He also loved to ride but they rode more for pleasure not on working ranches. They often **spent weekends riding in the south hills** near Twin Falls, or the mountains north of Ketchum. Often they went with friends to the Three Creek area for overnight rides. She was fondly remembered by Lola Blossom from that area, as they were invited to stay at their ranch so they could ride several days in a row.

One of Frances's stories of an exciting ride she describes in the following.

"It was in the Three Creek canyons in the spring when some of the areas around a high running creek are often very soft. Shenne's horse attempted to cross at a flooded area where water was about knee deep. The horse began to sink up past his knees and then as the horse panicked and lunged to get out he sank deeper in the bog. Shene slid off to lighten the horse and he too sank in over his knees. Fighting the mud pulling strongly at his feet, he jumped to get out and only sank deeper. Now in above his waist, he looked around for help. His horse was lunging forward and in one jump that Shene made, he was able to grab the horse's saddle strings and the horse pulled him out to dry ground. It frightened us enough that we now take caution around these places and urge others to do the same."

When Frances was still in her eighties, she rode short rides with Marcia Chojnacky and this is where Frances eventually left her horse to be cared for and ridden by Marcia and Mike who later bought the horse.

I wrote the following in a diary I had been keeping the year Frances gave up riding.

And so we lift ourselves upon our horse's back on Thursday morning and join not her alone, but all the women and all the horses that have run together since the dawn of beginning.

+++++

Chief Joseph Trail Ride

The Appaloosa Horse Association with headquarters in Moscow, each year sponsors a trail ride that is called the <u>Chief Joseph Trail Ride</u>. This ride commemorates the Nez Perce route that this tribe used while fleeing from the U.S. Army. The one hundred mile ride, across Idaho, takes five days, leaving from Spencer with West Yellowstone as the destination. A portion of the historical trail used is a part of the Lewis and Clark route.

One of the requirements to ride with this group is that you must be riding a registered Appaloosa horse.

My friend, Phyllis, will tell you about her participation on one of these historic rides in her story.

Phyllis Barnes: Jerome

Three Generations Riding

Over the years I watched Phyllis ride young quarter horses; however, I found out she saddled up and rode these horses with much confidence, as her skills and knowledge she gained from her younger days, gave her courage.

Riding as a young teen, she spent most of her summer days saddling up and riding with her school friends. She competed for **Queen** at rodeos—winning, and years later, became a part of the women's riding group called the **Thursday Sage Riders**. In 1965 Phyllis was **one of thirteen charter members** that started this group. This association gave her a lot of years experience on the trails as she rode with them most every Thursday (in the months of March though November) for more than three decades. She is spoken of as a very good mentor to many whom she sponsored in the TSR club.

I knew Phyllis in high school, but we really got acquainted on the Thursday rides several years later. We have enjoyed each other's company, moving cattle at Fish Creek as well as over night rides in the Sawtooth Mountains. This is one of those rides.

Early one summer day she loaded her mare, Bell into the trailer, then picked up Adria and her horse. They left at four AM in order to get to the Redfish Lake trailhead in time to leave for the twenty-six mile ride to the Grandjean resort. This destination is reached by going on a very, scenic trail heading west in the Sawtooth Wilderness area. The trail takes you by four lakes, goes over three passes and then it drops down into a long valley. From there you follow a dirt road for about four miles to the lodge. It's a full day's ride.

While on the trail, several other riders did not wish to lead up the steep and **precarious switch-back trail** above the large Sawtooth Lake, Phyllis took Bell up to be the lead horse. They did a marvelous job getting us the rest of the way to the resort on time for a steak dinner.

The other event I remember about Phyllis's giving personality was when we got to the Grandjean lodge, she and Adria were given the small cabin with the only shower, and for an hour before dinner we (five riders) were running in and out taking showers there. We had a lot of fun together those two days and I will never forget the generosity she and Adria showed to us invaders.

This is a story Phyllis gave me. "My most memorable ride was when I had the privilege to go on the **Historical Chief Joseph, 100 mile trail ride** across the Idaho panhandle. We rode it in four days with our own horses. My friends, Vonnie Jones and Kathy Kerley and I had to be riding registered Appaloosas as the Appaloosa horse is the designated horse for this State. We also had to provide our own sleeping place at night; we slept in our trailers that someone else brought up the other roads for us. Those hosting the ride provided great breakfasts, sack lunches, and steak and salmon for supper meals. It was great weather and **I saw country I will never see again."**

Besides a tribute to the charm and courage I see in Phyllis, she is also leaving a heritage of love for horses to her daughter, Patty and granddaughter, Lindsey who along with their husbands, train and ride their own colts they raise on their Quarter Horse ranches south of Kimberly. However, they will have to ride many years to catch up with Phyllis's lifelong dedication of going horseback riding.

+++++

Lois Claire Peterson: Jerome

A Family of Talented Horsewomen

Many times along the way I'm dizzied by the sense of the benevolent, nudging hand of God, this was one of those special days. It was the day I became aware of a women's riding group called Thursday Sage Riders and this happened because of a school friend whose name is Lois. Lois and I were in the same grade in high school where we had many of the same classes. We sometimes managed to get together as girlfriends at events at school as well as for slumber parties. Sometimes we skipped school and you might have seen us riding off in Lois's 48 Chrysler. We both married Jerome men and had our homes there in the country. We often saw each other when our kids had events at school or horse related events in the summer.

At an event Lois and I were both attending, Lois told me she had been riding with a group of women in Magic Valley who rode their horses every Thursday in the local deserts or up some trails in the South Hills. I questioned her more about where they rode, how long they ride and asked what it took to get asked to go along sometime. She told me next Thursday to jump my horse, Scout, into the rack of our pickup bed and meet her in the desert north of Jerome. I became very excited about the invite and could hardly wait to join the Thursday Sage Riders. Lois and I had several rides together that year with them. I want to thank Lois for thinking of me as a companion on the trails—what an honor it has been.

The following is a story Lois gave about her association with horses.

"As kids growing up in rural homes, the chief mode of transportation was our horse. Sometimes our car didn't work, but we always had a corral of horses. In the summertime, leaving from our house, we would saddle up, put a sandwich in a flour sack and be gone all day. My sister and I were often joined by neighborhood friends. **We rode out north in the desert all day.** When it got hot we jumped in the canal. In the winter we rode bareback to keep warm. When on our way to the pond to ice skate we hung the skates over the horse's withers. Those were the days! And this continued through high school."

"Our family belonged to the Jerome Riding Club. We rode on Sunday rides with them down to Blue Lakes and the canyon area. **We had a jamboree team** that competed against neighboring towns in water races, sucker races, many other relays and timed barrel events. It was a lot of fun. And the reward was that we always got to stop for a milk shake on the way home."

"When I married Ted, I had a chestnut mare named Desert Sage and he owned a big black gelding. We continued to barrel race Ted's horse. My mare was the start of our raising colts. Some of our favorite horses were Kitten, Stubbard a Shetland pony and another named Dukie that I gave to Win Mobley."

"Our four children all liked to ride. They competed in horse shows, rodeos and **all three daughters were rodeo queens, just as I was** my senior year in high school."

"In 1968 my neighbor Frances Callen asked me to ride with the women's group called the Thursday Sage Riders where I managed to ride occasionally that year. I really enjoyed these rides but as we farmed and with the family activities I did not get my pin for several years."

"I still ride around the farm for an hour or so, but my arthritis has kept me from longer rides. I find a horse is a good companion and **I've spent many happy hours with my horses, riding and caring for them.**"

I would like to add that Lois has been very modest in telling her horse story. I know this because of the many awards she and her daughters, Brenda, Christi, and Heidi have received over the years. They competed in 4-H—and won often. They showed in valley horse shows—and placed high. They are all great horsewomen in many fields of this association. I have been proud seeing her accomplishments and I am fortunate to know Lois and call her my friend.

+++++

I cannot build a mountain
Or catch a rainbow fair
But let me be what I know best-
A friend who's always there.

Lonna Smith: Jerome

Because she was a member of the TSR club, I got acquainted with Lonna almost three decades ago. One special ride just the two of us took then, was a journey up Deer Creek. It was the beginning of a special friendship of which I am very thankful to call her my good friend. Lona is a good rider and has a lot of respect for her horse. She has owned many good horses that have taken her and Ron, her husband, on many wild game hunts, as well as pleasure riding with close friends. Their cabin was next Jack and Marleen Sears, and when Bill and I were invited up to stay at their Place to ride for the six of us enjoyed many happy trails together. What fun it was!

"Spending Time and Doing the Important Things that Really Count"

Some of the most rewarding time Lonna and I spent riding together was when we were giving our three year old colts some experience on the trails in the Sawtooth Mountains near her summer home. Lonna was on Irsa and I rode Braddo. As **we rode toward Abe's Chair**, the toothy peaks dominate the skyline. Along the trail we began to read the dark letters carved on the nearby aspen trees where lonely shepherds had left their names and the date they were there. As far as we could decide seven decades ago, these men were here on this same ridge we were on today. We reached a well worn trail and picked up the horses gait that allowed us to listen to the four beat sounds our Peruvian Paso horse's hooves made on the hard earth. Lonna and my goal was that when we allowed it, we let our horses' gait, but also made them walk when we asked them to. The young horses needed to be worked every day that we could ride. We found this work was better accomplished with just our two horses on the trail as they had just come off of four weeks of training. We felt they lacked experience on the wilderness trails. The Smiths beautiful log cabin was at Smiley Creek located over Galena summit, about sixty miles north of Sun Valley.

As we neared the cabin, Lonna said, "Let's ride to **Hell Roaring Lake** tomorrow." I replied, "It sounds good to me. It is a good trail with little elevation that shouldn't tire the horses much."

The next day, we rode our young horses the five miles into Hell Roaring Lake. They were real good steeds and we had a super ride to the lake. We rested there at noon then after eating lunch we headed back. We were talking about the good journey we had and were riding alongside of Hell Roaring Creek listing to the water fall on the rocks of many small falls. The flat trail went in and out of the tall pines. Suddenly, Lonna's mare made two high jumps and on the last jump, came down on all fours so hard it pitched her off. Lonna was on the ground before I could even say a word and she just laid there not moving. I yelled at her to speak to me. Then her mare began to take off so I rode alongside to get hold of her bridle. I then stepped off my horse to quickly tie both of the horses to a tree, I went back to see about Lonna just as she rolled over in the dirt. The dazed look in her eyes frightened me.

"Lay still," I commanded. She obeyed as I reached her.

She whispered, "Oh, my head hurts." And further examination I found there was a large bump on her head. She had hit the only rock on the trail for many feet. "I don't know what happened; Irsa just kicked up like she was trying to get out of trouble." Lonna replied.

"Just stay still until you are sure you can get up and I'll get you some water." I commanded. On my walk over to the horses, a bee flew up out of the ground on the path. On examination I saw many more holes where these ground bees reside. "Lona here is our answer for Irsa acting up." I exclaimed to her. And on further examination of searching under Irsa's belly, we decided she was stung more than once, but the horse seemed calm now, only switching her tail.

When Lonna was ready, I suggested she walk her horse a ways but Lonna knew she couldn't do that with her vision blurring. She looked into Irsa's eyes then Lonna said, "**The soft look in her eyes tells me she's fine.**" So I held her while Lonna stepped up and got in the saddle. "Let's go back at a walk and I'll be all right," Lonna said.

Riding behind, I watched as the horse settled into a walk with her head moving up and down to the rocking, rhythm of her feet. The afternoon sun was slanting down through the trees shinning on Lonna as she was balanced bravely in the saddle while she led us back to the trailers.

After we got back to the cabin and put ice on the injury, Lona was resting better. Within a few weeks of taking it easy, Lonna's headaches began to cease. Although thrown for the first time when she got hurt, Lonna refused to quit riding and these are the qualities that made us friends. We have ridden many miles since then.

When Lonna took full custody of her infant great-grandson her riding days were few, but she and her husband, Ron have loved Buddy since they first saw him at a custody holding home. They knew they must do something to help. The child is five now, and a loving part of their home and now, during the day, is in day care.

"For a few years my riding days were limited—just finding kind neighbors like Barbara and my daughter and her daughters as they watched Buddy to give me some time off. But I do not regret doing what I could to for Buddy. And now that Buddy is older, I ride more, spending some time with the knowledge that I can take my busy life to a place to be alone and find serenity in the Sawtooth Mountains. Here as well as there, I am still doing the important things that really count."

And sometimes we call when a special sunset stirs our souls—and we go riding together

We may not have met if it wasn't for a love we share for horseback riding.

"He gives me Living Water and I thirst no more. The joy of the Lord is my strength." John 4:13-14

+++++

Carol Sobotka: Jerome

A salute to Carol's home town; the town of Challis got its start in 1876 as a supply base for the gold mining camps. Today it serves as a gateway to the wilderness. Whatever your preferred brand of outdoor recreation—be it hiking, camping, fishing, rafting or simply sight-seeing, you'll find plenty of opportunities in and around Challis. Just outside of Challis is the **Land of the Yankee Fork Interpretive Center**, a free museum filled with artifacts from the 'glory days'. Visit and learn how to pan for gold.

Occasionally Carol Crane Sobotka, returns where her roots are, to her hometown of Challis and rides into the Big Horn Crags and Mosquito Flats.

"Are we having fun yet?"

When you have known friends of the Thursday Sage Riders club for more than thirty years it is sometimes hard to describe their true character as we often take their generosity and faithfulness for granted. And in the last fifteen years, Carol has **been faithful** to come and **be our Trail Boss,** in the true western spirit. But, although Carol can be "busier than a huntin' dog," she still comes to help new riders and encourage others as well as guiding them up the trail and bringing them back safely to their trailers and at a reasonable time. I'm not sure I can give, in writing, a rightful tribute to Carol, as she was there many, many times for the women in our Thursday Sage Riders club. When we had one injured, (as it did occasionally happen over the last twenty years) she was knowledgeable and stayed with the person, being the last one to leave the mountain. I remember Carol riding her Tennessee Walking horse cross named, Tess. They were a great pair—so willing to go on down the long trails they loved. Carol would often warn those in the group that day, that if they didn't wish to ride an all day ride, they could go back anytime as long as they had someone to return with them.

As she leads our riding group we often hear her asking the women, **"Are we having fun yet?"**

Then she gets a hoop and a joyful holler reply from the riders and Carol has been answered.

One summer day, Carol, Becky Petterson, Connie Wolcott, Shirley Williams and I proudly rode down the main street of **our** home town in the **Jerome Centennial parade** representing the Thursday Sage Riders. Yes, Carol gave generously of her time and is faithful to show up when she said she would and not just because she is one of the leaders. She served because **she has a true western spirit** that not many others possess.

Now for more of her personal story.

Carol was born a first child to parents Cliff & Vilena Crane. To say Carol grew up in rural Idaho is a miss-statement. The town was Challis, but her home was many miles from town and up a mountain road eighteen miles.

"As kids, my brothers and I were so free; free to roam all over the area exploring and fishing to our hearts content. This of course was after the days work was done. When we did get to play, we always brought home enough trout for the next meal. I lived at a time when my brothers and I walked down the long road to meet the school bus."

"I did not miss the Challis area to the point of getting homesick to go back, as I had begun upper level school and was anxious to move on with my life. However, my years spent in and near Challis is the reason for my love of the mountains and why **I seem to have no fear of things regarding the great outdoors.**"

And this is proven by Carol's adventurous treks into the Big Smoky Mountains as she goes hunting with her son, and many of her family members as well as her friend Faye Redd. On these hunts, Carol has killed her own share of bucks even claiming many in her golden years. The Smokies is her favorite place to ride. One summer, Carol asked me to accompany her to the Canyon Campground for an overnight ride. It was the first time I had ever been there. The beauty and bigness of the area captivated me as we rode along the Big Smokie Creek for several miles. We came to the Big Peak trail and darted in and out of narrow canyons along a small creek. Belva Knight and her husband, Bob, rode with us. We saw this big valley for two more days with Carol leading the way. This is just one of the many ways Carol shares her life.

She still rides her new, easy riding horse all day and the next morning **rises early to treat** those in camp **with her great Spanish eggs and sour cream coffee cake**, in the true spirit that a friend like Carol possesses.

Carol now rides a Peruvian Paso cross named, Shiloh. She always took good care of her horses and their chores came before her breakfast. She has kept them in shape for the long rides in the summer months. In fact, the **long rides are what Carol lives for** often going into the Sawtooth

Wilderness areas and the Frank Church Wilderness. She enjoys rides with her granddaughters as well as her two daughters and daughter-in-law, Stacy,—all good horse riders.

A really fun ride Carol and I had together was in the Bitterroot Mountains of Montana when we asked our husbands to go with us and camp at a guest lodge there. We rode three great days to lakes, old cabins, and along ridges with fantastic views. What good sports they were and what fun we had and we were really spoiled eating dinner at that lodge while enjoying the beautiful, summer evenings in Montana.

Even after age sixty-three, Carol sometimes rode a three year old colt on the shorter rides. I am not surprised that this horse has turned out to be **a good trail horse with Carol in the saddle.** My tribute to Carol could go on and on as she has accompanied us on many great camping and riding outings. There is much beauty of the outdoors to appreciate and experience together. Thank you, Carol, for showing us (the TSR) the way and for keeping us safe, and most of all for being our friend.

(Ruth Staley's tribute to her friend) . . . *"Carol is so willing and helpful—To one and all a friend—adventure is her forte, We hope that it will never end."*

+++++

Ruth Staley: Twin Falls

A Dedicated Trail Boss

I cannot close this chapter without writing about Ruth Staley she has been one of our faithful members for three decades and was our designated **Trail Boss for fifteen years**. She led us well and is a great rider who never complained. At this time she rode a very nice Quarter Horse that got his muscles 'tied up,' as the vet called it, when he ate too many apples from a tree in their pasture.

When we go to the South Hills (an area up Rock Creek Road, south of Twin Falls,) we often rely on Ruth to lead us to the prefect spot. Ruth is a friendly woman who is always there to encourage us and is anxious for her friends to enjoy the ride. She promotes safety and welcomes new members with a smile.

At the time when Ruth lived in Hansen, my husband and I had some great wilderness rides with her and her spouse; we became good friends. Even after Ruth recovered from a serious aneurism, she returned to her love for riding.

I wish to thank **Ruth for her dedication** to the Thursday Sage Riders and as she still continues to ride with us as she is asked to guide our TSR Club. She now she rides a Tobino, Fox Trotter mare that she calls Tobi.

I appreciate her very much and am grateful she is my friend. Happy trails.

Ruth is our really talented **music** rider, often **composing a song** that she shares with us, like this one.

Thursday Sagebrush riders—blessed from up above,
Nothing can get any better—than riding with friends you love.
Golden girls, we thank you—your idea was so sure
To ride your beautiful horses with friends that ever endures.

+++++

Loraine Jones: Twin Falls

Second Generation Rider

Loraine's history with the Thursday Sage Riders goes way back to 1975. She rides a registered Quarter Horse, mare called Miss Lonesome Badger, a pretty red dun. She is most often one of our faithful friends as we travel the South Hills area. She now helps Carol with the leadership in our group. Recently we saw the need for someone to be a **liaison with the Forest Service and BLM to help keep our trails open** for horseback riding and Loraine volunteered for the job. Thank you Loraine, for spending your time to further our future in good riding,

I would like to add that Loraine also has the honor of having **a second generation** TSR member as her daughter, Kimberly Minter, joined last year. Happy Trails to you both.

+++++

Darlene Kiser: Jerome

A Hard Lesson to Learn

Darlene's association with the TSR club has been a long and fun one. Darlene often showed up to ride—rain or shine. For this I greatly admire her love to get on her pretty paint, Fox Trotter mare, Carley, and ride the miles.

She told my granddaughter and me of her **saddest time** with a horse.

"When I acquired Melodia, I knew she was going to be just right for me being I am so short. Her breed was, Icelandic Pony, and she was a pretty bay, well mannered and easy to ride. She had raised several great colts. We had some great rides together."

"Every time I now go out to the corral to get my horse I remember the day I forgot to **connect the snap on the gate.** Yes, Melodia **did get out** that fateful time. She knew how to get hold of the chain, wiggle it and take it off the hook. Well, that evening, she wondered out on our busy road and **was hit by a truck**. I felt so bad losing her and of course for the accident I had caused. This is one time that if I could go back, I would do things differently. What a lesson."

When I learned of this accident, I too was saddened for Darlene's loss. Melodia was a great horse, and Darlene **is** a good caretaker of all the animals she has on her farm.

Thank you for telling us of this incident Darlene, and I pray it will remind us all of the **importance to secure that gate.**

+++++

In the winter time we go
Riding in the fields of snow:
Let us ride in the white snow—in soundless space.

Lisa Callen: Jerome
2009 up Rock Creek Road

Catching Snowflakes

On this snowy Thursday winter morning, we Thursday Sage Riders circled our trailers at the Porcupine Springs campground and unloaded our horses. Through the falling snow we watched the tree stumps turn into snowmen as the snow quickly piled upon them. What else did we expect on the twentieth of November? For our last ride of the year it was a good thing we all had our long, riding coats with us. Six brave souls rode our already furry-covered, horses as they blew out their breath that steamed in the fresh, cold air. We started off in a snow storm with the trail covered with light, new snow. Linda Hine led us down the track that was lined with tall pines already heavily laden with snow. At the bottom of the canyon the trail forked into what was for us, a new canyon that we planned to explore. As the snow fell down in huge flakes soon our hats brim became piled high with it. I had snow in my lap and on my shoulders.

Within an hour we could not see where the trail was. I looked around and not one of the riders seemed concerned—only me. The smiles the women wore earlier were still on their faces, and Lisa, thrilled to be riding and enjoying the moment, **caught snowflakes on her tongue.** I will never forget the picture of Lisa on her pretty horse, T J, enjoying the ride.

On another day when Carol and I rode in the South Hills with Lisa, we asked our horses to pick up the pace and move out faster. I was in the lead in this wide, smooth canyon and Lisa's big, grey, T J, responded well. Being a registered Fox Trotter, I was not surprised that he traveled at that speed for about half a mile. Lisa told me the following remembering that day.

"I have enjoyed T J for seven years, and he has never given me any sign that he runs out of energy. The more I ask of him, the more he gives."

This is how I would describe Lisa—she gives. It is great to know fun, horsewomen like Lisa. I am looking forward in the future to following her lead on our Idaho trails. She is dependable and I appreciate her willingness to saddle up and go and keep the Thursday Sage Riders alive. This is a typical story about Lisa and when she is astride a great horse like T J, she has a positive attitude and a bounce of energy. Here's hoping your riding trail is a long one, Lisa.

Thou hast made summer and winter.—Ps: 119:17

+++++

Plain and easy to ride
May your dry camps be few
And health ride with you
To the pass on the Big Divide. C M Russell

Helen Marshall: Twin Falls

Truly a Woman of Western Heritage

The Pinter Mountain Range in Southern Montana is a grand place to meet horse riding friends and acquaintances. When, Bill and I and Helen Marshall, arrived at the Sundance Ranch in Montana, there were several reserved places for us to camp next to the lodge and corrals for the horses. Susan Mitgang was there to welcome us. Helen jumped out of the truck to hug Susan who had been her friend and neighbor when she lived in Twin Falls (now Susan lives in Montana.)

"Ready to ride? Dear friend," Susan asks.

"Yes, bring it on," Helen replied excitedly.

And the three day weekend went on like that for Helen who had come to ride. She was up early every morning for breakfast, saddled, and with hat in hand she mounted up for the long rides. It was a privilege to ride and see the beautiful lakes in that Montana range. The lakes seemed to be hidden beyond the mountain we climbed; we finally arrived there for our lunch break. It was a superb three days with nature all around us. I hope we can all go back soon.

In her mid-seventies, Helen was an enthused rider on this wilderness trip, never complaining. She was a fun person to have as our riding partner. Born in 1918, she was a daughter to Russell and Mary Thomas from Richfield, where her dad had farmed. Helen and I have been friends and riding pals for more than thirty years. Her wide, friendly smile began to charm me as she recalled memories of bygone days.

Helen continues, "Dad liked horses, used them for field work. He often let me ride them when I was very young. I remember a white horse I rode by myself in a round corral. By the time I was twelve we got a sorrel mustang from Nevada, he was smaller. He would only trot down the road for if I let him go faster, he would run away along the railroad track on the way to town. I often rode down that road when the train came in as the conductor would wave at me. Sometime I rode him to Sunday school. I very seldom rode him to school, I walked to the bus. Often times my school friend, Lucille Bickett rode with me after I was a teen." (Helen became an accomplished rider before she was sixteen.)

"When I went to the University Of Idaho, I never got a chance to ride; besides I met Ken and after we were married we moved in 1969 to **Castleford to farm**. We had five children who kept me very busy raising them and with the big gardens and chores I never had time to ride. Some time later my father-in-law bought a riding horse for the older grandkids. That is when I began to ride again. My daughter, Jean, loved to ride as a young girl and teen. Besides 4-H, she often competed in many horse shows. At this time, I joined the TSR group."

"In 1966 I met Marlene Sears who sponsored me in the TSR club. It wasn't too long after that I sponsored Virginia Spafford. I had met her at the 4-H fair where some of her sons were in the program. We became good friends and enjoyed many trail rides in the south hills together. My Rocky horse was the last horse I rode with the TSR's and used him for many years. I still kept him even after I retired from riding; I was 79 years old."

I was honored for more than thirty years to also be one of their riding friends.

+++++

Twig Schutte: Twin Falls & Jerome
(In an April, 11, 1997 journal, I wrote—)

"Twig was on Annie. I was on Bingo, we rode Deer Canyon where the coyotes, hawks and deer play, and we had a very nice day."

Without a Good Horse You're in a World of Hurt

My first memory of Twig was in the spring of 1970 on a Thursday Sage Riders trip to the South Hills. She rode a horse named Bill and they made a sharp looking pair. Bill, her well built quarter horse, took her everywhere with safety and enjoyment in those days.

We Thursday Sage Riders knew our safety depended upon a well fitted horse. Twig Schutte had many things that were required for great rides. However, when she sold Bill, the one thing she needed was a horse she picked for herself that would give her enjoyable riding. The following will explain what I mean.

Several years later when many of us were beginning to look for the "easier" gaited horses to ride, Twig came to a Thursday ride with a pretty grey Peruvian Paso named Pecoso. She reported to us that her husband, Bob, had just given him to her as a Valentine gift.

The following is a reference from Twig about this horse and her time with him.

"He was a beautiful dappled grey but with a **'cold back'**. When I first got on him he tried to buck, but after ten minutes of warming him up or sitting on him, you could do anything with him. We went to the White Clouds to camp and ride shortly after Pecoso became my trail horse. He was a great moving horse for long rides as he was easy to sit. I enjoyed riding him for several years until finally I had enough of that behavior. I sold him to a man who had experience with horses of this habit and the day he came to buy him, Pecoso bucked him off after he rode him a short distance. This horse I had put up with did the same thing to this experienced rider—he just bogged his head and threw him off in the barrow pit. This man still bought the horse. He said he was going to give Pecoso to his wife—hmmm, well you never know about horses or people do you?" Twig laughed.

Well, laughter heals and the heartier the laughter the better the cure.

Twig is a loving mother of three older children, Larry, Rob and Karla—all who have been horse oriented at a young age. Today all of her family ride, raise, or train Quarter Horses.

More about Twig.

In Bonanza, Colorado, Dora Branch—Twig Schutte was born in the depression years. She left home at an early age to attend high school and met Bob Schutte whom she later married. When they moved their family to the Twin Falls Salmon Track, Bob sold four of their Quarter Horse mares and kept a number of riding horses to use on their farm and to work with the cattle. His buying and selling of horses were his hobby. That is how Twig began riding many of his 'finds'. You might say this is how many horses came into Twig's life at an early age. Twig continued, "**I now ride an easy gaited horse** named, Jet, and jet power he is. He was only three when Bob bought him and we have come a long way in nine years. He is still full of vim and vinegar, but without a good horse you're in a world of hurt."

I asked Twig if she would do it all again, and her reply was, "After all these years and the aches and pains I have had with these horses and some I have not named, I would do it all again—you bet. You see it brought me in association with the Thursday Sage Riders. I never considered myself a horse woman with much ability, but I called it **'Therapy Thursday'** as I eventually joined the club where I didn't often miss a Thursday ride or overnighter. I have met so many great ladies all those years while riding horses with the club. Many are my best friends. When after riding with this club for 25 years, I became a **'Trail Boss'** for five years. I have many good memories."

Through the years, Twig and I have ridden together in Nevada and Wyoming where we had beautiful times. Only a woman rider with more than four decades under her belt can know what a long ride can do for the soul, and Twig still continues to ride them. **"It gives me nothing but pleasure,"** Twig said with a twinkle in her eye.

+++++

Adria Blair: Jerome

A Special Woman Who Rescues Hurting Horses

Not all these horse riding women claim to be 'cowgirls,' for there is a varied history of these spunky women who rode in rodeos. Yet, a cowgirl might be the woman next door fixing fences for a new horse she just acquired—like Adria Blair who has worked with many wounded or mistreated animals that others have given up as not trainable, which she expects to turn into good riding horses. She keeps them until they recover, finds them new homes, or comfort them as they go to horse heaven. This natural talent was given to Adria as she was born to a **skilled equestrian** father and she learned much from him. Her big Quarter Horse named Zip was an example of one of the most abused horses she had acquired in several years. In her warm voice she told me about this big gelding story as follows.

"He had been beaten so badly many of his teeth were missing, and he shied so naughtily it was nearly impossible to touch his head or even to brush his neck. He was a real challenge to catch and I used to sit out in the pasture with a pan of grain waiting for him to trust me enough to come up and with his long neck, reach into it and take a mouthful."

Adria's horses have had a life filled with love. Zip was an example of that love, for after Adria worked with him, he became a great mount and she rode him with the Thursday Sage Riders for several years.

The new equine love of Adria's life is the **miniature horses that she cares for.** When a small colt in her barn was born to a miniature mare, there were many children who came to her place to see the beautiful, tiny colt that was about puppy size. Adria shares her miniature horses with many others when she gives demonstrations with them at schools and special occasions.

Adria was raised on a ranch south of Jackpot, Nevada at Knoll Mountain by parents Carl and Martha Hice. Adria told me the following story of when she was a young girl.

"At one time the small town had nearly 3,000 people in the area and the need for working horses was great which called for many to be caught off the desert and trained. Father was an early *Horse Whisperer*. He came to this area in 1907 and gentled many horses even the dangerous ones with very bad habits."

The youngest of the family, Adair's grandpa often said of her that she was so independent that "if she fell into Knell Creek, they would look for her upstream." She was ideally situated to understand and convey the practices of her father at an earlier age to an era rapidly leaving their own mythology.

"One of my earliest memories of a lesson I learned happened one summer day in southern Nevada when I was out riding my horse Ribbon. I stayed out most of the day riding through a valley and up to a ridge. I returned at a fast pace into the yard where Dad was. I dismounted then began to tie up the horse. After unsaddling him, Dad told me to walk the horse as he needed to be cooled down. Which I did—around and around the farm yard I walked. Each rotation I would look at Dad for permission to tie him up, but he only signaled for me to go around again so the horse would be **completely cooled** down. About thirty minutes later I was able to

129

quit. I learned a big lesson on that day out, my dad saw to it I always took proper care of all the animals."

After Adria married and began to have a family she continued to work with horses by riding and training many horses for horse owners in Reno. It was a good 'out' for her, but she felt her work with the horses often went to no avail as the owners didn't do as she had suggested with the younger equine.

In 1980 as a single woman, Adria moved to Magic Valley and worked at a veterinary clinic where she met and eventually married Joe Blair. They moved to their ranch near Jerome. The first time I met Adria it was springtime and several of us TSR women were riding in the desert near Jerome. A lightening storm was brewing in the west and many were loping their horses back to the trailers trying to get there before it hit us. Adria came upon a young rider who was afraid her horse was going to run off with her if she joined the others in a fast gallop. Adria was riding her horse named Zip that had been used for coming alongside young horses as a rodeo pick up horse—and this is what Adria did; she took control by **ponying** the excited horse all the way back. And yes, they got rained on, but this was typical of Adria. She is one of the most thoughtful riders I know. In the three decades I have known Adria I have only known her to be full of sharing and helping others. Since that memorable time our friendship has grown and every time we meet and ride off together, I sit a little straighter, listen more attentively as our hearts incline toward each other.

One summer we were on a twenty seven mile ride into Grandjean where I had several small incidents that needed attention. Adria was there to help me recover. One time, with a smile on her face, she handed me a small screw with which I repaired my broken rein. She remarked, "Win, one more screw up and we'll need to send you back—as I am out of screws." This is Adria, full of good fun. We got a good laugh out of this. Laughter filled the air and lingered in all our hearts for a week until we met the next Thursday.

The following is what Adria thought about one of the rides we took together.

"I knew I needed to get away and clear my head and I realized I was tired and needed a time to myself. Therefore I signed up to go on the Grandjean ride with the TSR group. The next day out on the trail, I looked over at my riding partner and smiled; she winked and smiled back as we saw the trail head. It lit up my world and I felt that faint and familiar **sense of anticipation that the adventures** of the next few days would bring us. Once in the saddle I tried to wipe a youthful grin off my face so the bugs wouldn't end up staining my teeth. We laughed a lot, talked horses, and it was a time to renew old friendships and make some lasting new ones in the three days that we six riders were together. You would think I would have been exhausted, but I wasn't, instead I received much needed clarity that gave me a renewed sense of purpose. I hope we don't loose sight of the sense of freedom we have to recreate and enjoy our great outdoors it is one of those important things that make this county a good place for all of us to live in."

Good luck Adria. You are a free spirited cowgirl I am proud to know.

+++++

From Mackay to Challis you will pass Idaho's highest mountain, Mt. Borah at 12,662 ft. It is in the Big Lost River Valley. In the early days after Mackay was established, it was a railhead for copper mines. As the railroads closed the ranching became strong helping the town to stay. It had a newspaper with a linotype machine and presses. It now houses the **Lost River Museum** in a century-old church. If you ever travel through make sure you stop there and see the vintage collection of this town's past.

Blanch Lanier: Jerome

A Lady of Many Horses

In Mackay, the mid morning sun climbed a cloudless sky behind barren winter trees. The ground was still covered with snow and its glazed veneer was broken in patches from horses being fed a pitchfork of hay under a blue-blanketed sky. This described a warm, spring Saturday in the life of Blanch and her brother Jerry, as they often went out to the pasture to catch a horse of their choice to ride.

"I would often choose a pretty, pinto gelding we called Cricket that I rode in hometown parades and as a teenager, **a queen contest**. Cricket would move without question, and was an easy ride for me to learn on. When he and several other horses were hit by a car and killed, it nearly broke my heart. When I needed a dependable horse for events, I rode a mare named Tiny Lass that my sister Marilyn used."

The ranch where young Blanch Twitchell was raised was a home where her dad was once hired to pack hunters into the back country. They raised cattle and horses, a few sheep and even some pigs. It was a self sufficient ranch with hay for the stock and the garden was large and cared for by her loving mother who often put up with her oldest daughter being outside most of the time. They all helped with the household chores and there was plenty to eat and "we did not think we were deprived of any thrills as we did most of the fun things other friends did." Blanch's dad recognized her desire to ride a horse her brother had green-broke and most often allowed it. She knew that her dad preferred a lively horse over a quiet one and others said she was a lot like him. Therefore, most of the young equine she got to pick were full of "buck, and running", and were often a challenge to ride. There was an exception. It was an older mare Blanch and a school friend would ride bareback and often double. She remembered one Halloween after dark they had gone out with her brother and his friend, to 'trick' at a neighbors house. They did not intend to ask for a treat, just wanted to soap windows and—do a little mischief. However, the thing the girls did not think about was getting back on the big Quarter Horse mare bareback. When the occupants of the house realized someone was outside they came out to invite the kids in. The kids thought they were being yelled at for their mischief and being frightened, tried to run away. The last one on the horse nearly got left behind and ran alongside down the dark road until they found a place to mount up. "We never did that again, we were afraid our folks would find out," Blanch recalled.

"From that time forward, I have had a saddle horse to ride. One of my favorite horses I owned was Prisy. She had a heart as big as all outdoors and **I used her for barrel racing.** She loved to meet that challenge. She would get so excited she would buck at a dead run on the way out. Only one time did she throw me and I got hurt. I was unable to ride for several weeks," Blanch recalled. "Some of our horses were good for the kids to ride. Our son used a black named Bolly Mare in the kids' buckaroo rodeos for a number of years. Only one of our three daughters cared for horses."

"When we moved from that home, I looked for a place to keep the Gypsy mare as this mare gave me Rebel—a nice gelding that I kept into his old age," Blanch said. "When I had to put him down, I cried around the house for a week and I still miss Rebel. He was a horse easy to ride anywhere. We had spent time in the Copper Basin, Big Timber, Montana and many times chasing cattle at my daughters place in Bellevue on this horse. One summer several of us women planned a three day camp out. How beautiful were the lakes, early morning breakfasts and camaraderie with sisters and good friends."

"My new horse I call, Kiawai Mi, (meaning **kind gentleman**,) is a **Missouri Fox Trotter** that replaced Sam that I rode for many years. Mi is a pretty Tobino color that makes him all the more adorable. I love to ride this horse with my sisters as with, 'Trotter,' we are able to cover a lot of country in the Fairfield area during the summer months. I hope to be able to ride him a lot in the years ahead."

Blanch is a real cowgirl and is a recent **cancer survivor** and I wish her great rides in the years to come.

+++++

Karen Ambrose: Buhl

Creatures of the Wind

The more I was around Karen the more I learned that she was a giving person. Karen and I became friends several years ago when she and her husband Jim moved back to Buhl and she became a member of the Thursday Sage Riders. She came to visit me about the time I was down with a broken leg. She said, "**Our scars do matter**, as they tell us that we have lived and that we haven't hidden from life." I realized that the confidence and strength that Karen displayed came from a strong faith in God. She too has overcome some bad accidents and has scars to prove it.

Karen has made a great contribution to the sport of horseback riding through teaching lessons to many adults and children. There have been rewards as she watched her students compete in many shows and rodeos. Perhaps she won hearts with her dimpled smile as well as being a **successful equine teacher**. Maybe this coaching was natural to a person who was a teacher in the public school system for more than thirty years, or maybe it was her love for horses as she said—"ruined me, right there," and this love she wished to share.

"'Mommy, mommy, I rode the horsey and I rode in the front seat.' Those were the words I said to my mother as I, at the age of three, was removed from my great uncle's horse on his ranch in East Texas near where I was born. There my love affair with the *Creature of the Wind* began. Not just I want a horse, but more like—ride the horse, or is the horse in the barn? Or exercise the horse, feed the horse and so forth—you get the idea."

"I begged my parents for a horse every day until they were sick of the word, horse. I was raised in the era when every cereal box had a contest to win a pony and, of course I tried to win every one of those contests. My parents wondered where I would put a horse. And I would reply, 'In my bedroom, of course.' I thought in my child's mind, that it could live there with me and we would both be oh, so happy sharing a room. I never won a free pony and never gave up trying until I found my Goldie, a wild Mustang that had been formerly owned by my neighbor in Grand Junction, Colorado. Goldie was a Palomino and the most beautiful horse in the world, for to me, she looked like Trigger. She cost one hundred fifty dollars and I had to agree to raise a third of it even if I was only eleven. I kept her at a friend's place where I got some free hands-on-learning along with the five dollars a month rent. I did baby sitting and ironing to keep up with the stable boarding. My wonderful parents had a saddle, bridle and breast collar made for me in Mexico and also paid for the shoeing and vet bills."

"After I was able to keep my own horse, riding was a natural choice for me. I was able to ride a lot when I was young and this forever **changed my life in a positive way**. By the time **I was eleven**, I was riding with the **Rim Rock Riders Club** on trails where we often had contests. It was rewarding and a chance to ride together once a month. I was one of the youngest in the group and did not know there was a competition going on, but at the end of the first year, I had acquired the most points in my age division. At an awards ceremony, I was presented a brass and ivory trophy and a belt with my name engraved on it."

"I was in my first horse show at Mesa County fair that was held each summer. Goldie and **I won some ribbons** and I was so proud of my first horse."

"I still have that feeling each day as I look out the windows at my current horses, Tess, Taffy and Abbey. Taffy and I were a part of the Silver State Silverado drill team in Nevada. We performed in parades and rodeos in other states."

"I had Tess for twenty-two years and rode in **competition doing western pleasure, trail, working cow horse and equitation**. I was so proud when **she won top places** in these classes, and I give Tess most of the credit as a great horse doing all that I asked. Also I often gave lessons to young children on Tess."

"Today, I love riding Abbey (my new horse) in the deserts, plains and mountains of Idaho. There have been many other horses in my life, and I have great respect for them and all the things they have taught me. They truly are *Creatures of the Wind.*"

+++++

Shirley Williams: Filer
Our overnight ride together

A Ride with Many Surprises

Bear gulch is a good camping place with plenty of tie up places for the horses and trees to park our campers under. This June, as Shirley and I pulled into the camp there were already eight riders setting up. We unloaded our horses and secured them on lines between some tall trees.

Opening the camper door, we were greeted inside by a **surprise** visitor. Bridgett, Shirley's dog came bounding out. She was glad to have the outside to run in.

"She must have gotten in after we finished packing." Shirley apologized.

"It's ok, it will be just like staying at your house for her; we'll leave her in the camper while we're gone riding," I added.

That day as we rode our horses down the south fork of Shoshone Creek, we came onto the humming birds feeding place where feeders were hanging in the trees. We saw bright green birds; some red necked with white wings and some nearly white ones flitting around the feeders. Their distinct long, needlelike beak is perfectly adapted for siphoning the nectar of sugar water from the feeders. I identified some of them as Anna's Hummingbirds because they were cloaked in iridescent feathers that flash green in the sunlight. Their throat and crown were embellished with a lustrous, rosy hue. What a **surprise** to see the parade of flashing feathers.

The next day riding along Pole Creek we surprised a pair of ducks with seven, noisy ducklings, or should I say that **they surprised us.** The pretty feathered, sandy brown mother of the babies had the familiar mottled orange on her bill and she had patches of blue on her wings. The noise the Mallard female made let us know to stay away. The familiar *quack* was a loud and resounding warning that we had certainly upset them.

To conclude a great time riding out in the south hills, we were **surprised** to see a mule deer buck with a large doe, like a statue, watching us as they hid behind some tall brush. They had been drinking in Bone Springs where the light pink geraniums were blooming everywhere and the western distort flagged in the afternoon breeze. What a beautiful sight. I recall that we often see these brown deer with the dark accents late in the afternoons. I feel they know most hunters' hunting time and move more during mid-afternoon.

I had a great time camping with Shirley. I thought of the narrow line of meeting good people like Shirley and the **surprise** I got when she asked me to accompany her in her camper for this camp out. Even though she was raised in Jerome, a younger sister of one of my classmates, I had not met her before this summer. I am glad she became my friend.

Shirley also has a long history of horsemanship while living out of state. She has several young horses she rides and rides them well. There in Nevada she raised her family but **came back to Idaho** to retire and plans to continue **to ride where she was born.** Welcome back, friend.

+++++

Connie Wolcott: Idaho Falls

This humorous story is given to me by a fun, new Thursday Sage Rider that I enjoyed riding with for several years before she moved. Connie has enjoyed horses for many years and it is just like Connie to get on her Arabian horse for a ride in the desert at a time when she is upset as she often said, "Riding helps me too recover from bad times."

Out of My Head

Connie's story continues. "About ten years ago on a Sunday afternoon I was riding in the desert near Emmet when I decided to have a lunch break. I tied my horse up at a small tree and sat down to eat. The melancholy mood I was in when I left home caused me to put my marriage license in my pocket. There was a slight east wind, but considering the mood I was in, I decided to go ahead with my plans. With a set mouth, I reached into my pocket and pulled out the official document. Wadding it up with a tight squeeze, I threw it on a small, dry shrub, and then threw some dried cheat grass on top. I took my match-book and lit the paper wad on fire. This last week in August had been a very hot, dry week and the flames exploded. The first thing I knew I had to move out of the way of some hot moving fire coming right at me. Then I realized as the fire went beyond me that I needed to try to stomp it out. And stomp I did—fast and furious. But the fire was moving too fast. Franticly, I chased after it continuing to beat at the hot flames, but to no avail."

"I realized I must get help and I ran back to my horse, grabbed the reins, jumped on and cantered home. As I was moving toward the house I heard a BLM plane circle above me. Ohhh, I'm in real trouble I moaned as I rushed into the house and grabbed the phone to call the sheriff about the fire problem. Fire! I yelled as the operator came on. After I hung up I was crying as I told my mom what I did." "'You're going to jail,' she said while we listened to the siren of the Middleton fire truck as it went out."

"An hour later the sheriff called back and wanted to know what happened. I told him the whole story, marriage license and all—and praying that he would be lenient, but I was ready to step up and take the ticket."

"He listens then tells me that forty acres were burned. "I'm sorry, but all things heal in time," he added. I thanked him then hung up. Then I waited for the axe to fall, but I never received a ticket. I guess he felt sorry for me on the day that I was most certainly out of my head."

4-H Leaders & Members

Desert Wind Riders 4-H Club

4-H Jerome County Fair Parade

Diane & Shanna Tolley

Megan Kelsch

I pledge my head to clearer thinking,
My heart to greater loyalty,
My hands to larger service,
My health to better living,
For my Club, my community, my country, and my world.

Diane Tolley: Boise
4-H: Rewarding and Fulfilling

Nothing Compares to the Great Outdoors

"A little over ten years ago I became the leader of a 4-H horse club named Vaqueros. During this time I have acquired a couple of 4-H kids that are like my own who have been in my club for six and seven years. I have watched them learn, grow up and blossom."

These are the words Diane said to me when we met at the Idaho Horse Council meeting where she was attending as a delegate. I listened with interest to this enthusiastic horse lady and I knew I wanted to share her story. She was there to report some of the work that the Idaho Humane Society Rescue Ranch had been doing. We learned that this ranch had been very busy placing equines in safe homes after they had been abused, neglected or abandoned. Diane did this work on top of being active in county, district and state 4-H horse groups and their functions.

This is Diane's story in association with 4-H.

"The 4-H horse program uses the horse as a vehicle to instill in a child, confidence, respect, honesty, responsibility and much more. As the leaders, we are preparing them to be honorable, respectful citizens in our community with hope they will make their world a better place. We plan to show them by example, with various community service projects and events that they compete in to **learn sportsmanship** and how to recognize and control their feelings. Keep in mind that each child is unique and learns differently. However, I think one of the best lessons is compassion for humans and animals."

"I ride the range in a different way with our children—as a leader, teacher, mentor, friend, organizer and a stable influence in their lives. It's very rewarding and fulfilling. I would do this again, but I would start younger in life so it would last longer and I could have absorbed more of life's precious knowledge faster."

"I was raised on a 240 acre dairy farm in a family of all girls. I started working on our farm at a young age and always loved horses. During the haying harvest, at the age of twelve, I drove a team of work horses named Snip and Snap. But I very seldom got to ride a saddle horse out of the corral because my parents didn't want us to get hurt. Once a year I did get to ride out to do roundup with the yearling cattle. If I could go back I would have hounded my dad for a horse to ride while we were on the farm so I could take a horse to the county fair instead of Holstein heifers," Diane said with a smile.

"But sometimes I did take riding lessons. In one lesson, our teacher used an older black mustang gelding named Trinity. Trinity had a sway back and the teacher was teaching us emergency dismounts while on bareback. When I threw my leg over his neck to dismount, my leg got caught and I was hurled to the ground. When I hit, I heard some cracking and wasn't sure what it was. I asked my instructor, *did you hear that?* But she dismissed it and so I proceeded to ride another horse with an English saddle. Later that night I couldn't sleep or get comfortable and it was hard to move my right side. When I went to the doctor, I found I had three broken ribs. Well, of course this isn't the story *I tell,* for in my opinion it was a rodeo and I stayed on as long as I could before I bailed—ha," Diane added.

"My first horse was bought late in my life. We got a nice Quarter Horse in 2002 named Black Satin. Blackie could stop on a dime and was a great trail horse. She was very successful in Western and English pleasure, English jumping, and showmanship and reining and on top of all of this, she was a lover. She was also very smart. One summer she learned to load in and back out of a straight loading trailer with only a few tries. Blackie died a few years after that at the age of ten. I like to think that she is now resting in peace with her mane and tail flowing in the wind giving little kids that had never been on a horse before a glorious ride."

"During the years that we had her, Blackie and my daughter, Shanna, had their picture on the front page of the Idaho Statesman. It was a story about fair time. (There will be more of Shanna's story following this chapter.) This horse was very photogenic and we miss her greatly."

"Today I currently go on trail rides with my daughter, friends and our 4-H club. Our favorite place to do this is **Celebration Park along the Snake River and Birds of Prey.** This park was established in 1989. You can explore this area's high desert flora and discover the rock-face petroglyphs of Native Americans and early settlers of long ago. Here there are so many interesting landscapes, wild animals, birds and of course the river. This area was a wintering ground for Paiute Indians along the Snake River. We also like to ride at Eagle Island and the Eagle foothills."

"The experience of working with these young people and their animals has been a learning experience as I have found the students are also the teachers. They have taught me more of life's skills than I could have imagined before they came into my life. The 4-H leadership has been work, but as I said before, very rewarding and fulfilling."

I want to thank you Diane for taking time for giving us your story and telling us about your riding involvement with the 'Vaqueros,' as well as your leadership in all 4-H programs.

+++++

Shanna Tolley: Boise
Age 17: 4-H member

S-sassy; I-intelligent; E-intelligent; R-rough; R-rugged; A-athletic;
Describes my horse Sierra; by Shanna Tolley.

From Goldie to Blackie

Shanna Tolley was eight years old when she joined the Vaqueros 4-H club. She didn't have her own horse at the time, but leased a horse to use for two years.

"My first horse Gold Flame, I helped purchase with $200.00 that I had saved up for just this purpose. Goldie, I called him from his color, was a registered Arabian gelding. He really had a personality as an escape artist and he wasn't without some bad habits like the time he bucked me off. After I got used to him, I took him to a horse camp in Donnelly. We had a great time and I entered the **mountain orienteering, roping, horse nutrition and hoof care classes**. I began teaching the pivot for the showmanship class to Goldie the first year which for an older horse it took him a while to master."

"Within a few months Goldie was my favorite horse, a horse I can count on. When my other horse Blackie got injured, Goldie was the horse that I rode. Even though he was an older horse,

I took a lot of caution on him—going easy. I learned a lot riding him and **gained a lot of trust over the years** that I had him."

"Several years later I retired Goldie and began riding Blackie. She was a real smart horse and knew what I wanted from her. Her bad habit was her pawing. She began doing this one day when she was tied to the trailer. It got so fierce that she caught her foot in the area between the tire and the fender. Before we could rescue her she was bleeding so much we had to get help. Fortunately, she did get well, but I had to give her time off. I learned that we should have hobbled her."

"I did more eventing with Blackie and the great experiences have taught me a lot as this horse was very smart and **I hoped to unlock more of her secrets** as we went along. We learned skills I now use in horsemanship classes such as side-passing. It is exciting reaching many goals with her already learned skills."

"Then, five years later Blackie died. I will always cherish her memory. Her death caused me to have to lease a horse named Sierra, a registered paint mare, for my last few years in 4-H. I enjoy showmanship, western riding, English, gymkhana, trail and reining."

"I hope to achieve a career in animal science and become a vet. I love horses and would like to have horses all my life. **I enjoyed Teen Conference** and <u>Know Your Government</u> programs at the camps I attended. I feel so privileged to have attended these 4-H events. There have been many others who have helped me to be successful in 4-H, and I would like to thank them: Carmen Graham, Kristen Gilmore, Dana Holstad and most of all, my mother.

I volunteered to help at County, District and state events. I helped in many fundraising activities and a dozen other community service projects working hard throughout the year".

Shanna concludes her story; "Then I started something new. For the last two years, a **registered miniature pinto horse** I call Jose, became my next project along with two others. With Jose, **I do in hand jumping**, **in hand trail** and **miniature driving**. I believe that amazing things can happen if you change it and if you believe in yourself as a horse handler as well as a horseback rider."

"I am grateful for the opportunities the 4-H program has afforded me over these ten years. I have also **made many life long friends** along the way. I have learned horsemanship and how to care for my project animals. I learned how to speak in public as I build confidence and how to do interviews, but 4-H has helped me to mature and learn responsibility and if I had it to do it over I would practice more and not just have fun riding, but take opportunities that 4-H has to offer a little more serious."

Thank you Shanna for your story and I believe your passion and kind, gentle heart for animals and people will take you many places in life and bring you great success. Good luck to a very sweet young lady.

+++++

Megan Kelsch: Meridian
4-H Member

Horses Have Helped Me Learn Many Life Lessons

"All horses deserve, at least once in their lives, to be loved by a little girl."

Here is Megan's story in her own words.

"My name is Megan Kelsch. I now live in Meridian and ride my eight year old Half-Arabian mare, Party Hearty, and my eleven year old Arabian gelding, Mica, in most of the 4-H events.

I started taking riding lessons when I was eight years old. Then we purchased my first horse when I was nine. He was a two year old Arabian gelding named Mica."

"During my horse show career I have made many friends and lost some due to the nature of competition, I will explain; a friend that I had been close with since elementary school had just joined my 4-H club, The Desert Wind Riders. Unfortunately, jealousy ruined our relationship. I was fourteen at the time and didn't understand why someone's success should affect a friendship in a negative way. I had achieved, by hard work, an award in Showmanship and also performed well in an oral quiz. However, I used this experience to write an essay to win an award called the Idaho 4-H Horse of the Year. I wrote about how my horse had positively affected my life and the lives of others and about how my horse, Mica, was always there when I needed someone to talk to and always offered **a mane to cry on**. He was the reason I still continued on with showing after my experience. I knew that if I kept working with him and my other horses I could possibly be successful and in competition; friends would come and go. I received a letter that I had won the award during the summer and I was ecstatic. It was amazing how such **a bad experience could turn into something fantastic**. I received a Peter Stone model of my horse and **a horse blanket** for Mica. I now try to promote good sportsmanship to my peers and even the younger youth. Sportsmanship is a life lesson that if practiced well or not, can change the way you view yourself and how others view you."

"A humorous story that happened to me while riding is as follows. In the 2009 Western Idaho Fair I dressed my horse, Mica as a bride for gymkhana. I wore a blue 1980's style prom dress and I was supposed to be his "Maid of Honor". Well the dress was strapless and I was running back through the keyhole timer and I looked down and the top of the dress was at my waist. I was so embarrassed! But later I was running barrels (after putting a shirt on over the dress) and Mica refused to stop. We got to the rail where I was expecting him to halt when he darted to the right and I dropped to the left. I was still attempting to hang on, but as I was hanging upside down with my toe trying to pull myself up on the horn, I remembered I was in a dress and everyone was getting a show, even more embarrassing!"

"I ride my horse Party Hearty in the Arabian shows all across the Nation. I compete in Equitation, Hunter Pleasure, and Showmanship. I went to Nevada, New Mexico, and Utah in 2009. In Nevada, I competed in the Region 3 Championship Show where I became **Unanimous Regional Showmanship Champion**, and in New Mexico I attended the Youth National Championships where I didn't place, but felt I did well."

"I use Mica for 4-H events and local horse shows. He does Western Pleasure, Hunter Pleasure, Equitation, Horsemanship, Reining, Trail, Showmanship, and Gymkhana. Mica is going to reining training this spring to compete in the Arabian shows. I compete at the local and national level as often as I can."

"I hope to use my knowledge of sportsmanship to educate others. I would do it again. Even if I ended up losing a friend, I learned a lot from an experience that will benefit me in the community."

"Other horses I ride besides Mica, my eleven year old Arabian gelding, is Party, an eight year old Half-Arabian Mare, Sami, a twenty year old Half-Arabian mare, and M&M a fourteen year old Morgan gelding."

"Since I joined 4-H in 2002, I have competed in multiple events at the county, district, state, and national level. I also won the senior individual division at the county, district, and state levels.

One competition that I compete in is horse judging. In 2009 **our 4-H judging team placed first at the county, district, and state levels**. Those that attended with me were **Carina Marsh, Chelsea Bagby, Kiarra Rothwell and Shelby Miller**. We continued on to **attend the Western National Round-up in Denver, CO** in January 2010, for the **National Horse Judging**. We had never competed in national contests, so we were very nervous. We placed third in performance class judging, but w**e ended up placing fifth place overall**."

"I often ride about four to five times a week on Party Hearty or Mica. My friend Chelsea boards her horses out at my place so I ride with her."

"If I could go back I would want to get started earlier as I feel that I would be a better and more experienced horsewoman. Horses have helped me learn many life lessons and mature more quickly."

I learned that this **Desert Wind Riders 4-H club** managed to raise $4,000 in donations for the trip to Denver. I am sure proud of this club. I also learned that Megan is attending Oregon State University in Corvallis, Oregon as a freshman this year. Good luck Megan and happy trails.

+++++

Stacie Monaghan: Nampa

"I Have Learned Enough to Change Me."

"I don't like to think about my life without horses as this impact has made a big difference in my life."

When I first interviewed Stacie I could tell she was a big giver—especially in her relationship involving horses. I learned she has given her support and expertise of teaching to many young people helping them to understand their horse and giving them proper care. Perhaps the years she spent in the 4-H program gave her the desire to share. Stacie credits her knowledge in horsemanship from this curriculum as she excelled in English riding, Western pleasure, and Working Ranch Horse in her six years of being in the club.

This is her story.

"When I was seven we began taking annual trips to my uncle's ranch in Oregon. While there I was able to ride an older gelding named Red—plus this started my love for horses. I still have a picture on my wall of this memorable horse."

"When I was eleven we moved to a larger acreage learning to be 'country people' and soon were able to purchase several horses. The one I settled on for my 4-H project was a mare I called Sugar. Even though this horse was not well trained, my leader said I would grow with her and she was a good choice. Her beauty and conformation made me admire her even though she was a challenge. You would have thought I would have thought twice after she bucked me off on our first ride, but I continued to ride and train her with consistency and it paid off most of the time."

"The year when I competed in our next to the last show of the year, I decided to ride in the bareback class. Now, before this time I had not been successful in this event and should have known better. We started out at a walk, and then, at the request of a lope, Sugar began to crow-hop and as I gently pulled back she then reared up causing me to loosen up. Sugar began prancing around and I realized we were out of control. It was all I could do to stay on. The ring steward had a panicked expression for my safety as well as the others in the arena so she signaled for us to slow to a walk. We did a lot of walk trot until the judge placed all of us according to our performance and of course I got last. The judge praised me for just staying on the deck. I did not do the bareback class the next day as my mom reminded me with a smile that it was best to just live to ride another day."

Stacie said her most memorable reward was at the Western Idaho Fair when she was sixteen. She had spent a lot of time working with Sugar during the summer months. "It paid off as I finished second in my age group in showmanship. This gave me the ticket to compete in the senior championship run-off. Competing against me were others who had expensive registered horses with silver trimmed halters. So with typical western wear that was recommended by 4-H leaders, I went into the show ring and vowed to do my best and to enjoy what I was doing. With a smile, I entered the arena with the others proud to be chosen to compete with these peers. I knew my family was watching and I prayed I wouldn't make any mistakes. The judge gave us the pattern and as it was, I was next to the last to show. This was good as it gave me time to watch and remember all that I had learned the last five years. While moving up in the line I practiced with Sugar to do the forehand pivot. Sugar was a fast learner and when it came our turn she obeyed as I asked her. When the winning numbers were called—lo and behold it was mine, I couldn't believe it. I got a huge ovation as I believe the audience was glad a typical 4-H horse had won."

Stacie told me it just goes to show how unpredictable life and horses can be, and we talked about how her attitude had a lot to do with her winning. This is explained in her closing thoughts.

She said, "I learned when things look hopeless, to **do my best** anyway. When my best wasn't good enough, I learned to **lose graciously**, receive instruction and **work harder**. I never realized at the time what horses were doing for me, but I realize I have grown from being shy, to a fun-loving healthier girl who is willing to try something new. Or to shoot for the moon even when it looks impossible and shoot why not give it a try and enjoy the journey? I enjoy sharing what I know to the shy person who comes for horse related help. I tell them to be firm and yet soft—be decisive yet flexible—demanding yet understanding—loving but not a pushover when working with their horse. These are the things I learned working with Sugar. Oh, I have not learned all there is to know, just enough to change me and it came with my association working with the equine as well as trying to help others."

Stacie shared that her nursing studies have restricted her riding time, but she gets on her horses every chance she gets. She is thankful for the opportunity to start her nursing career and without learning persistence she might not have received good enough grades and been accepted into the program.

"You'll always fail if you never try," she said. I am sure she was thinking of the times she got bucked off Sugar and still got back on. Good luck Stacie and Happy Trails.

Back Country Horsemen

Jo Heiss

Mary Beth Conger

Chasing Dreams

"There are things that give you a sense of accomplishments. Things like clearing the trail, pruning a section of woods that needs to be done . . . . Then you go at it." ^former President, Ronald Reagan^

Seven decades ago many opportunities for a family to enjoy pack and stock travels to go into most any forest areas was readily available. Today, for example, in our National Forests there are less and less campsites that we can camp with horses. I support minimum regulation as needed to protect the resource, but humans are a part of this environment also.

The one service organization that does a lot to insure and make this privilege of back country riding possible is the **Back Country Horsemen of America**.

I recommend if you share the goals and interests of this hard working group of horse riding and packing-in horse people that you get in touch with a club in your area and join them.

Also see the story of Kathy Kerley (chapter 11) for a club in the Magic Valley area.

Jo Heiss: Hailey
Sawtooth Back Country Horse Club President;

Join a Club to Protect Your Right to Ride

"To educate, encourage and solicit active participation in the use of the back country resource by stock users and the general public commensurate with our heritage is one of our goals, and this pamphlet gives out good information to the general public," Jo said as she placed the colorful brochures in their holder and put it on the shelf.

"You really believe in this information and want to see it get out to the horse users, don't you?" I asked the back country mountain rider. Jo smiled her big smile, nodded in agreement. "Thank you for placing them in the office," she replied.

We talked a while of the importance of keeping the trails open in all public lands.

Since then I have learned that Jo Heiss is the president of the Sawtooth Back Country Horseman organization for the Wood River Valley area. It is a service club dedicated to educating all recreation trails users and **keeping all trails open to all user groups** as well as, cooperation between the different recreation user groups, with courtesy to all. And I know she works hard to assist the various government, state and private agencies in their maintenance and management of the resources.

She and her friend, Lisa Lintner, often attend the hearings that the Forest Service holds, in the Ketchum area. They are also interested in other state organizations that may have connection with horseback riding on trails that overlap other public lands.

The following is in Jo's words.

"The Back Country Horseman of Idaho, as a charter organization of the Backcountry Horsemen of America, has continually tried to get Federal legislation to pass <u>The Right to Ride</u> in order to keep stock on all backcountry and urban trails and have access to these trails. **Horses have historically been used on all trails** and should continue to be allowed to do so. In parts of the country some National Forests have been trying to close some of their trails to stock use. The Backcountry Horsemen of America has successfully fought with lawsuits and lobbying to keep all trails open. It is so important for all stock users to **join these organizations on a local, state and federal level,**"

"We horse people are outnumbered by the mountain bikers, and hikers that are using many trails north of Ketchum. Education is necessary for us who wish to continue to be able to ride our horses in many areas. All need to get involved and attend these open hearings and workshops to give input for our cause. And I encourage you, the reader, to join a group like the BCHC in your area and be active in the agenda to keep these trails open for all to enjoy."

Jo rides weekly when the trails open in the spring to late fall. She has since she was able to hang on to most any horse her mother (Marge Heiss) put her on. It's in her blood, and this is why it is so important to her, to continue with the working clubs that wish to keep the trails open in the Sawtooth Mountain Range.

Taking an Element of Adventure

"I remember before I was in grade school I have loved to be on a horse. Even when my mother put me on a big black horse, that was part Tennessee Walking Horse. She ponies me alongside of her horse and this made me mad. I wanted *my* horse, which I did get when I was five; my parents brought me a pinto grade horse. We had a cabin in Ketchum and my friends and I would ride every day or drive our buggy's and have buggy races down the main street of Ketchum, playing cowboys and Indians all day long. What a great babysitter that pinto was."

"Riding bareback was common for us sisters. Our only challenge was staying on when we jumped the creeks, or when running the horse as it often stopped fast. Growing up we had many summer rides where Elkhorn resort is now located. All this open country behind our second home in Ketchum, was our arena of learning to be a horseman. Also, at least once a week, we went out on trail rides with our mother and friends."

"As an adult, I have had the privilege to own some good trail horses. I know most all the Sawtooth Mountain trails like the back of my hand. We have packed in and stayed most of a week at some beautiful, remote lakes during the summer and fall months. And I have also enjoyed riding horses on trails in other states."

"A ride I recently took with my sisters, Cheryl Hymas and Lynn Christensen was up Trail Creek Summit just east of Sun Valley. I do not recommend it for beginners as it was a challenge for us to complete the trail's circle. We often had to get off to lead horses down paths that were so steep I had to rely on my horse to hold me back—but what new country! I feel riding is an element of adventure and often not knowing when you'll be back."

"I would not trade my riding days for anything, in fact, because of a back problem, I gave up skiing that I also enjoyed for many years, to continue trail riding."

Good work Jo. You are a very giving woman that I'm privileged to know. See you on the trails.

+++++

Mary Beth Conger: Emmett
Back Country Horseman Club in the Western Idaho area

The **Squaw Butte Back Country Horsemen** of Idaho is a very active club. They sponsor clinics to teach and inform folks who attend. At their event this year, the students were challenged to learn new skills that would make them safer and more confident horseman. Attendees from five chapters along with non-members left with a better understanding of the BCH club and the importance of getting involved to preserve our heritage of back country stock use. The hands on day consisted of courses of <u>Safe Trail Riding</u>, <u>Defensive Horsemanship</u> and <u>Beginning and Advanced Packing.</u>

At this clinic, Marybeth Conger, and her husband, taught different hitch methods. The comments were that this was outstanding as they learned that there are many ways to pack stock and every packer will have their own methods. **Check them out at, sbbchidaho.org.**

Another talent that I know Marybeth has a great ability to write stories of their adventures which are very interesting and informing. This and their years of riding and packing in are the reasons I asked her for her story.

Always Enjoying the Trail with my Horses and Mules

"The trail is the thing, not the end of the trail. Travel too fast and you miss all you are traveling for." Louis L'Amour

"When I was three, my journey began riding a donkey at Knott's Berry Farm, Ca. I remember how fun it was, traversing the ground, without moving my feet, until I lost one of my black patent leather shoes, which my dad eventually retrieved for me. Moving across the U.S. was a way of life for me, but my dad finally retired in New England when I was twelve. **English riding lessons, led to Three Day Eventing** and my first riding horse, which was a big, bay thoroughbred gelding named Rebel (for those that know me, no comments)."

"Throughout the years, I continued to ride, compete & then at age thirty; I moved to Washington State where I meet my husband Bill. He introduced me to a Western Saddle and took me on my first pack trip into the Bob Marshall Wilderness. We were still dating then and I admit there were times on that trip, I was thinking about ending my relationship with him, as I gazed down a 500ft steep embankment while riding on a trail that was maybe six inches wide. Finally after my stomach settled, I got hooked on the beauty around me and **began having fun riding in the backcountry**. But I knew I had to learn more."

Never Loose Your Cool. "So, I joined the Back Country Horseman Organization to learn and been an active member for twenty plus years. With their education programs, I became a more knowledgeable and confident horseman. With their trail projects, I put my mighty muscles to work to keep trails open. After all, **I want my grandkids to have the same choices I do on where to ride,** at least that is the goal. I have discovered some awesome riding areas in Montana, Oregon, Idaho, Washington and even the Grand Canyon. I have ridden many horses over the years but by far my **most enjoyable ride was on our first Mule Joe.** He patiently taught me the distinct differences between a horse and mule and the importance of making a few extra pancakes for him at camp breakfast."

"Bill & I began to take others on pack trips so I looked at ways to reduce weight and bulk on our stock. Simple actions such as repackaging items, using lighter equipment and dehydrating some of our meals made the difference. In fact, I took the later to the next level and **co-wrote a cookbook, *Easy Dehydrating Meals*.**"

"Presently, I am settled in Emmett, Idaho and riding a Quarter horse gelding named, Fred who has been a member of my family for years. He has thousands of backcountry miles and is by far, the best at leading our mule string. Bill is still my main riding partner and I continue to be involved with Back Country Horseman. While I still learn on the trial, **now I teach others who are just beginning on their journey**, so the cycle continues."

"I ride as much as possible trying for at least two pack trips a year with lots of riding in between to keep myself and my stock in good shape. My motto is a simple one—be safe by being prepared, always have fun, and no matter what happens never loose you're cool."

Warmbloods / Dressage

Melanie Nevins

Danielle Thomason

Kathleen Thomason

Marleen Thomason

Jacqueline Kennedy (1929-1994)

I Want to Live my Life

I would like to share with you part of a tribute to Jacqueline Kennedy that I recently read in <u>Peoples Weekly</u>. The article stated that Jackie, at the age of ten, proved that she was ready for equestrian competition. I learned that she entered many events at South Hampton with her horse, Danseuse. Jackie was described as the brain of her family, but was a daredevil horseback rider. Jackie gave this sport a lot of hard work, and her self reliance proved to give her much success.

Then as First Lady she was referred to as **an energetic equestrian**. And at her time as the wife of the country's 35th president, Jackie became the best known woman in the world. She was quoted as saying—**"I'd rather spend my time feeling a galloping horse under me**—not writing in a journal. **I want to live my life, not record it, as life is too precious."**

When Mary O'Hara wrote her short chapter in *My Friend Flicka,* she titled it—Flicka is Halter Broken. It is a beautiful gentle story of Kim, a youngster, who learned that once you gain a horse's confidence it will follow you anywhere. The author wrote that, "Flicka never felt the touch of her owner's hands except in gentleness and affection making an easy lead."

Melanie Nevins: Hailey
2009

GOOD FOR THE SOUL

On this early winter afternoon, Silver Bell Ranch is nestled in trees that are laden with snow. The new white fence outlines the pastures where a dozen horses wrapped in their blankets look up as we drive into the driveway at the beautiful ranch house. I remember it was well groomed, one summer when I visited, as Melanie Nevins loves to line the yards of her ranch with many summer flowers. Several months later when I returned, the ranch seemed to burn with colors of fall—truly a paradise on earth. I am looking forward to visiting in the spring as I come to see one of many events that take place at their **huge indoor arena.**

This seventeen acre equestrian ranch was purchased by Jeff and Melanie Nevins in 1996. It was a **dream of Melanie's** to have a place to keep her horses to be trained, ridden and shown. Today, they promote the Dutch Warmblood horses she and Jeff invest in. Many of the yearlings have been trained by Danielle Thomason. Also, this lovely place is shared with many others and not just boarding customers, but clubs such as Pony Club and 4-H clubs as Melanie shares what she has—doing a lot of volunteer Community Service around her home town of Hailey. She and her friend Del often take their miniature horses to events and public places where others, especially children, can enjoy them.

As we talked, I told Melanie I remembered seeing her on a black horse at the Horse Expo in Boise several years ago. She was assisting in a **demonstration of dressage** on this big beautiful horse that performed well. Melanie is tall, lean, well dressed with sparkling brown eyes and dark hair. In her riding outfit she looked super but the more I learn about Melanie, it is her big, generous heart that I most admire about her.

One story she recalled in her early days of riding is as follows.

"When I was eleven we moved to where I could attend a working cattle ranch in Arizona. There I got a real chance to have the hands on experience of taking care of my first horse, a Morgan cross. He was a fun horse that I grew up with along the southern California coast where we could trot along the beach with other friends on their horses. From these younger years with a horse, I knew I would be very happy if I had one to ride and take care of."

"When I moved to Idaho, I guess I began to see that maybe I could get my dream horse. When I began to associate with some dressage riders and I took some lessons, I knew **I wanted to have** a part of this sport. I enjoyed riding, but it was the horses that were used for this sport that attracted me. The warmbloods and especially the Hanoverian breed was often used in the events that I watched, therefore I was interested in them. A gentleman I met in Hailey, told me of a place in Germany that I could look for these equine and gave me an introduction to this special place that raised and trained them. When I went there, I got a full tour and was very impressed. Today, the German government has taken over the development of this breed and because of this they are very high priced and my attention was later drawn to the warmbloods **raised in Holland**. The Dutch people produced a quality horse with a similar appearance of the Hanoverian breed—attractive head, long and well-conformed neck, a wide deep chest, nicely sloping shoulders, a long straight back with muscular quarters and a well-set tail. The legs are strong with broad joints and hard hooves. But the most important to me is their good temperament and active movement."

When Melanie told me of this, I recalled our visit with her Dutch Warmblood horse she called Piet. He was in his stall when we entered the barn. As Melanie opened his stall door, Piet stepped up to greet us but did not seem anxious around strangers or attempt to get out. This

16.2 hh gentle gelding was a beauty to see and we enjoyed his friendliness.

"Even though he is now older he is very sensitive and a tough competitor," Melanie proudly expressed.

Melanie has not ridden in competition for several years giving her time to their son Jordan as he is active in the art & music classes at high school, as well as the time it takes of her managing the Silver Bell Ranch.

Melanie also has a registered Quarter horse named Zippo. She has had this gentle horse for several years and he is the horse that her son Jordan occasionally rides. Zippo is ridden by Melanie's nieces when they come to Silver Bell ranch for the summer months. Melanie enjoys riding when she can with her friends and mentors Danielle and Kathleen Thomason and Marlene Thomason. Melanie belongs to several equestrian organizations: the U.S. Dressage Foundation and the North American Dutch Breeders origination (KWPN) to name a few. Melanie said she has enjoyed her time spent here at Silver Bell. "The only thing I would do different would be to, not let others tell me what to do with my horses. And indeed this sport is good for the soul," Melanie concluded with a smile.

Best to you Melanie and I'll see you at the Silver Bell Ranch arena for the next fun and exciting horse event.

+++++

The Idaho Dressage and Eventing Association today have between one hundred fifty to two hundred members. They put on about six dressage shows, plus Derby ones and events during the year. Kathleen Thomason of Jerome has been an active member of IDEA serving on the Board and held offices over the years. Dressage is their forte'. Marleen and her sister Darleen's story are as follows.

Marleen Thomason: Twin Falls
Kathleen Thomason & Danielle Thomason: Jerome
Exerts by Bernice Richardson (mom)

Riding Keeps You Fit and Young

Those of us who are introduced to horses are far fortunate—but with it comes responsibility.

I met Bernice, Marleen and Kathleen Thomason's mother, at a writers meeting and told her I was having a hard time getting a hold of her daughters. She said she would help me with their stories. We talked a while and I found out that this family had an early history of riding horses. The following is from an interview I did with Bernice Richardson.

"When I found that the children were interested in horses, I went to a stable and we all began basic lessons. However, the girls were so avid to have their own horses that they worked baby sitting and doing other odd jobs for extra money. We went on overnight stays at horse camps together, as there were trails in parks that had stalls. Our young girls wanted another horse, so they could be together. Pepper was the first horse we got when the twins were 14, then Freckles, an Appaloosa mare named, Show Girl that had a filly named, Pollyanna. As teens they were active in FFA and were proud members, wearing the blue jackets of the organization. Marleen and Kathleen had no rebellion about work."

I found this still true for them as grown up women when I read an article of their interest to further the equine sport of Dressage. This equestrian sport has grown statewide and some of this **credit goes to** Marleen and Kathleen for their clinics they have put on.

Bernice continues their memories of the early days with horses.

"When we sold our house in California, things just seemed to fall in place. It was a big event moving here to the Magic valley. We had three horses, four dogs and a flock of sheep to load. We left our furniture to get at a later date as moving the animals were of great importance to us all. When we stayed in the higher elevations, we blanked the horses, stabled them, and made sure they were traveling well."

"We moved to Kimberly in 1973, and I have enjoyed having my daughters and grandkids live close to me. This way I could watch their progress in dressage, also."

Kathleen continues their story.

"When we moved here, we rode with the hunter/jumper girls for several years, as we had been introduced to dressage by a friend in San Diego. Several years after we married, my sister and I began taking lessons from Ernest Herrmann, a European instructor in Boise. We've been hooked ever since. For me the appeal of dressage is that it's a series of progressive logical techniques to develop a horse's muscular system."

I learned that riders apply certain subtle aids with legs, hands, and seat at a certain time to get the horse to walk, trot, and canter and execute progressively more complex movements in an elegant and powerful manner. The top level of dressage is called Grand Prix, which is seen at the Olympics. Today Kathleen has made the arenas at her place, a riding home for dressage by hosting recognized shows and clinics there. Danielle is training at the barn in Jerome.

"It is rewarding to train an animal and develop a relationship with it so it responds appropriately. Dressage training not only makes a horse stronger, it also keeps a rider fit and in shape. It can be a lifetime sport and riders of ages 12 to 75 can equally be competitive. We're 60 and training dressage horses makes us feel great. I feel riding keeps you fit and young—as well as the mind nimble, because it requires a great deal of concentration. We recommend once you begin serious training that you ride at least four times a week," Kathleen said.

Two years ago, Marleen, riding her nine year old Rhinelander gelding, Amaretto, which was imported from Holland, was named the Idaho Dressage and Eventing Association's Second Level **Adult Amateur Champions.** (This is awarded on test scores at the conclusion of the dressage show season.) She had also been awarded, **Rider of the Year** at second level and above and has won this award several years.

Kathleen's horse is a young, Dutch Warmblood, gelding named, Under Par-DG (Bogey) and they are progressing to compete at first level. "Bogey turned up at Silver Bell in Hailey and was offered to me at a very affordable price. He's 16.2hh, a beautiful grey. He was pretty 'broncus'. I had him ridden by Danny for two weeks and then gradually I began to train him. In 2009, his first show season, he was Training Level and First Level **horse of the year**, also Rookie horse of the year. My next step with him will to be to teach, strengthen and develop his collection that's needed for Second Level."

The Twins are willing to share their expertise and are supportive of anyone who is interested in dressage. What is ahead in rewards, Kathleen and Marleen have no idea, but rewards or not, they will continue training their dressage horses because this is the real appeal to them. Marleen and Kathleen are both very humble women and I have enjoyed getting to know them during this time of writing their memoirs. I wish them Happy Trails, and I know it is rewarding to them to know they have handed down this heritage to Danielle.

+++++

Danielle Thomason: Jerome

Danielle has trained with several international trainers in the U.S. and Europe. She is competent to teach horses and students through the 4th level dressage at Sugar Loaf Arenas. There are indoor as well as outdoor facilities available east of Jerome and horses can be boarded and exercised with her at the full size dressage arena. It is a clean, safe facility and they plan on having shows and events there. She went to the Seattle Symposium and she was chosen out of 75 applicants to be a demonstration rider for the Symposium. She rode Ameretto, Marleen's horse).

Great riding Danielle, I have heard great things of your talents.

+++++

Specialty Riding

Lucille Bickett & Friends

Jeane Miller
Helping Hands

Joining in helping
Jumping
Jockey

Jeane Kulm Miller: Jerome
Helping Hands secretary and assisting

Jeane gave me the following quote, *"Worry doesn't empty tomorrow of its sorrow, it empties today of its strength."*

Helping Others

Helping Hands Freedom Trails is a campout with horses for special needs individuals and their caregivers. And 'caregiver' fits Jeane completely as she is very friendly to others and I often hear her ask, "How can I help you?" In 1991, she became a part of this wonderful group of caring people who for three days in the summer camp near a lake in the Sawtooth forests with their guests—**special needs children and adults**. Jeane has been the secretary for the Magic Valley group for six years keeping people informed and also participates in the camp out by taking one of her gentle horses for these special guests to ride.

The following is about one of those campouts.

"As we work all year collecting donations to enable us to take 'special needs individuals' to this three day camp, I wish to tell you a story of a special young lady that came to camp one year. She was very shy and couldn't speak so you could understand her at all, but she was the sweetest one. We were at Pettit Lake and for quite a few years we have had a country church service on Sunday morning. We sing old time church songs and have a good time. This special lady asked if she could sing this one song, and of course we agreed. She went up to where the band was and stood with her back to us and started singing the words loud and clear. As she sang, she turned around to face all of us and finished the song, not missing a word. We were so surprised and felt very honored and humble because she did so well. And when the hymn was over she reverted back to the way she was most of the time. In the sixteen years I have been associated with Helping Hands, there have been many wonderful moments. Never know do we?"

Jeane continues the story.

"All of the activities at the camp-out are things these special needs people don't usually get to do. We have **special made saddles** for those who can't sit up by themselves that have straps on the saddles tall back with an emergency release. There are old fashioned pioneer looking wagons that are equipped for wheel chairs. There is a special rodeo night where the guests may ride a 'rolling bull barrel,' or ride stick horses around barrels, and at the end of the weekend, kings and queens are chosen. We have added a karaoke contest that makes it possible for more to join in. There are prizes given by local merchants for each contestant. On Saturday night we hold a big dance so all can join in. Sunday, after brunch, a **cowboy church service** is available. I'll tell you—many tears are shed that weekend, mostly by us volunteers as we see how much these special people affect our lives."

Jeane told me that this organization works all year gathering food items, door prizes, raffle prizes and many other things needed, and if you wish to help with any needed items you can call Jeane. Their camping times together are usually in mid August and have been at F.S. Flats beyond the Magic Mountain ski area. She extended her thanks to everyone who contributed.

Jeanie tells of the first time she took a horse up to the Helping Hands Camp.

"Poco was a very gentle horse I felt would be a good equine to share with the special needs group at the camp near Alturas Lake near Stanley. I readied her for the two hour session that morning with unsure emotions. When Tina, one of the guests, walked up and wanted to ride Poco, I was more relaxed since it was her first time here also. I led Poco while Tina rode and we (the other caregiver who was helping me) visited with Tina to get acquainted as well as teaching the inexperienced Tina about horseback riding. She had never been near a horse before. She wanted to pet Poco like you would a cat, but soon stroked the horses neck properly and I believe Poco relaxed. Tina was a special person and as the horse lowered her head for more affection, I feel Poco realized Tina was gentle and loving. To see her touch and ride for the first time in her life is something that really pulls at your heart. Through the day, the special needs students stood in line to get to ride and Tina always waited for her turn to ride only on Poco. Tina passed away several years ago at age 40, but we still talk about how she was one in a million as she never met a stranger nor passed up an opportunity to do something new. I have been very fortunate to be a part of a group that saw to the needs of others first. If I could do it over again, I would have participated in this program sooner."

More about my friend Jeane's early days of riding horses.

Jeane Brannon Miller was born and raised in Idaho where she met her husband Kenneth Kulm, but after 30 years of marriage she became widowed at a young age loosing him to a long battle with cancer. To help ease the loneliness and give her more to do, her friend Lynette gave her an Arabian-Quarter horse cross to ride.

"She was a bay horse with four white socks and a wide blaze that I thought made her very classy looking. This mare's name was Fahri and in the spring her foal Keema was born. She was a nice colt but didn't have as much chrome as her mother," Jeanie said with a smile remembering the pretty horse. As soon as I could separate them I began riding Fahri in the south hills and it was there after having a great day so far my story of the accident happened."

"Lynette, my riding friend, and I were coming back down 3rd fork and were less than a mile from the trailers, when Fahri planted her feet to a quick stop then jumped around. (As I look back I believe she had heard a snake nearby.) Her sudden commotion caused me to loose my balance as I was turned in the saddle looking back and down I went landing on my back on top of two large rocks. I still had the reins in my hand and Fahri just stood there looking down at me. I felt a lot of pain and was unable to even turn over without Lynette's help. After a while with her help I was able to crawl upon the horse and come on out. Again with the help of a nice young man at the trailers, I got into the pickup then they loaded the horses and Lynette and I went home. However, the next morning I had much pain and because I could not walk I realized that I had not just pulled and bruised a muscle. It was then I called an ambulance to take me to the hospital; lo and behold they diagnosed that I had a **crushed socket of my left hip.** This was why I could not move my left side. One pinning procedure was unsuccessful and then I needed a hip replacement in 1994. Today I am blessed with being able to go back to horseback riding, dancing, bowling, and wearing high healed shoes. I ride as much as I can with good friends Twig, Jan and Kathy who I met on the trails with the Thursday Sage Riders Club. I ride a mare named Poco, a black registered Quarter Horse. My faithful horse, Nugget, I have retired after riding him for several years. He's a pretty sorrel with a wide blaze and two white stocking feet. I love horses. They have been good for me just as they have been for the disabled that our Helping Hands group takes to the camps where they too are able to ride."

+++++

Jumping horses

The Missouri Fox Trotter is one of America's oldest breed. In 1820 the Morgan, Arab and Thoroughbred were crossed to produce a horse with speed, but was later used for its endurance and smooth gait. A fox trot is a gait where the horse walks in the front and has a sliding trot action behind. The Fox Trotter is a pleasure horse for trail riding and an excellent cow horse. Their temperament is good for the youthful rider to enjoy. There is a record of a winning Fox Trotter that won 350 harness trotting races. Wow, what a horse.

Lucille Bickett: Gooding
Fox Trotter, Country Gentleman took on a new meaning.

Take Things as they Come

Coming from a house in Dietrich where she had her first horse race, to riding a camel in Egypt or an elephant in India, then back to Gooding where at age ninety-four she was featured in a newspaper article riding her horse in a parade, Lucille has certainly gone full circle.

Lucille was raised on a farm ranch in a district named Marley, near Richfield. When she was young, she rode a horse named Fanny that was used to pull wagons for farm work.

By age twelve, Lucille's dad bought her and her brother a bay horse named Sparky; however, her brother would rather ride his bicycle to school so Sparky was all hers.

"Of course in the winters we often drove a team with a wagon or a sled to school, but even my girlfriends couldn't ride Sparky as he liked to run."

And run away he would, every chance he got. Lucille explains this in the story.

"I had stopped at a store after school to get something to take home, and had not put Sparky's bridle on him yet. Then, when I came out, I had a sack in one hand and I just took the halter rope he was tied with and put it around his neck and hauled up on him. Well, before I was seated, he began to walk away. The saddle tipped with my weight on one side and I was afraid it would turn under his belly. I scrambled upon his neck in front of the saddle and by then he began to trot—then as I was unable to make him stop, he began running faster down the road. Well, it was miles before we would get home and I thought if I turned him up a road away from our home, he would slow and maybe even stop. After he jumped a few ditches, nearly losing me, he went upon a rock pile and did stop because he lost the saddle. However, on the rest of the way, he began a fast trot then a lope and was going too fast to turn into our lane. I let him run straight ahead where my brother was bringing in the cows. I thought when we met he would stop and follow them home, but a big cow charged us and hit us so hard Sparky fell with me. We recovered well enough to make it home where my brother and I went in the car to get the saddle. But the next day I was so sore I couldn't sit or climb stairs at school. This is just one incident with Sparky as he was one running horse but I never rode again without my bridle. I rode Sparky to school until the eighth grade. We got along fine, but the teacher had to hold him when I got on."

"There were rodeos in the small towns, and quarter mile races that my cousin and I would enter. Often I won first place and my cousin second."

"I remember the stock market crash although the effects were not felt as much on the family farm as we had chickens, pigs, sheep and cows as well as we raised our own vegetables and fruit which we canned. In those days, every town had a grange hall and dances were held there. That is were I met Harvey, a young widower with two children who I married at age nineteen."

"After I married, I let Sparky, the pretty sorrel horse go to Dad's to help the herders in the sheep. Dad soon returned him as he was too fast for the slow moving sheep. (He probably ran off with the herder,)" Lucille said with a smile. "I rode him for fourteen years. With all his running in his younger years he won in the seven-barrel race held at Carey, and we enjoyed competing in the gymkhana races. This horse taught me many things and thus began my love and learning about horses. Oh, I liked to go to the mountains with the horses to camp and often we would shoot our guns."

"I guess I was meant to work with horses when a two year old buckskin was offered to me at a price I couldn't turn down. He had great conformation and I felt he could do anything in which I might want to compete in. I learned to take things as they come and did lots of training with him until he matured more. He rewarded me with a first in the Magic Valley horse show in the trail class. That was in 1949 and I competed for another fifteen years on him. I often rode him with a side saddle in some parades. At a show in 1955, I watched some **jumping events** and decided to try it with Snooper. This seemed successful with him, but I could feel hesitation and I always had to push him up as he didn't seem a natural jumper. With some advice from others like a Presbyterian minister from Wendell, who was experienced, after that we did quite well—often placing high. **I did this competition for a total of twenty-four years.**"

"I trained my own horses till I was sixty-five then decided to not do it anymore."

When I asked Lucille what horse brought her the most personal rewards of all the horses she trained she told me; "The horse I really liked I called Silver Fox as I could enjoy his natural **talent in jumping**. He was **my Missouri Fox Trotter horse, The Country Gentleman.** I went to Missouri to get him. And he is the one who won me so many trophies and ribbons that you see some of them in my house."

Yes, I saw hundreds of ribbons made up into not one but two bedspreads that were on her beds. The trophies lined her shelves in most every room and I know she gave many of them away to be reused.

After Lucille was widowed, she said she went on many fun trail rides to several other states including Texas, Montana and Utah. One she did at the age of eighty. This was just before she lost most of her eyesight. She has also ridden in Australia and in Argentina—the Brazilian way—flat saddle and all, as she explained to me. "It was a lot of fun," she exclaimed.

"I also had a Peruvian Paso I called Red Fox that I bought to **ride with the Thursday Sage Riders** on the trails of Idaho. This was in 1977. Here I met many good friends who today visit me and take me with them to luncheons. The places we went together were a sweet treat in my life and I still cherish their friendships."

And I cherish *your* friendship and thank you Lucille for sharing your stories and teaching us to 'take things as they come,' as you most often did.

"I've had a good life," Lucille said with a smile, "I've traveled very extensively—far more than I've dreamed of. I've been all over the world—on six continents, so I think I'm ready to stay home. But I just love horses. **It's just the thing I do.**"

Born 1914, Lucille celebrated her ninety-seventh birthday at the senior center in Gooding January, 2011. There were thirteen guests who knew her in her horse riding days and we had fun talking to her about her lifetime journeys on a horse, of course.

+++++

Racing Appaloosas /Jockey

Idaho has declared the Appaloosa the states horse; this is some of the history of that horse.

The Appaloosa is descended from horses imported to America by the Spanish conquistadores in the 16th century. The breed was further developed by the Nez Perce Indians of Northwest America and the name, Appaloosa is derived from the Palouse River which ran through the Indians' territory. They bred the Appaloosa not only for its attractive spotted markings, which were excellent camouflage, but also for its qualities of stamina, endurance, speed and athleticism. The skin must display one of six markings to be in the National Registry for Appaloosas. They generally have a sparse mane and tail. The Appaloosa makes an excellent riding horse, being both docile and quiet, but also energetic.

Jockey career

In the earlier days, racing was the most popular event at western rodeos, and champions won the acclaim of the crowd and exceptional prize money. This was inspired by the country's fascination with the short-lived pony express. There was a woman named Ruth Webster who was tutored by an express rider, that won ladies' races at Cheyenne in 1916 and repeated the winning streak in Denver at Frontier Days. She rode thoroughbreds, raised and jockeyed them. She was known as the "Mother of Thoroughbred Racing."

Do you give the horse his strength or clothe his neck with a flowing mane?
Do you make him leap like a locust, striking terror with his proud snorting?
He paws fiercely, rejoicing in his strength, and charges into the fray.
He laughs at fear, afraid at nothing; he does not shy away from the sword.
In frenzied excitement he eats up the ground: he cannot stand still when the trumpet sounds.
Job 39:19-24

Diana Smith: Blackfoot

A Lesson in Planning for Success

"This quote is not made by me, it was made *for* me:"

> *Riding a horse is not a gentle hobby, to be picked up and laid down like a game of solitaire. It is a grand passion. It seizes a person whole and, once it has done so, he will have to accept that his life will radically be changed.—Ralph Waldo Emerson*

I met Diana at the Idaho Horse Council annual meeting held in Caldwell. I wish to thank her for giving me a super story. I was impressed with her enthusiastic attitude to be a delegate as a younger person. She represents the future of the horse industries for our state. I hope you enjoy her story and pray the young people who love horses will learn from her memoir that she tells in her own words.

"Appaloosas became a part of my life due to the influence my dad had to the **Appaloosa Horse Racing Industry.** I like the Appaloosa's smart, athletic abilities, dispositions, and character. They have lots of character."

"Our family has many horses. Some of my special ones are Bucky, BJ, Tri Star, and Turner Classic Moves (nicknamed TURNER). Turner is the best! Out of over sixty of them though, I love each one in different ways and know each one by name. Our family owned horses before I was born and as soon as I could, I started associating with them. The first Appaloosa Dad gave to me was nicknamed, BJ. Her registered name was J&K's Barbi Jet. The second horse I received, was nicknamed, Bucky and her registered name was JK Street Cash. Bucky is actually a Red Dun Appaloosa. Because she is not buckskin, one would think she got the name Bucky from bucking, but that was never the case with her. The name came from the late talented Rod Grant. He was training Bucky for horse racing at the time and the name just stuck with her."

"As I learned to exercise racehorses and **as a licensed jockey**, I have had many accidents with horses. The most brutal one was a **traumatic brain injury** that fractured my skull and caused severe brain bruising and swelling. The accident left me with what the doctors guessed would be a three year healing period and the end results of how well I got, was up to me. The horse I had the accident on was my own horse that I took to a track to give a schooling race in like company. I was her trainer and at the time and I felt she was ready. Unfortunately, we tripped twice on the track while hustling to catch up to the other racehorse. The other racehorse, happened to be the one, that I rode in a race eleven months prior and ended up breaking off my pelvic bone. (ironic, isn't it?) Anyway, my horse tripped while racing and that threw me up on her neck. This really imbalanced her and she tripped the second time which is when I landed on my head. I do not blame her. I think she probably tried to stay under me as best she could and the accident happened for a reason. I am doing really well, still able to work with horses."

"I'm getting to work with my dad in his tax preparation office, (it's an amazing opportunity for me to learn how to manage a business.) I'm learning different software programs, and getting to know the many wonderful clients that come in year round! Another aspect of how well I'm doing is that instead of traveling to the various places that the races took me, the accident brought me back to my home town where I met and fell in love with my future husband. We love spending our extra time together playing with our Appaloosa colt, Turner, and enjoying the wonders of what a horse can do for a person!""I do not compete in horse events today like I did before the accident. When younger, I tried barrel racing and pole bending. I exercised horses on the race track and was a licensed jockey. I show horses at the Keeneland Thoroughbred sales, Ocala Sales, Saratoga Sales, and once at the Timonium Sale."

"A rewarding experience happened when I was exercising horses. A friend came and asked me to help him with his mare. Her name is Derby Cat. I helped that day by working her with the race gates. About one or two weeks later he asked me if I would gallop her. After I galloped her he told me he wished I would get my jockey license and ride her in her first race. I told him there was nothing more in the world that I wanted and that I would get my license right away. Derby Cat and I approached the race gates one week later. We were in the ten hole out. We ran third that day and two weeks later we tried it again. Out of the third gate, we swept out, fought for the front and by the end of the turn we were past everyone and still gaining ground. **We won by what seemed like ten lengths** that day and I have rarely felt anything as thrilling and gratifying as that moment. I remember riding her on the back stretch as we caught our breaths and feeling so overjoyed that I thought I would just fall right out of the racing irons! Would I do this again? I would love to do it again and often do in my dreams!"

"I am a member of the Idaho Horse Council and I am proud to serve on its board of directors with some of the most talented people I have met. Their efforts and accomplishments drive me to better myself and work as hard as I can to make a difference for the better in the equine industry in Idaho."

"I am also a member of the Intermountain Appaloosa Club. This is a great club that, through them, I am learning a lot. My goal is to join the American Appaloosa Club in 2011. "I do not ride as often as I used to. The Traumatic Brain Injury left me as a candidate for worse injury results if I were to have another accident to my head. I still like to ride for pleasure either in the mountains when I can or just on our ranch. I am hoping to take my future husband riding very soon and I believe he will be my riding partner for the rest of my life. Otherwise, one can't ask for a better riding partner than my dad, or brother, Mike. They are fun and safe to ride with and have taught me most everything important that I know about horses and enjoying life. I wish to thank you two! If I could go back in the years, what would I do different? I have always been strong willed and this is probably why I have been in so many accidents. I do not wish to go back because I love my life as it has been, but I do plan in future horse endeavors to **always take time and plan for success instead of just acting and finding out what happens.**"

"Watch how your horse interacts with one another and realize how you interact with those around you. Then ask yourself, are you a helpful member to the herd or a hindrance?"—Diana L. Smith

Drill Teams

Brandi

Brandi Horsley Krajnik & Heather Miner

Erica Greenwood

Myra Beck

Echo & Aigana

Sitting bareback astride a horse, touching his warm sides along the full length of our legs, feeling movements up the length of our backs and into our heads, sensing in our hands as we hold the rein strap, we tap into the physical nature of the horse and become aware of our bodies the way a horse is. Increasing our body awareness increases our ability to experience the ride to its fullness.

EhCapa History

The EhCapa Bareback Riders were created in 1956 as an inexpensive way for children to ride and enjoy their horses. EhCapa is a family-oriented horseback riding club for boys and girls, and has performed in many western states, including Idaho, Wyoming, Nevada, Oregon, Washington, California, Montana as well as British Columbia and Ohio. Most riders average six years with EhCapa. The horses are of every shape, color and breed, with no specific qualification except that they are trained and loved by the children who ride them. The group consists of forty to fifty motivated young people.

Their performances vary from season to season, but they always include an exercise of maneuvers and jumps that even few experienced riders can handle—all without the aid of saddles or bridles. This is done with the riders having a unique relationship with their horses based on sound horsemanship principles. The program emphasizes commitment, patience with self, consistent practice, active team participation and mentoring others.

The club's style of riding is reminiscent of Native Americans. The name Apache was selected to be spelled in reverse, thus the name EhCapa. The organization rides in the hope of bringing honor to Native Americans, from their beautiful handmade clothing to the traditional native symbols painted on the horses.

(An Eh Capa performance at Ketchum; September 2010.)

Apache Riders

This group of young horseback riders has performed all throughout the Northwest the 2010 season, in California in 2009, Ohio in 2003 and into British Columbia, Canada in 2000. This fine group of young people has had a very busy summer last year. They have been asked to perform at many rodeos and celebrations. Their horses are in show shape—clean, trimmed, shinning and well mannered.

The twenty-seven members were proud of their performance at the pole-fenced pasture one morning in Ketchum, Idaho. Afterward they came along the rail and visited with the many spectators. They scarcely had time to eat lunch before they lined up for the Wagon Days Parade in Ketchum. They were led by their beautiful Queen, Erica Greenwood. What troopers they all were, never complaining of the 80 degree temperature in those dark, hot wigs, leather pants, and beautiful, heavily beaded shirts and headdress—especially the long feathered headdress the teenage men wore. The march in the parade was very impressive with the long lineup, the swift turns and the colorful outfits. They accomplished their goal of another "feather in their cap." The crowd cheered and clapped for them. I should not have been surprised at their nice attitudes, even as these young riders enjoyed the praise they received.

These Apache style riders do all the drill, including jumping at a very fast pace **bareback** and **do not have any bridles** on their horses. The only tack you see is a tack rein around the horse's neck. It was enjoyable watching the riders direct their horses with leg cues at the lower girth and using soft voice commands. Brandi Horsley, their leader, told me they ride in honor of the Native American way of horsemanship. I visited with several members who said they enjoyed going to the different places to perform and would otherwise not get to travel like this club offers them.

I learned that some have been members for about eight years and there has not been one serious accident from performing in the arena or traveling to and from on the road. They are a great group and I am proud we can claim them as Idahoans.

One of the mothers, Gina Price, has two daughters that ride in the club; Aiyana is eleven and is their Mini Princess. Jessika, age sixteen, has been in the club six years and will run as the 2011 Queen. They are most certainly serious horse lovers.

Karmel Laursen's, daughter Echo is the Reigning Princess riding a nice Arabian bay horse and has been with the Eh Capa for eight years. I asked her mother if it was a big commitment to be here. Karmel answered, "Yes, we parents live and breathe this life all summer. We get to travel a lot and we feel it keeps them busy and out of trouble—when they love it—it's OK and much worth it."

Brandi Krajnik stated that **past leader, Janis Wisten Gram** kept the EhCapa Club performing through thick and thin for thirty years and much credit should go to her for her great leadership and dedication. In this group I met courteous, young people that are, responsible, and appreciative. I wish them health, and good riding.

EhCapa is a nonprofit, charitable organization and is financed by its participation in horse-related events, as well as through sponsors and fundraisers. Performance fees are negotiated on the basis of number of performances and distance traveled.

+++++

Brandi Horsley Krajnik; Nampa
Leader, Teacher, Friend & Parent

"There are too many good horses to put up with a bad one."

Most of the credit of the great performances of the EhCapa group goes to their leader and her assistant as well as the parents of the riders. I have visited with Brandi Horsley Krajnik who has been their leader for eight years. I can understand this group's success after meeting with her. She is a friendly, smiling lady and a dedicated leader with a lot of hands-on experience to lead the more than thirty-five members, which includes her daughter. She told me she enjoys the kids very much and the only hurdle *she* has had to jump is getting parents to realize all members must follow the rules. I learned that the club travels together and camps together just as families do. They practice once a week starting in March and then ride twice a week from June to September. The following is Brandi's story.

In It for the Long Haul

"I was raised in Nampa by a 'horse crazy mom' who had a horse named Snip. After a lot of lessons for all of us, Mom realized I too thought only of riding horses and looked for me a good horse I could grow up with. We found Fella, that was a rescue horse and after giving him much care—which included good food, grooming and some time, I was able to ride him. I rode him around our place bareback when I was eight years old. It was like trot around and then bounce down his neck when I wanted off or when he was tired of me. I guess this prepared me for the Eh Cappa team," Brandi said with a big smile as she remembered those days.

"As a youth, I belonged to EhCapa for eight years and had wonderful times. I had a love for horses and was looking for something to be involved in and EhCapa filled the gap. I was a very shy kid and the riding with EhCapa taught me confidence in myself. I started coming out of my shell and enjoyed doing things with my many horse, loving friends. When I was a teen I achieved the Liberty Team, which means I could ride in the program without the horse's neck strap, nothing at all for the horse's guidance. This club is where I met some of my best friends today. Heather for one, for as a young girl and teen, she was a close friend that rode most of the years that I did."

"To add a little humor, when I was eleven I had just joined the Eh Cappa riders. We were performing at my hometown rodeo, The Snake River Stampede. I was on a Quarter Horse named Socki and she was a Welsh/Arab small mare. I was slight myself and I was supposed to come riding into the arena in uniform. This humorous part of the performance was practiced often where I broke out of the line and made it look like I wasn't supposed to—as our leader Janis would chase me saying *I was too little to jump*. Well, I guess my horse thought the same thing because she refused the jump—just put on the brakes, and I went off. It turned out okay, but I was embarrassed at that time. Socki was a great first time horse for me to ride in the youth drill team, she taught me a lot and I missed her when she died. Then I rode a quaterhorse named Snip. He turned into a great horse. He had a very likeable personality."

"When I was too old to be with the Eh Cappa, I was honored to wear the Caldwell queen title when I rode for the Nampa Stampede. I took public speaking and modeling lessons that helped me achieve my goals. One of my fondest memories was that I was invited to ride in the **Rose Parade in Portland**, Oregon."

"I was also in 4-H several years and I *learned more about winning when I lost*. It was good for me. The horse I rode was a three year old mare I called Socki, then we bought a four year old with a registered name of Charm Me Dry, that I called Shimmy that has served me well for many years. Some of my horses could have competed with me in other horse related events such as racing barrels etc, and if I could go back I wish I had competed in these events when I was younger."

"My current EhCapa horse is Shimmy. She is a pretty, prissy buckskin quaterhorse. Before becoming the leader of EhCapa, I was a volunteer who helped many young riders learn the way of bonding with their horse. As their leader, I hope today to pass the same confidence and enjoyment that I had as a young rider. I know what EhCapa did for me, for today it is very dear to my heart. Watching the group of new riders' progress is rewarding to me."

"A quick story as the leader, I will tell you. One evening while we were performing at the John Day Rodeo, in the middle of the drill, one of our riders was jumping when the jarring landing of the horse caused her wig to fall off her head. Jessica just caught it, but then continuing the drill, she did not know what to do with it. I signaled for her to put it back on her head and keep in the drill. So she did, but now she had 3 braids instead of one when her own braided hair came down. She was embarrassed but continued as I asked. We all had a good laugh at her three braids. However, these kids and their parents are the best sports. We have a lot of returning riders every year. I am so proud of them. Today, we as a family often ride in the Owyhee County area or go to Celebration Park for the day. With my daughter enjoying riding, I guess I'm in it for the long haul."

"I have enjoyed traveling with the troop. We have some very good riders—including two young men, some have been with us for more than eight years and some that just joined us." Thank you, Brandi for sharing. Good luck and happy trails to you and your daughter. It was special to get to know your hard working assistant, Heather Miner. I asked her for a word about this fine group of young people. Heather said, "We work with them every week, and there are many challenges to overcome, but it is a good feeling to see the ones who want this membership and work very hard to achieve and perform."

+++++

Myra Beck: Burley
Drill leader:
Story also under Mule Riders

Memories from the Past/ Visions for the Future . . .

This was the theme for the Cassia County Fair and Rodeo as they celebrated **100 years** in 2010. The **Friday night rodeo** was a lot of fun to watch—from the mad cow riding race to the top cowboys and girls competing in their events, along with the very pretty reining Queen Tanisha Adams and her attendants. I was there to also watch the performance of the women's drill team. This large drill team was led by **Myra Beck.** I spoke to Myra before the performance even though she was completing final details for the event; she was smiling and friendly to me when I met her granddaughter who was also one of the team members. Their horses were brightly saddled and they waited anxiously for their turn to participate.

As previously mentioned, I truly enjoyed watching this hard riding group of women present their drill program with Myra always in the center blowing the whistle and keeping the drill in movement. The large audience clapped heartily for the entertainment. Great work girls! I too give a round of applause to you.

Friends

Freddie
Hopkins

Marcia Chojnacky

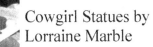

Bridger Wilderness,
WY

Cowgirl Statues by
Lorraine Marble

Lorraine Marble

*If you don't understand the phrase, "it's just a horse" then you will probably not understand phrases like—**just a friend.***

May your horse never stumble,
Your cinch never break
Your belly never grumble,
Your heart never ache.

Freddie Hopkins: Jerome

Chance Meeting?

In being human there are only beginnings, and the good work of being friends and good neighbors is the unique ability which can set us free.

In the early 1980's a special blessing happened to me. A new neighbor moved in next door. I yelled, *hurrah,* when they unloaded horses into their pasture. I hoped they would become new friends and we could ride horses together. And my hopes were proven, because within a few weeks I met Freddie Hopkins, **one of my best friends today,** and right from the start we began planning where we would ride our horses.

Freddie told me her riding aspirations began when she was in junior high school. Her dad bought a Fox Trotter they called Trigger. They lived in the town of Mountain Grove, Mo. but kept their first horse, Trigger, and her brother's horse, Buttermilk, on a farm just outside of town.

Freddie began to relate her first memories. "We rode our bikes out to get the horse's, carrying their bridles on our handlebars. We rode bareback back into town to meet others we rode with. Thus began my love for the beautiful animals. As an adult, I was a single mom, (after divorce) but I never gave up the desire to have a nice riding horse. When I remarried, my daughter Tracy and I moved to Idaho; we each had a horse and were anxious to ride the trails of Idaho. **Having good riding horses has been such an inspiration to me.**"

And so our friendship began in 1981. I invited Freddie to come with me on some trail rides with the **Thursday Sage Riders** where we rode in the south mountains near the Nevada border as well as the Sawtooth Range. We rode together a lot on Thursdays—she on Brandy and I on Bingo. Soon, Freddie became a member of our club.

We also took some hunting trips together in the Wood River Range and it was there where this story began. It was in the days when the law was looking for a wanted murderer named, Dallas. One day we were five miles from camp when we approached a tent set up in a cluster of trees. There were no horses around and not a sign of life. As we rode closer, a bearded man came out the tent door that resembled this criminal. I said, "Let's ride!" But Freddie just pulled her jacket back revealing her 44 and said, "What for?" At the time, she worked for the Department of Correction and had just obtained her concealed weapon permit and I knew she was a good shot. We laugh about this and insist it was "him," even though Dallas was thought to be in Nevada at the time.

Freddie is a very pretty woman with a friendly manor; you first notice her dark watchful eyes, as well as she is always handsomely dressed. She sits her horse well and as our friendship developed, I was proud to call her my adopted little sister. Today, Bill and I often go to new places with Freddie and her long-time friend, Terry. They are good sports to pull their horse trailer up some of Idaho's dirt roads into old towns where we ride. Last year we camped near Atlanta along the South Fork of the Boise River. As we rode through the **old mining town** we talked of the olden days and what it must have been like to have lived when the town was new. On the way to a mountain lake we rode on an old trace of a road that was 100 years old and went to some of the old mining digs. It was a fun three days.

I asked Freddie for a story on which she learned a big lesson. The following is her story.

"One fall, Terry and his son Torry and I were elk hunting in the Pioneer Mountains. We were riding down narrow switchbacks near a place called P.K. Pass with an elevation of 9500 feet. It is on Iron Mountain and Mine Creek was below. It was toward the end of the day and we were loaded with our elk carcass and rifle in scabbard, besides packing enough food to sustain us for a long day. I was on a palomino mare named Tandy; she was not experienced at such narrow trails. When we come upon a place in the trail that was obstructed by a sweeper branch protruding over most of the path, it struck some of our equipment, pushing us out on the edge. Tansy slipped to close to the perimeter and as she lost her footing she began to panic. She scrambled for all of her feet to remain on solid ground. It was a very steep drop off with no area to regain her footing. She began to slide, so I got off hoping it would help her recover and she did. But, it was steep and I went sliding and tumbling out of control. I tried to protect my face, but my legs slid out from under me and as I hit a fallen log, my face and left side scrapped the hard rocky earth and after another tumble, I came to a stop beside a tree. I thought I might have some broken bones and stayed still for a while. With some help I finally was able to sit up. Terry helped me bandage some cuts, gave me some pain pills and helped me back upon the trail above. With his help I got on another horse and was able to ride back to the trailers. It was several weeks before I could ride again. After that lesson, when I come to a dangerous place in the trail, I now get off and lead my horse. Except for the accident I would do it all again. I do not ride today as much as I wish to, but go when I can."

I see Freddie with implicit courage, a very good sport and we still have a barrel of laughs. She now rides a great trail horse and recently we have journeyed into the White Clouds together for a weekend stay, enjoying the beauty of the Idaho Mountains that thirty years ago she came to see.

+++++

Yes, compared to Lewis and Clark we were doing this the easy way. However the mountains are still as high and jagged. The wind blows just as hard, and the rain is just as chilling and many of the rivers we cross are just as deep and deceptive.

Shirley (Lee) Straley: Jerome her mother **Shirley Young** and her sister **Edith May Maxey**

Shirley and I grew up together. It was her family that invited me to their summer home north of Ketchum to ride horses with them. I credit the Young's friendliness for giving me the desire to ride horse-back during my teenage years.

I asked Shirley Young Straley (known as Lee) to give me her story of events with the horses in her life. One late summer, she cordially invited Bill and me plus five Thursday Sage Riders to **Wyoming** to ride in the Bridger National Forrest with her. We had a wonderful three days staying at her home, riding to the beautiful mountain lakes, and the enjoyable hospitality was unmatched by Lee and her husband, Jim. Thank you for all.

I asked Lee to tell early history of their love for horses and include her mother, Shirley Young and sister Edith Maxey.

Shirley Gorman Young

Early Idaho Pioneer

"Shirley Gorman Young, was born at the turn of the twentieth century. When she was nine years old she moved with her family to Jerome where her father and uncle had opened their general merchandise store, Gorman Brothers. Their building still remains on Main Street. In those days, transportation was still the rail system along with horses. I was told of a story about Mother, in her youth, trying to control a mare that she had hooked up to her buggy. When bees attacked the horse at a bridge crossing, she won the battle."

"Shirley persuaded her siblings to join her in **purchasing an Indian pony** from a school teacher. The boys soon lost interest and she bought their shares and eventually her sister's who always left riding but returned leading the horse. I never heard of falls or mishaps. Shirley went on her first date with Leonard Young (who later became her husband) in a buggy pulled by his mare, Dixie Princess. They had two daughters, my sister Edith May and six years later I was born. Women were very involved with horses in the first third of the 1900's, but not necessarily just for pleasure. They operated horse drawn farm equipment and were using them as their main mode of transportation. Shirley went off to get her diploma at the University of California, Berkeley. While there, she lived with cousins and an uncle who was one of Teddy Roosevelt's Rough Riders. Shirley, her husband, Leonard, and daughter Edith May **returned to Jerome** before I was born. They lived on a farm south and west of town. It was during the depression and times were hard. Although my father had horses, none were suitable for my mother and with a little girl, a baby and cooking for thrashing crews, etc. there would have been no time for pleasure riding."

"After twenty-one years of teaching and caring for the family, Shirley Sr. bought a matched pair of Pintos for us. She said it was in self defense so she could ride with us in the mountains instead of wondering where we were. Not surprisingly **her daughters were horse lovers. Edith May rode any horse she had an opportunity to.** Many were not the best horses but she rode anyway. Because of their great horse program, Edith May went to Stephens College in Missouri and later raised and showed Arabians with the help of her husband John, as well as our mother."

"I was a part of a junior posse for girls that were living in Jerome County; with my horse back riding friends, we raced, played in the canals and once were caught in a very bad thunder and rain storm east of town. A farmer saw us coming and waved us into his big barn for shelter."

"During my grade school years, I was fortunate to spend my summers at Graham's Ranch about seven miles north of Ketchum, Mr. Graham had a sorrel gelding named Tommy that I rode bareback. He loved to run and was not greatly influenced by a mosquito like me on board. My mother said she always held her breath until we made the 90 degree turn from the old road onto the lane. We managed to always make it without mishap until the day my dad was behind a willow-lined ditch and when he came out, Tommy side-stepped to the other side of the road but I did not."

"My mother bought my Pinto mare, Dixie Queen, for me when I was twelve and the mare was five. She was **not exactly a model kid's horse** as she had been raced as a two year old. I used a curb chain on her when I rode with the other kids. I rode mostly with my sister and mother and other adults in the mountains, so there wasn't much opportunity for going fast. It was fortunate that I spent horse time with my mother because she was not just an expert rider, but **she was knowledgeable and wise about horses.** She could pull a loose shoe or teach a horse not to pull back and break halters. Dixie was a kicker, but **Mother taught me safety and respect for horses**."

"Our property was the last before the national forest lands so we could ride out the back gate to Oregon Gulch and to Baker Creek, Fox Creek and others. We also could cross the river to go up North Fork. We also rode with the Jerome, Twin Falls and Gooding riding clubs when they came for overnight rides in the mountains. We didn't have a horse trailer therefore, I had more miles riding and leading one to the camping spots to the start of the rides than many of the actual rides were."

"The summer of 1955 Marge Heiss organized a ride from Jerome to Ketchum. Mother and Edith May and I, took turns riding the two horses and driving a pickup with a horse trailer for emergencies.

Twenty-one young women made the ride, camping north of Shoshone about six miles at an old CCC camp the first night. A new road was under construction and made a beautiful bridle path between that camp and Timmerman Hill. The second night we camped just north of Timmerman Hill and rode from there to the Hiess place in Ketchum, for a total of seventy-five miles."

"My senior year I was selected to go to Ogden, Utah to compete for queen of the Ogden Pioneer Days, where girls from Nevada, Idaho and Utah competed. We eight girls were judged on riding, scholarship and personality. I had a great time as first runner-up staying in the Ben Loman Hotel, eating at fine restaurants, riding in parades and grand entries."

"Following in my sister's footsteps I attended Stephens College and **spent every free minute at their beautiful stables.** My riding classes were all taken in English gear. I rode three and five gaited horses but regret not taking advantage of the jumping. I transferred to the University of Wyoming and met my skiing cowboy, Jim Straley. After marriage we were fortunate enough to be assigned to Pinedale, Wyoming. Pinedale is at 7100 feet elevation situated between a high mesa of sage brush and grazing land on the south and the Bridger Wilderness to the north."

"We had three sons Monte, Zane and Latner. When they were in school I was able to go with Jim on many rides. Our boys also rode, trained their own horse, showed them and worked on ranches. **I led the 4H horse club for six years** and Jim did the horse science group. We had a drill team, horse shows, a competitive trail ride and every summer a three day camp-out and mountain rides. Twenty two horses and riders is quite an experience, but fortunately nothing earth shattering ever happened."

"All my rides were meaningful to me, but one really great one was a four day pack trip with my youngest son Lat. At twelve Lat rode his gelding, Suraman, and we packed on Tasmara. I was riding Springtime, an Arab mare; this was her first trip. We went into the Bridger Wilderness from Elk Hat Park. A couple of days out, we stopped for lunch on the top of Hat Pass. There was no place to tie the horses so I held Suraman. I didn't think the mares would leave him so we turned them loose in front of us with our backs to the trail we'd come up. They kept edging around us and I told Lat to catch them. The trail down from there was not really rideable nor was there space to lead two horses at once, so Lat took Taz down and tied her to a small bush. Lat and I started down with the other two horses, but before we reached Taz, she had pulled loose and started up the trail and managed to get around us. Lat and I had to keep going to a place where

I could hold both Suraman and Springtime. Fortunately Lat was a very fit cross-country skier and managed to run her down so we could continue. The last night we camped at Coyote Lake, I tied Taz close to the tent. She stood so quiet that I kept thinking she must be gone and **I spent the night peeking out the tent**. We made it out of the mountains in good time."

"In later years I returned to live part-time in Idaho having a second home near Hammett. I enjoyed riding my mare I kept at my sister's place. I was sponsored by Lenore Mobley to join **the Thursday Sage Riders** and I had many pleasurable rides with them including a twenty mile ride in the Sawtooth Range. All winter long in the snows of Wyoming I'd count the weeks until I'd be back to Idaho and do some spring riding. Even after I lost both of my mares I kept in Idaho, I often rode there as the wonderful ladies in the TSR group loaned me a horse for the day. I wish to thank those for hauling extra horses for me to ride."

+++++

Lorraine Zimmerman Marble: Fairfield

A Cowgirl Who Creates Cowgirls

When The Going Gets Tough—the Tough Get Going

Lorraine and her family moved to Idaho in 1970. I met them at that time, where events involved cattle or horses. Her winning smile gave me a welcome each time we met. Today, she and her husband have a nice log home in Fairfield where Lorraine was keeping her horse. She often rode with some of my friends and even after Lorraine was unable to ride (from an accident) my husband and I would go by their mountain home and have supper with Lorraine and her husband, Jeff. I learned she was a giving person as you will read in her story. Also this is where I realized **Lorraine had talent in sculpturing.** As you can see in her picture she produced very beautiful and intriguing statues.

"When I was nine years old, I started riding my dad's work horse, Dick. I was born in Canada and there were plenty of places to ride on the farm. When I was sixteen, on weekends I rode a 16 hh Irish hunter that I exercised for a friend's mother."

"I never owned my own horse until after I married and lived on our ranch in California. Then we purchased a Three Bar Quarter Horse mare that was in foal. The stallion was Brush Mount that was from a ranch near Pendleton. The pretty foal, Irish Miss was born on St. Patrick's Day in the middle of a horrific Santa Anna wind. **I trained her myself** for my personal mount and for twenty-six years I enjoyed riding her. In our early years together, I rode her in a bozal hackamore and often bareback."

"I became a 4-H leader when my children could join and after I outfitted them I couldn't afford a saddle for myself. We rode to the meetings round trip, fifteen miles—yes, I rode there bareback."

"I enjoyed riding many horses as we rode many miles on the high desert in Lullen Valley. Besides the seasoned horses for the children, we bought cross bred heifers off the range in Nevada, fed them on the ranch and sold them back as bred heifers with a nice finish on them. We raised six cuttings of hay and spent mornings moving pipe to water it; often walking up to six miles a day. We then spent the afternoons at the swimming pool to cool us off. We had a rewarding life there—**rattlesnakes and all.** We were an isolated ranch with no TV or phone. The children would, once a week, take a trip to the library when they ran out of something to read."

"We had a chance to board horses from Big Bear and the owners came down to ride in the winter. Our care included giving some of the horses exercise as well as the feed we grew there. I rode mostly in the evenings because it was cooler then. One early evening I was riding in the arena. My youngest daughter was playing with her yellow dish set in the back of a hay wagon. She was singing to herself. I glanced over and saw, to my horror, **a large coiled rattlesnake** on the wagon's wheel. I bailed off my horse and vaulted the corral fence and scooped up my daughter and took off for the house. When I returned the snake was gone. I believe the child's singing kept the snake from striking."

"We entertained large gatherings at our ranch, as cross country rides was positioned near our place and the Vet check was held here. Some of those barbeque lunches were a lot of fun, as interesting people often stayed with us. **We took in many teenagers that were aimless and gave them a horse and put them to work. These kids are still in touch with us today** as we consider them part of our family. They say that the experience was the best of their lives."

"When the water for the ranch was dropping we decided to move someplace with lots of water. In 1970, we ended up in Idaho on a farm with sprinklers for irrigation. This is where we raised our children until they went away to college. We again did 4-H as our place attracted them to ride the big open spaces of the desert east of us. Our club grew to thirty-five kids. We enjoyed this farm that was near BLM ground and the children and their friends would ride off to explore. We often had family rides into the Hunt area that would take all day."

"I really enjoyed my riding experiences in the last forty years, even the Cowboying I did in Nevada one fall. I wish I was still riding and raising horses because I loved training the younger ones."

"I do sculpt horses occasionally and have since I was nine years old; it was my father who taught me. I should do more, as I love it, but traveling and quilting take over my extra time, not to mention our four children, grandchildren and all the other kids that have been this family's home at either Fairfield or in Arizona in the winters."

Best in all you do Lorraine. And **no** she does not sell her beautiful statues—darn it!

+++++

A Horse will be Honest with You and Tell You How He Feels.

Four Generations of Horse Riders

Yes, these are stories of 4th generation women riding horses. This winter when I visited with Marsha's mother, Ann, she too said she had long relationships with many a good horse on the farm where she was raised when she was younger. What a nice lady, and one that has raised a super daughter that has been a special neighbor and long time friend to me, Marcia Chojnacky.

Marcia Chojnacky: Jerome
Ann Schwarting
Kirstin Short and **Samantha**
Emma Jaro

Tomorrow the Sun will Shine and We will Ride . . .

"Come on Marcia," I yelled. "Our horses, Bingo and Sonny are loaded up and the mountains are waiting." We had prepared to leave for a **three day vacation in the Jarbidge range**, sixty-five miles south of Twin Falls.

We had our camp on top of the ridge where many tall pines protected it from the summer sun. It is at 8000 feet elevation. There is a small stream that runs nearby where we can water the horses. Just below us is the **Pole Creek Guard Station**. There is a more wooded area near us to the west where some campers could park. We six Thursday Sage Riders had our camp-area to ourselves.

It was a beautiful night, with a full moon coming up. The horses were content as we gave them their grain and we could hear them crunching the last of their hay. We devoured our pot luck supper, and were able to build a bon-fire for the evening visiting time (something we women do a lot of). It was a lovely evening spent by Cheryl Hymas, Virginia Spafford, Ruth Stanger Staley, Twig Schutte and Marcia and me.

In the morning we found that the trail leading down the canyon was unlike any we had seen in Idaho. The smaller trees were mostly mahogany and scrub pine. Along the hillside, the rock formations were a red color and places were shadowed as we rode closely under them. We loved its uniqueness, we had wonderful rides and we want to go back someday.

Marcia tells the story.

"The first morning we rode up Hummingbird Springs and below God's Pocket. What incredible scenery! The wildflowers were totally awesome. And the riders were such great company."

"We thought our group of riders was the only group camped up in those mountains, but one evening after the ride, Win and I were out walking, and two men appeared from nowhere and came up an adjoining trail to us and said, "Mai tai's anyone?"

"They were clad in sandals, shorts and Hawaiian print shirts and carrying a drink. My goodness, we just about fell over and had many, many laughs about the surprise itself and the folks that were hidden amongst the trees in the mountain camps."

Oh yes, our rides were definitely filled with laughter but they also afforded us that awesome slower pace in life to discuss whatever might be on our minds. Our rides were precious bonding times. This trip began a lifetime friendship for Marcia and me, of horseback trips over central

Idaho. I call her my friend, not only because she has often saddled my horse for me when I was not up to it, but in many areas of our friendship she has 'just been there for me.' Yes, we have been to the mountain tops together as well as down in the valleys.

When Marsha and her husband moved to Idaho they settled on a farm next to ours. They have raised their family, Kristin and Cliff, here and it is a privilege to get to know them through their school years; Cliff after college settled nearby with his nice family. Like Marcia, their children became horse enthusiasts—thus giving her two granddaughters who also like to ride.

Renewed Interest in Riding Horses

First, I can't continue without introducing you to Anne Schwarting, Marcia's mother.

When Anne visits Idaho, we enjoy getting re-acquainted over lunch or coffee and I have called it a privilege to have her as my out-of-state friend. I have asked her to tell of her association with horse riding in Idaho—plus some history of her love for the equine.

This is Anne's story.

"Some time ago my husband and I visited my daughter, Marcia, who had recently moved to Idaho. **My interest in horses became renewed** with this visit. It appeared that almost everyone, from the very young to the very old, had a horse and that they were able to ride. I found that very fascinating and felt that it would be just great to be able to ride through the countryside once again."

"I had not ridden a horse for many years back and during that time, I would rent a horse for a dollar from a stable and ride around a lake in an English saddle. I loved it."

"In time, I purchased one of their horses named, Dee Bar a registered twelve year old quaterhorse that was well trained; I felt if I bought this horse, I could relate to my family in Idaho. I rode Dee for many years. Marcia and I continually compared our days out riding—one of us from the East and one of us from the West. We often wondered how many years we would be blessed with two great horses, as Marcia had Sonny at the time."

"Whenever I visited my Idaho family, **we would saddle up and ride**. Not only did Marcia enjoy riding, but so did her children. The sagebrush desert was near their farm and I had the pleasure of riding with them. This is where I met their neighbor, Lenore, as we enjoyed the friendship and scenery together. I was hoping one thing—that I would never see was a rattlesnake while riding there—and I never did!"

"Many good memories were made while riding in Idaho with my daughter and granddaughter. One never knows, I may have the opportunity to ride once with my great-granddaughters. How fortunate to have four generations of gals who love to ride!"

Now more of Marcia's story.

"I grew up on Long island along the shores of Morches Bay on a farm with my two sisters. We had the freedom of running through the fields catching box turtles in the woods as well as catching blue claw crabs in the bay."

"I was instilled with an excellent work ethic along with play. I had two girlfriends with horses and we spent great times together. I really enjoyed this and I guess with my mothers love for horses, I had it 'in my genes'!"

"After college, I married and we moved to Idaho in 1971. Before I delivered my first child, I finally had **my very own horse, Sonny** Kid Red; he was an awesome sorrel quaterhorse, was seven and well schooled."

"This was the beginning of an incredible relationship that none other horse can compare. I rode him for twenty-one years. He was tender with babies on his back, yet he could carry Miss Rodeo USA in our local parade; he would barrel race and do well shown in many horse shows and was enjoyable in the mountains. I could not have had a more perfect relationship with a horse and along with this, so did my two children. The farm and desert was a perfect playground for all with horses. There is no question that my Sonny was my favorite riding horse. It was a sad day in my life when the vet told me he had a thyroid cancerous growth and surgery again was not an option."

"One evening after a ride to Alice Lake I noticed Sonny had not eaten his grain. I reached up on his neck and knew that this was the last trail that we would enjoy together again. I cried over such a loving and faithful horse, my companion on hundreds of miles of trails. To me he became a legend. It took some time before I found Jake. He had good trail sense. I rode him for about seven years. Some of my most perfect moments were the rides my kids and I took right from my home in the BLM desert."

"When I think of some of my times on horseback, I think of two special people. One, my longtime friend and riding partner, W. Lenore Mobley. With a phone call we would report that the sun was shining, the desert was waiting and the horses were anxious. Her daughter, Willann, often rode her black, Shetland Pony, Dukie, down to my house. She would tie him up, sit under my apricot trees, write some poems, and enjoy brownies that I had baked."

"Win and I also rode together with the Thursday Sage Riders and what rides we had! There were times it rained, times the wind blew, times were cold and times we saw rattlesnakes and many times we witnessed fellow riders dumped off their horses. But as we witnessed the first spring wildflowers **while on horseback we would just smile**. We rode because we were good friends."

"Another special person in my riding days was Frances Sheneberger. She was one of our TSR leaders when I joined. I enjoyed riding with her, as Frances would say, "Honey, it's a beautiful day to ride." And off we would go to the Red Bridge Road, or the desert by Notch Butte or the desert by my house. She loved the desert and I credit her with the love I also have for the beauty there. Sharing childhood stories, history of Idaho pointing out the wagon tracks along the canyon and even listing to the meadowlark sing, was common for Frances. The bird sang just for her, as she would repeat that it chirped, 'Twin Falls, pretty little city,' then she would laugh. We had many great rides together and I truly respected her as a great horsewoman."

"When Frances was eighty-four, she called and said that I have to buy her Clipper horse as it was time she quit riding. I knew that that time would have to come when I'd lose my riding pal, but I was not prepared for it. I did buy Clipper, and my husband, Mike loved and enjoyed riding him, along with Jake and me. We often rode to some hunting grounds where I had never been. Clipper was a great horse for our family to enjoy when we took those adventurous rides. I am always in search of the wildflowers and those high pristine alpine lakes and if I have to I will hike to them."

"**We are blessed to be four generations of women** and girls riding horses. We have all had our bedrooms filled with books and magazines of horse stories. We have stared at catalogues filled with boots, spurs, chaps, saddles and horse pajamas. We have fallen asleep with a smile dreaming about—"tomorrow the sun will shine and we will ride again."

+++++

Kristin Jaro Short
Marcia's daughter

Kristin took to horses from the start. She was a small girl with a strong desire to be a good rider. It was very fortunate that her family had, Sonny, just the right horse for her. She knew how to sit a horse even before she became active in 4-H, so it was not a surprise to me that she did so well in every event she entered.

After Kristin was married, horses were a love she just had to continue with. Today she shows, raises, and trains some of the best Quarter Horses in the west. I know this because I have seen her many **trophies**—some from big **national shows**. They also enjoy the **Cowboy Shooting** origination that they do as a family. Good luck Kristin and may you and your talented daughter, Samantha, have great rides together.

Samantha Short
Marcia's granddaughter's story is as follows.

In the summer, Samantha, at eleven, shows many animals in 4-H, they are projects that take up a lot of her time. This year she spent part of her summer with her grandmother, Marcia, therefore, she has not showed her horse Scooter because of other timely projects. She hopes to be able to go with her parents to the Cowboy Shooting competitions next year when she is twelve, a required age. I practice the routine without the gun, and know I am going to enjoy being a part of this sport. Maybe I out-grew the showmanship classes even though **I acquired grand reserve awards** with Tiny my Quarter Horse that I often ride."

"My first horse, named Buck, was given to me by my grandpa Short. After Buck died Dan was the horse I rode until we retired him at the age of twenty-seven. I loved him and miss him very much."

"The incident I had on the horse I ride now is he often gets big eyes, and takes off bucking all the way across the arena. I just bale off him when he gets like that."

"I enjoy riding and look forward to doing more with my family as they all like to ride."

+++++

Emma Jaro: Jerome
age 6 (daughter of Cliff, Marcia's son)

Born to Ride

When you visit Emma while she is riding her new horse Brownie, you will see her smiling all the time. They have built an arena for the purpose to teach Emma to ride; it is beside their home north of Jerome.

"I feel happy when I ride," Emma said. She reined her big Quarter Horse into me and added, "I was born to do this."

She grew up on a horse and rode as a small infant with Dad in the saddle. As she grew, her dad led her around the driveway at her grandma Marcia's on a good kid's horse called Biscuit.

"Biscuit loved kids," she said.

When Emma talked about the fact that last year she also lost her horse, Wilson, she said sadly, "I sure missed him."

When Emma didn't have a horse to ride in an arena she went to riding those mutton busters at the county rodeos. She was used to riding with her legs tight around her horse, because of this she won a belt buckle at the age of three for mutton busting. She told me, "I had the longest time and won, but **the buckle was so big** it would pull my pants down. It was heavier than my pants! But I won a smaller one later and I can wear it in a walk trot class," she said proudly.

This is Emma's horse story in her own words.

"The story I would tell you about was the day last summer when my dad and I loaded up our camp things, and our two horses to go up to Little Smokie campground. We camped that night, and the next day after breakfast we started off for Warwick hot springs. While we were still near camp, dad's horse, Cowboy, started acting up. Now Dad usually kicks his butt when he gets goosy. That morning the horse really, really acted up and started bucking. Dad got off to settle him down; and was just getting back on when Cowboy really came uncorked. He probably got scarred as he hadn't been ridden for a while. He lacked experience and was what Dad calls green broke. When Cowboy reared up he went all the way over and fell on the ground. Dad had his leg under the horse and when the horse got up—Dad didn't. He said he was hurt and I said whoa to Wilson, and he did. Then I hopped off to help Dad. Then both horses took off down the road. But I wanted to help Dad."

"I got some things he needed to wrap his leg. He couldn't walk and I had to pick up camp and did most of the work. Then when we were ready, we got in the pickup and went down the road to get the horses that had run off. Dad could drive with his other foot. We saw the horse tracks and I had to go down where we saw them to get them. I walked up to Wilson and grabbed his reins. I pulled on Cowboy and he came too. We got them ready for the trailer and Dad hopped around trying to help, when a man came along to help us. But I did most of the loading."

"We took off for home, and when we got to a town we went to the hospital so Dad could get his leg in a cast. This woman there wanted to cut Dad's boot off, but Dad said no. And after a while they got it off. It was a long day".

"I was so disappointed, I love the mountains. I want to go to the mountains every day.

You see, after it happened, I was not afraid. Dad could just ride on back of my horse and I thought we could just put his leg up and go ride."

"Dad let's go riding it's a nice day."

Working Horses

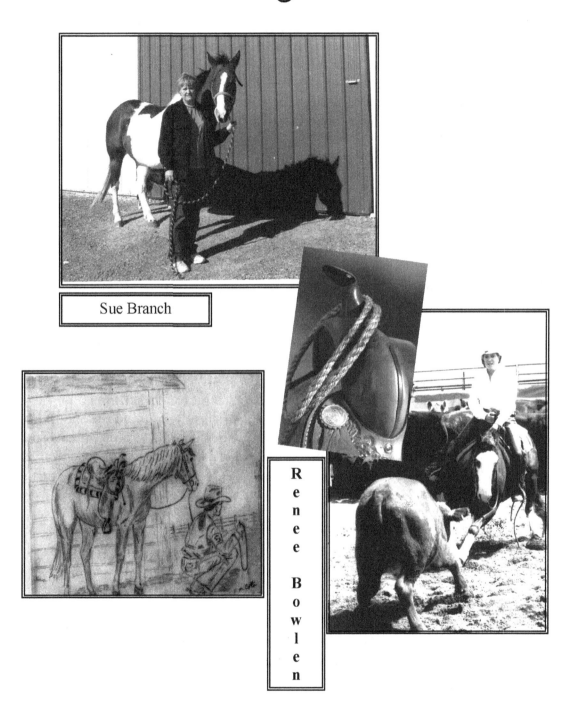

Sue Branch

Renee Bowlen

The Quarter Horse is one of America's oldest and possibly its most popular breed of horse. The early Quarter Horse was a solidly built small horse, standing at approximately 15hh, and was notable for its tremendously powerful hindquarters. It was quickly realized that the Quarter Horse was far superior over short distances to the Thoroughbred types and it is still noted today. Racing in short distances they excelled especially in the quarter-of-a-mile races and this how they got their breed name.

Among their other impressive talents, the Quarter Horse is a natural ranch animal possessing 'cow sense' to a very great degree. A modern cowboy's favorite mount, this horse also possessed great agility, speed and tenacity, as well as intelligence.

In the 1800's as people moved west, the Quarter Horse was favored to pull a wagon, as well as used to help complete all the chores around the early settlers' homesteads. This versatility is perhaps unequalled by any other breed and is due to their quite exceptional temperaments.

+++++

Sue Scheer Branch: Jerome
Jamboree

Braveheart

Three times down, but Sue got up again. I read somewhere that to test the real worth of people, look past appearances and go to performance. These are testaments to quality and it is performance that sets Sue apart that shows her brave heart. Driving down the long lane to visit her at her beautiful log home, I recall many of the highlights in her life. I should have put Sue in the TSR chapter however; her first riding days were with jamboree teams where she leaned to become the good rider that she is now.

When I first got acquainted with Sue she had just lost her husband Mike from a long illness. Widowed with two pre teens, it seemed dark clouds pass silently overhead for Sue. But Sue gathered up her courage and as much as possible continued her life as it had been with her family. They continued to ride their horses, go camping and being a family again. What Sue got from the comfort of her horse was priceless although she and Mike had ridden weekly in Jamboree meetings. She was fortunate to have experienced many areas of Cowgirl life for when Mike was in the all men's posse she was allowed to participate in their jamboree games.

Sue described some events and her horses she rode.

"In the late 1970's the jamboree groups were plenty and very competitive. I rode a black Quarter Horse named Snooks, she was a mustang cross. She was fast enough—a game horse that loved to run. Then when this mare's grandson, I called Levi, was a three year old, I trained him for the events as well as pleasure rides. We called our team the Regulators; it consisted of Mike, our two children, Steve and Danielle, and a few friends. The host team determined what races we used that evening. There was the 7 barrel, Spud Race, Flag race, figure 8 race, barrel race, scurry clover leaf race, pole bending, ride, lead race, rescue race, three horse race, hand holding and water races. We competed with other Magic Valley teams and by the end of the year we usually **placed in the top place** or at least third. It was given to those with high points in weekly events. The association with these horse loving families, enjoying their fellowship at pot luck dinners around bon fires and children playing together was lots of fun."

184

There were more times of tragedy for Sue when she was seriously injured one evening. This accident left her unable to compete, as it took more than a year for her to be able to mount and dismount without help. But with nerves of steel she continued to go to the events mounted on her horse while the family competed.

Several years after the jamboree teams disbanded, Sue rode with the Thursday Sage Riders. This was where I became acquainted with her and her teen children. After they lost their father Sue felt it was still important for the three to ride together. Then one dark day, as she walked around her pickup, Sue was hit by a motor cycle which nearly took her life. Concussion, internal injuries, broken bones, loss of sight in one eye and many surgeries were needed for several years. These became a part of Sue's life, but **Sue is a courageous woman**, she fought for her health. Now on some days, she still rides one of her four good saddle horses for an hour. She has retired old Levi, he was 29. Sue also hosts some of the get-togethers of the T.S.R. club in her log home that she has styled with western art. It is a delightful place to go. Sue and a friend often come out in their pickup to find us for desert or canyon rides plus join us for lunch.

As Sue got stronger, she and her husband, Les, often ride together in the Mountains—sometimes for an hour and on her **new Quarter Horse mare** she sometimes can extend the ride for two hours without too much pain. They are raising some very nice colts and this has been Sue's touch with the equine that she loves. She said if she had it to do over, she would ride more with the TSR group because she loved our mountain rides. I salute you Sue, because you have shown over the years that you do indeed have a brave heart.

+++++

On the first of March, spring was trying to break in Southern Idaho. The indoor arena was the best place for the first **Grass Roots Cutting Horse Club**'s event of 2010. As Bill and I walked into the building the first thing you noticed was the steam rising from the bodies of the many colored horses as work-out on them had begun. Cowgirls were moving their horses at every pace getting them ready for the event in which they had come to compete. Oh, there were other cowboys there, but the only ones I could see were several women I so greatly admire.

People may talk of first love, but give me the glorious sweat of a first ride. You see, this brought me back to the first time I rode my horse down an open canyon in the South Hills near Twin Falls, Idaho where we pushed a gathering of cows that often tried to get buy us. What fun it was!!

Today, a lot of action was going on in the arena. I saw the anxiety on the face of the cowgirl as Becky and her horse entered the arena to cut one young steer out of a small herd. Did she feel as I did, thinking that this is the real west? A smile lit her face as she and her Quarter Horse faced the steer—eyeball to eyeball. The horse moved with quickness as if there were hot coals under its hooves. **Becky Petterson** stuck to the saddle with expert grace. I have known her since she was in Jerome High School. Good luck to you Becky, have a great ride on that pretty Paint that I know you trained yourself. I also enjoyed visiting with **Denise Shoemaker** an old friend I met with the TSR club. She was riding a nice Quarter Horse getting ready for competition later in the day. Denise led our TSR group on many long rides in the South Hills—and I do say long, as she enjoyed being out in the hills. She often rode open range to take care of many animals. Good riding to you both.

+++++

Renee Bowlen: Jerome
Reigning cutting horse
A cowgirl that overcame serious accidents and a bout with cancer.

Watching Renee Bowlen on her beautiful Quarter Horse compete in the cutting events at the arena that day, I realized how much she truly enjoyed the sport. Her draw on the steer was not the best, as the animal wanted to run back and forth and not face off with her and her steed or try to get by them to go back to the rest of the herd. I could hear her laugh, in dismissal as the steer ran again to the other side away from her. Renee's having fun, I thought and now I see why. She said she liked speed and 'wild things' even though this draw might not give her a lot of points. The big liver colored horse seemed to be bowing in the loose dirt of the arena each time it moved to turn the steer to keep it from going past them. Even though her 1300 pound horse was only seven, I could tell he enjoyed the race with the opponent. His white, bald nose and those four white stocking legs against his dark skin made him enjoyable to watch.

"I gave him the experience he needs and for today I am satisfied with the way he worked," Renee told me at lunch. I found out why Renee called this "wild things."

Wild Things

Renee is a third generation cowgirl. She was born on a ranch where horses were the family's livelihood, just as Renee and her husbands business in Jerome today is. They have several acres of corrals full of working Quaterhorse that they work in an indoor arena. Often I have seen them work the horses among the small herd of buffalo in the adjoining corral. Renee also enjoys keeping her lovely home surrounded by a beautiful yard. Where she finds time to do all this I do not know as she is also the mother of two sons.

This day in February at her place, Renee had just ridden ten horses to get them in shape and gentle those for the training needed to compete as reigning cutting horses. Many of the Bowlen's close friends are thirty year repeat customers. I know they do a fantastic job winning many trophies as well as saddles and other gear which I saw in their house. She just returned from Elko, Nevada where she was awarded first place in a bridal class.

Renee grew up riding young horses that were not broke. She tells of colts she rode that were snubbed close to a gentle riding horse and taken to their hunting camps.

"By the time we returned from camp," she said, "these young horses were pretty well broke. Then often we would ride them in gymkhana competition in town. It took a little more training for the horses my sister and I rode in the EhCapa type, shows. Oh, I was not without incidents. The two weeks I spent in the hospital at age ten was from an accident that nearly cost me my life. A big appaloosa we called Mr. Fred, dumped me when we were using him for a pack horse. My spleen was crushed and I had to have it removed before I bled to death. My recovery went well and I was back on a horse before summer ended. I guess **the thought of riding kept me going just like the bout with cancer I had a few years ago. I kept my dream alive.**"

"In the summer months, I would ride more than two miles to my friend's home and maybe stay most of the week. Other fun times I remember was going to nearby Stevensville, Montana to a two day party and parade. My girlfriends and I would wash up our ponies for the events. This one day, we decided they would look good with the long hair of their tails cut off. So we did it. We were so proud of them, but our parents did not like it. I think it was mostly because we did not ask them plus they explained horses use this length to switch the summer flies off their backs. We learned a lesson here. Our county fair times were different as a lot of us participated in horse races which my mother often won. I really enjoyed my youthful days with all our friends. There were sad times, when we lost several of our best riding horses. They were in an accident when they got out on the road because one of our horses could manage to open the gate and we did not watch him closely."

"After I married we still had horses. Our boys participated in local 4-h programs, but only one is interested in horses today, even though being a part of this program was very rewarding for them. One of my personal rewards was mentoring a young girl, just down the road from us that got to go to the Nationals in cutting horse competition. I enjoyed this very much."

(And seeing you compete in the cutting events has been rewarding to me also, Renee.)

Thank you for sharing your memoir's with me. I have enjoyed getting to know you and also your lovely sister Debbie. I know she too has many good horse stories being the great cowgirl she is. What a heritage you both have had. Congratulations on your great success.

+++++

The National Reined Cow Horse Association was formed to improve the quality of the western reined stock horse. One of their goals is to continue work to keep the vaquero tradition alive in equine industry, as history records the American cowboy of the late 19th century arose from the vaquero traditions of northern Mexico and became a figure of special significance and legend. One of the contests the club includes is the Hackamore Classic; another is the Snaffle Bit Futurity which is open to only three year old horses.

Christina Allen: Nampa
Reigned Cow horse Competitor

To learn you must want to be taught

When I met Christina, her friendliness made me want to visit with her more. We were at a Back Country Horse meeting the High Desert Club put on and Christina began talking about her work she does with horses. I asked her for her story and I really appreciate her willing spirit to oblige me even though she is a very busy horsewoman.

This is her story.

"I moved to Idaho before I was a year old. I currently live in Nampa, but home is wherever my family is. They all live near me with my parents in Indian Valley and sisters in Nampa. I feel that:

Having somewhere to go is home,
Having someone to love is family,
Having both is a blessing."

"I've never known a time without horses. My first horse was a Shetland pony named Spooky. However, the horse that I remember the most was a black and white paint pony named Domino that I did everything with. I tried to be like John Wayne and run up behind him and jump over his rear into the saddle and take off. I never made it. I hit in the middle of his butt every time.

He would just look at me every time I tried. It was later that I found out that many of the stunts had a trampoline to help them jump. I have many stories involving this horse."

I found that Christina shows horses each year in the summer months. This year the horse in which **she rides snaffle bit in** is, Sophy (Paloma Roo) in the **Reined Cow Horse events.**

"Next year I want to show her in the two-rein and bridle class. The thing I like most about the cow horse is the level of horsemanship required to be competitive. To be a partner with your horse is a feeling you can't describe. When you have felt it, you strive for it with each horse."

"My first horse show experience was on an Arabian gelding I called Challenger (AW Bay Challenger). It was when I was working for an Arabian breeding and training facility; I was in high school at the time cleaning stalls as well as taking care of horses. It was my way of working up to riding and showing. It was a great experience and harder than I thought it would be. To go from riding in a western saddle to an English saddle took a little adjusting. I learned a lot there and got to show quite a bit. The first time I showed Challenger he bucked and almost ran over the judge. We got 5th out of five showing, but—ha, who's counting."

"Before I left there I received a first and second on him. I was very proud that he had overcome many obstacles to become a great horse and for him to trust in me seemed to be the key. Time and patience paid off and I think about him now and then and wouldn't mind riding English but—I just love the cow horse."

"When I lived in King Hill I did teach 4-H, as I enjoy teaching and watching kids while they enjoyed their horses. But where I am now, I get to ride everyday and do the things I enjoy most—reined cow horses at my place in Caldwell. No, there isn't a whole lot that I would change. **I'm right where I always wanted to be—with horses."**

Christina is a dedicated cowgirl as her spirit and passion so reflects.

A quote she gave me I will share with you: "It is better to be slow tempered than famous; it is better to have self control than to control an army. We toss the coin, but it is the Lord who controls its decision."

Family

Bill & Lenore

Janell

Beth

Renee

Sara

Willann

Family

Bill & Lenore Mobley

Eric, Valerie, Skyler & Averi Auclaire

Dustin & Mandy Auclaire, Lenore & Bill

Mandy & Barb

Amber Hoy

Paige & Grandpa Bill

Family

Andrew

Melissa & Hillarie

Sean & Grandma

Alexis

Tirzah

Win Lenore Hull Mobley:
Born and raised in Jerome:

I have given you the following history of Southern Idaho because this is where I have lived since I was born. Both my mother and father came here at the beginning of the twentieth century to farm this high desert. It was a good life for them—and us. This is where we raised our family.

I love this part of Idaho—the desert as well as the surrounding mountains. I have found some wonderful places to ride my horse from early spring to late fall that is less than an hour's drive from my home in Jerome. It is the best of any world. I have shared many of these good rides with you in connecting stories. *Enjoy The Journey.*

Jerome history:

In the early 1900's, great men and women dreamed and schemed. We have them by the scores on the north and south sides of the great Snake, here in Magic Valley. They executed their plans and their visions and fashioned a path to a reality in this desert land. These great people were vital and necessary. Without them the conception would never have been possible.

But it remained yet for the people who came in droves, by wagon and by train load and automobiles to win the land. They took it from the brush, grubbed it off from the raw earth, furrowed the fields and brought the water to the very fertile earth. They were not families of wealth. They were common folks who cast their lot and came from almost every state to settle this land.

At the "North Side," of the Snake River Canyon, on October, 1907, over two million dollars in land was sold at the opening in one 24 hour period. Nearly 1800 persons filed for land, some for town lots and others needed acres for farming use. This drawing was used to protect the actual settlers from speculators.

This all happened because the I.B. Perrine family, who settled in the canyon along the Snake River, realized that with a dam upstream, and some canal system, the desert would flourish bringing many settlers to this Magic Valley. This precious water we got from the wild Snake River was guarded and guided so closely from the high mountain reaches. Many of the people in this book **had ancestors who settled here** then and many came later after seeing the beauty of Idaho. Most all came to **start a new life** on these high plains. To these who braved the raw west when the west was alive in its entire romantic lure, I salute.

Many of our historic travel systems here in south central Idaho, reconnect with the Oregon Trail. From Fort Hall site on the Snake River—some 250 miles west to Mountain Home. This route called the Goodale Cutoff was important to travel by many immigrants and by miners to new gold strikes in the mid 1800's. This Cutoff system runs across remote and undeveloped lands in south-central Idaho and is still preserved for historians and all who appreciate to visit and travel our historic trails. I hope you take the time as I did, to mark gaps in your curiosity and go locate this road.

Our family stories:

Since the beginning of time, people have lived in families.

Loving family relationships are the best defense we can have against the challenges of the world.

From tribes to clans, families over the years have eased out tensions, strengthened belief in our own abilities, helped ward off offenses and relieved anxiety. Modern living puts an enormous strain on family harmony. Often today's families are so fragmented and busy that they communicate with each other only through notes on the computer. By showing a willingness to spend time together and an appreciation for each other, we can begin to heal our families.

Children who are connected to a huge clan know they are thought of, cared about, and loved by a wide circle of people whom they are related to. Spending time together is important. It isn't always convenient for everyone, but taken seriously, perhaps we could form a bond that can surpass the normal conflicts and differences families must deal with. Enjoy your family this year, and know that this may be the last chance you have. Go camping, fishing or horseback riding as we do. And yes, family member—friend, you are invited.

Finding Faith in a Flower

"Sometimes when faith is running low
And I cannot fathom why things are so
I ride along among the flowers He grows
And learn the answers to all I would know!
For among the flowers I have come to see
Life's miracles and its mystery . . .
And standing in silence and reverie
My faith comes flooding back to me!"—Helen Steiner Rice

Win Lenore Mobley's story.

I have Enjoyed the Company of a Horse

I was born and raised in Jerome and we have made our home here.

When I was thirteen, I was asked to come to the barn for a surprise. Life at that time was still a delightful and mysterious dream. I felt the world was full of every imaginable kind of magnificence to be had. Running ahead of my dad, I entered the barn to see a bright red mare wearing a halter and tied up to the manger. She was small built just right for a young girl. She had an attractive head, bright eyes and alert ears, and she whinnied as she saw me. There was a narrow, white streak of hair down her nose; an abundance of forelock and mane down a neck that was short and muscular, typical of a Morgan bred horse.

"I don't believe it, is she really mine?" I smiled at my dad. "Yes, Mickey is your horse to ride—a gift from your mom and me," he replied.

Ever since that birthday, **I have enjoyed the company of a horse.** My earliest memories have been of horses, I remember when I mounted to ride this new gift, for **you never forget the freedom of riding your first horse**. I even remember what the day was like, and that the air was new and lovely to breathe. The feel of the horse moving under me was wonderful even though I was hanging on to her mane very tightly. I got her into a trot and found the gait fun and soft. I found her hard to stop at a lope, because she wanted to run. When I accomplished this task well enough, I was then able to visit at my girl friends' homes, at least a miles ride; each one gave me a new look of admiration and respect as I was a year younger then they were.

Rain or shine, I wanted to be out with Mickey. On days when I couldn't ride, I would go out to the barn and climb up the ladder to the old lookout floor and there between the rough slats of the ceiling, I could study the mare beneath me and imagine myself riding through space upon her. Lying on my stomach, I hung my head over the edge of the hole that was high above the floor where she stood. I would watch Mickey and talk to her so she would get used to my voice. She liked me, not just because I fed her sugar cubes, but it was a trust we developed from the beginning. Often I rode her in the desert next to our farm Oh, I went off her several times—mostly my fault. She was the horse I learned to ride on. She was quick, often shied and could stop real fast: Nothing like a first horse like this one—right? My sisters, Uvah and LaNeta did not care to ride and this gave me much time on Mickey.

I might not have continued on with horseback riding except for my high school girlfriends. Most of them had and rode horses: Carrie Dell, Pat, Shirley (Lee Straley), Jonnie and Sue—I was often invited to their places to join them in this sport. I feel my first 'hard to ride' horse was the reason I learned to expect almost anything from many of the well broke horses I have owned. And I have been fortunate as I have had only one horse accident where I had to go to a hospital in the sixty years that I have been riding. And this was caused **when a horse fell with me**.

When I find myself in a difficult spot, I go to the mountains to ride my horse. It works for me. It was what the mountains reveal to me that has lasting meaning. In early spring it is getting away to ride in the desert and having time to think, pray and sometimes cry.

In the last fifty-five years, Bill, my husband, and I have owned many good horses. He has always liked horses. I even wrote a children's story about how he trained the gentle horse that he now rides. The name of the book is *Calypso, Dark Horse.* We have enjoyed the horses that have taken us on mountain trails to hunt, as well as horses our daughters have enjoyed. There were Appaloosas that our daughters showed and rode at many events. We owned great Arabians that we used on the trails for twenty-five years. We had a Thoroughbred Quarter Horse cross we used for fifteen years for rodeo events and while hunting packing on trails. Yes, hunting brings our family together. This is when I can visit with Valerie, my grandson Eric Auclaire's wife, as we take the horses up to the mountain top on Soldier Mountain and wait for Bill, Eric, and Dustin to meet us and tell us where their kill is. I thank God for women like Valerie—such a good sport.

The horse I now ride and have enjoyed for seventeen years is a Peruvian Paso named Braddo. I felt that when a horse is started and trained correctly, it can bring much joy to the owner. **I have been blessed with great horses,** and wish to thank those who broke the great horses I owned, especially, the Joe Dawkins, Debbie Spencer, Carol Pugh, Mary Kimble and Michelle Hine Ruble.

I do not claim to be a great horsewoman. I have never trained a horse from the start or raised one, I just love them and riding horseback gives me a sense of freedom.

Braddo and I go everywhere; he is a tireless, dependable horse that has never bucked, kicked, or ran off with me. I love him and I guess I spoil him too. The first time I saw him at Cheryl Hymas's barn he was a day old. A few days later I went back and helped Cheryl move some of her colts. Braddo had on a halter and Cheryl asked me to lead him while she led his mother. We were walking a little behind his mother and Braddo wanted to catch up, I held him back and he kicked me in the leg. I wore a bruise for a month. Little did I know one day I would get even—so to speak. When it was time to wean this colt, Cheryl called and said she was looking at a picture of me with Braddo and it was an omen that I needed to own this horse. I laughed and never dreamed that Bill would later **buy this horse for me that Christmas**. I will never forget the days when Braddo allowed me to halter him, gently brush him, saddle him, and eventually let me climb upon him. By summer I rode him around the yard when he was three. Then that fall I was ready to hand him off to a professional trainer for the right finishing. Braddo was an easy starter in the mountains. As a colt Cheryl had let him tag along when she exercised the mares near her cabin in the Sawtooth Mountains. I wish to thank Cheryl for raising the perfect horse for me to own in my older years. I am in awe of my horse and very relaxed with him. I just appreciate a good horse and it has been a dream come true for me. (He is the horse in the picture.)

Bill and I have enjoyed horseback riding in five states. One of these rides was in Montana near the same mountain range where they filmed the movie *The Horse Whisper*. While riding there, I smiled as I kept expecting Robert Redford to be riding over the next ridge and join us. While there, we got to know some very enjoyable people like Susan Mitgang and Roy and Sandy Rose from Montana who were great hostesses. (Later I learned that Roy and Sandy were raised in the Burley area and Sandy was a former queen of the Cassia County Fair.) It's a small world, isn't it?

I credit the bond I have with, my granddaughters and two of my grandsons including one great granddaughter, to the horseback rides we have had together. I feel that horseback riding and camping, is an association that can bring loved ones close together, even the grandsons, Austin, Conner, and Joshua love to camp and fish with us. We love them all.

I have been blessed to have friendships with most of these horse loving people I have written about. And I am very thankful for the great camping and fellowship with the Thursday Sage Riders. But most of all, my favorite partner, these days, is my husband, Bill. **My spiritual Leader is my Lord and Savior Jesus Christ who has given me the words to write. I thank Him with love.**

+++++

Janell Mobley Pearson: Nampa

The Year I Joined the Drill Team

Our oldest daughter (of five daughters) should have started her story as such: Being raised by a horse-crazy mother, I was often put on a horse when either the horse was frightened or I was. One horse bucked me off, and another one just took off with me and when it turned sharply, I didn't. I did try a 4-H horse program with a young gelding, which I enjoyed. However, it rained the whole week of the Jerome County Fair. This horse did not like being wet and he rolled to cake his pretty, bay body with dry, corral dirt. With my dad's help, I was able to clean him up and get him ready for showing. I really needed help as the thought of me going out in the arena and showing this horse made me so nervous I threw up the hot chocolate that I had for breakfast all over my white shirt. This was my beginning in associating with horses.

This is the rest of Janell's story in her words:

"The fiddle begins and the circle forms a do-so-do with my partner and then we break off, weaving every other one. For a sixteen year old, it is both a frightening and exhilarating move because a collision could be fatal. My horse, **Scout, and I became one dancer**. We are square dancing at a gallop and occasionally a run, horses and riders forming patterns to music with memorized moves. Twelve women and their beasts . . . dancing!"

"I remember the day Prairie Scout came to our farm near Jerome where I was raised. As I ran outside, letting the porch door slam behind me, a friend, Lyle Crozier, had Scout unloaded and was leading him around the yard. He was a beautiful red quarter horse gelding with a "PS" branded on his rear flank. Taking Scout's lead rope, Lyle led him up to the back of the pickup, lowered the tail gate then, Lyle commanded Scout to, "get in." In what seemed like slow motion,

195

the big quarter horse raised his front legs like he was going to rear up and gracefully leaped into the bed of the pickup. Unbelievable as it seemed to me, there he was with his head hanging over the cab just waiting for an adventure. It was amazing. Since I didn't know how to pull a horse trailer I knew this would be the answer for me to take a horse beyond the few miles of the farm. Mom had suggested I try out a square dancing group that one of her trail riding friends was in as they needed another rider. The Square Dancers would be riding entertainment for nearby town rodeos and would also ride in some summer parades. This sounded like fun to me. It was the summer before my junior year and the times for practicing flew by. A few days before our first performance at the Gooding Rodeo, I was sewing a sparkling red vest and hat band for our costume. On the way to Gooding, I wasn't sure if we would get there as Scout rocked the pickup all the way. I didn't know if he was excited or didn't like the wind from the long drive. Everyone in the yard of the fair grounds stood frozen with their mouths open when I untied Scout and let down the tail gait to have Scout back out on his own. He settled quickly so I saddled him, and I dressed for our first show. All the other women were older than I was, yet they assured me that we would do great and they would watch out for us. We all lined up outside the gate . . . waiting. I was so nervous; I thought I was going to be sick. Then the music began, and we galloped out around the inside of the brightly lit arena. On the music cue, we paired up and broke off into two circles. Soon we split up weaving both circles into a fast paced figure eight crossing every other rider in the center. I think Scout had the moves memorized, too. Soon my fears subsided as I smiled to the audiences' applause. We danced to the music—Scout and I. (He is the horse in the picture)

+++++

Tirzah Pearson: Nampa
Age 21 Janell's daughter

Learning Lessons on Horseback

Living some distance from our farm, our granddaughter, TZ, as I call her, did not get to ride our horses as often as she would have liked. When her parents came for a weekend visit, she and I would often saddle up and ride at the farm or in our north desert.

She became a good rider as her desire was great to go other places with us. After she began to drive, it allowed her to accompany us to more trail rides.

A three day summer ride that TZ told me she enjoyed was going to Lona Smith's cabin at Smilie Creek. The spring rain did not stop her from riding every day. We had a great time and TZ today still talks about Grandpa showing her the new spring flowers and how I sang as we rode along. We had a great adventure those three days.

In her words, this is her story of her horseback riding days.

"Ever since I was three, the words "Grandma's" and "horses" were always paired. Often, when I went to Grandma's house, we would saddle up for **a ride around the farm**. Then, when I graduated from the "beginners program," the rides would be extended to the desert or to a friends' place in the mountains. This is when I enjoyed riding Bingo as he had a smooth, fast walk. Sometimes I would slow him up just so I could kick him and trot a little; this was a great feeling. Third Fork Canyon was one ride Grandma and I had taken. We got in trouble trying to cross a very fast creek when my horse, Charla, got her foot stuck in a pile of branches. It was wedged in so tight that I had to get off in the knee deep water to keep the horse from fighting the trap. Charla wouldn't move so Grandma got into the water, reached down to free her hoof. We both got pretty wet that day and laugh about it often."

"Another memory in 2006 of going with Grandma and her riding group was **not** as tame. On one early morning ride in Snake River Canyon, the wake up call was complete with a gorgeous sky. Watching the sky change colors and the clouds change shapes, we walked the horses along the sandy trail. We started off great until Lee's mare got into her mind that she was a bucking bronco. It seems the mare did not like being held up as we went single file through a narrow area. She arched her back, put her head down and started hopping. It was a strange but tense sight, and after a half a dozen "bounces", Lee went off. Luckily she was not seriously hurt, and she soon got back on her horse and we began again. The group of seven women were talking and laughing enjoying their ride to the end of the canyon to have lunch in some trees there.

I was riding Charla, and as we neared a hill, I held her back a little, since I was not as experienced as I am now. She did not like that at all, being made to go slow while the other horses rushed up the incline. I released my hold on the reins, and she bolted up the hill. As we reached the top, she **began jumping and with a forward hop, unseated me.** I grabbed at the saddle horn, but my feet were already out of the stirrups. Charla moved with quickness and I went off her. I couldn't believe it. It happened just like I watched Lee fall to the ground.

As the wind whooshed out of me, I was sure that Charla's front hooves would come crashing down on my ribs. Instead Grandma's anger came crashing down on the unruly horse and she quieted her. After this, on the way back after lunch, Grandma insisted we switch horses, which Grandma laughingly said was punishment enough for the unruly Charla. We left the lunch spot early with Lee accompanying us.

I was in the lead and as we came up to the gate, I heard Grandma shout. I looked back and saw to my horror that Charla was on the ground with Grandma under her. I dismounted and ran over, trying not to cry hysterically. Lee was already there beside her saying she had never seen a horse go down so fast and Grandma said she did not have time to pull her foot out of the stirrup and felt the fall had broken her leg. It seemed so unfair.

Grandma insisted we leave her lying beside the trail with her cell phone and that we take the horses to the trailers, load them up and return with the pickup and park near a locked gate that was just down the road. When we returned, Grandma had called Grandpa on her cell. He had arrived in his pickup to save the day. **He made a make-shift splint out of two pieces of sagebrush** and strapped it on Grandma's leg with their belts. We then carried her to the pickup and Grandpa drove her off to the hospital. I was picked up by my cousins Dustin and Mandy, who drove the horse trailer home and put away the horses

Later that week, Grandma told me, "The horse needs to be shod." (I thought she said **shot**) and that's why the horse acted up. Needless to say they didn't shoot her. They did trim her feet, though.

I felt sorry for Grandma as she missed riding most of the spring. But she was back on her horse before the end of May—cast and all. That's my grandma!"

Thank you TZ for your good story. I like riding with you and may we have many happy trails together; because of your bravery the day I got hurt, I would like you to lead me on the trails any day.

+++++

Beth Mobley Auclaire Swartz:
2nd daughter with 3 generations of horse lovers

Remarkable Gifts

Beth is our second daughter who has always loved animals. She showed Black Angus heifers in 4-H and did it well. As a teen she sometimes rode one of our many saddle horses around our farm or in the north desert near our house. I was not surprised when she and her husband moved to a ranch in the middle of the Nevada desert and began to enjoy riding horses. While visiting there, I have enjoyed riding with Beth and Sara at this ranch as several miles out we come to some old stone corrals, windmills, water tanks, and about five miles from her house, you arrive at the foothills of the Humbolt Mountain range that rise up to 12,000 feet. From there, you can head back on a dry river bed and it is safe to run the horse here—it seems that the horse's mane and tail dance from the wind you create—its fun times for my daughters and me.

This is Beth's story of "**remarkable gifts**".

When New Animals Arrive

"I saw the land at first light sixteen years ago in Railroad Valley near the foothills of the Quinn Canyon Range. It took my breath away then, as now. White snow capped peaks to the north, east and the south. On the west side lie the Pancake Range, with its flat tops and desert canyons. I never intended to be a farmer; even though my parents were farmers as were theirs. I remembered the land as if it were yesterday. Inch by inch I have devoted myself to bringing life to the farm. I knew I could never be depressed here. Afraid, perhaps overwhelmed, possibly frustrated, no doubt, but never depressed. A friend asked me if I was going to keep animals. Raising sheep and keeping horses had not occurred to me."

"One day, when the circumstances surrounding my life were about to come together, I was on my hands and knees working in the yard, when the phone rang. My good friend and neighbor (who live twenty five miles away,) said to me. "**I hear you are looking for a horse.**" Susie Fallini told me about the Paint gelding. I was very excited as it sounded like the Paint knew when he could get away with mischief and when he couldn't and I could relate to that behavior. While haying is an exciting time on the farm (if all goes well) the most exciting time for me is when new animals arrive. A new dimension of hope and possibilities always accompanies both the anticipation of the arrival and the onset of their stay. It never really fades, even after we are all settled in with one another. In a way they take care of me, giving me what I need to have in order to take care of them."

"When the Paint arrived he was everything I had hoped for. White with brown spots, they looked as if they had been stitched on by a very fine seamstress. Full of vim and vinegar, he could talk of course. I would go into the corral with halter and rope in hand, my friend would greet me and drop his head, and he knew his reward. We would ride the section of ground that I farmed. With pivot irrigation and sandy soil, we had a lot of gophers. I didn't let the Paint lope until we were on ground that was safe and packed firm. The third time out the Paint would anticipate this type of ground, moving faster and faster, when we hit these areas I would give him his head and let him move at his own pace. After we had played enough he would settle right back down and walk back to the corrals. I have a small frog pond next to the house. As soon as the Paint was unsaddled and brushed down I would lead him to the pond and let him go. The Paint would proceed with his bath. Water would be everywhere. Paint loved the water he would splash and play and when he had his fill, he would graze a little on the wild rice grass and then put himself back in the corral. The Paint lived on this farm with me for ten years; he had been a joy to me ever since he arrived. He was my first horse and **his memories shall bring me delight forever**."

"The stuff that dreams are made of comes in all manner of shapes, forms, textures and colors. For me, it was the white blaze, the little curved tips on her ears and that long black mane and tail she had. Charla was **a beautiful Paso mare, eager and loving**. The first sound of my voice at the corral would bring her running to me. It seemed she read my mind and would come to me when I've just thought of her name, before I can even call, she was always there. Charla is the only horse I picked and purchased, (but one my mother told me about.) I didn't realize it until now that when Charla lived here the farm felt more than perfect. I am glad I picked Charla for my horse. I had nothing to lose and everything to gain. These were ties that could be broken by death and even then continued. One day I will again find another like her. (Charla is the horse in the picture.)"

"After I lost Charla, I began to search for one with a soft gait. I acquired a Tennessee Walking mare that was at the Clarkson's ranch in Oakley. She arrived in the winter and I am hopeful that spring will come soon so that I can ride her. (Thank you, Chris and Jen) There have been and always will be beautiful horses on my farm. My decisions about choosing horses are often emotional ones. Most of the horses now on my farm are pension horses, ones no one could any longer afford or couldn't ride hard for their chosen job. Some are horses my mother found for me."

"My mother is a remarkable horse woman and writer. Her abilities are based on a natural ease, an inborn affinity and understanding of horses and writing. All of us sisters, I've come to understand, are the amazing products of varying degrees of appropriate parenting that we received. (And I don't want to leave my dad out.) One of the things I am so grateful to Mom for, is that I have an absolute unrestricted freedom in my life in regard to the elusive and misleading realm called creativity. If, indeed, our mothers hold such a powerful sway over that part of us then she certainly gave me a remarkable gift—**a remarkable gift from a remarkable woman**."

+++++

Mandy Auclaire: Jerome

A Family Riding Partner for Grandma

Mandy's history with horses goes way back as she too had a horse crazy mother (Barb). Therefore when Mandy came into our family I knew I had another riding partner. And I was correct—she is great. Mandy was there when I needed an adult to go with us when I took younger grandchildren riding. She rode Callie a lot when I asked her to give him a day of riding in the desert or in the south hills when he was just learning to be a trail horse. There was one time we even got, Dustin, (my grandson) her husband, on a horse for a day, and that was a great ride up North Soldier. Good memories with family.

This is Mandy's story.

"As a little girl visiting my grandparents in Kamiah, one early morning Grandpa Julius and I went out to feed the horses. I still remember the smell of the alfalfa and the musk horse smell, the horses seemed larger than life. I couldn't wait for horses to finish eating so they could be saddled—then came the waiting for them to be saddled. At last I was lifted up on my mother's horse. Though it was a short ride I was in heaven. **So began my love of horses.**"

"My first horse was an old pony named Belle. She was black and white. She let my little brother, Jarred, and I lead her around. We climbed on and off her back as she was a gentle pet. I then remember an Arabian/Quarter Horse named, Cherokee. He was red with white stockings. I rode him down the corn field behind my house in the winter with the wind blowing in my hair. In the summer my mother and I would ride in the south hills. Our favorite trail was the Third Fork canyon."

"A ride that stands out in my mind is a ride I took a few years ago with my two favorite horsewomen, Grandmother Win, and my mother, Barb. My mom was visiting from her home in Cascade and she brought, Lady, her own horse to ride with us. I had, Charla and Grandma brought Braddo. When we pulled into Third Fork trailhead, it began to rain. We prepared our horses, put on our rain gear, pulled protectors over our hats and mounted up. Nothing was going to stop us. The pitter-patter of the rain on our hats and coats created a wonderful noise along with the horse's hoof beats. We wondered in and out of trees going up and down the trail that ran alongside of Third Fork creek. What a beautiful, fall ride it turned out to be."

+++++

Alexis Auclaire:
Age 9—my great granddaughter;
Daughter of Mandy and Dustin Auclaire;
Alexis wrote the following.

"When I was little, I used to ride a horse named Bingo where my mom, riding Callie, ponies us alongside. And then I started to ride by myself. **Now I love to ride horses**. I have fun riding my horse at my grandma's house. I like to ride horses a lot. I want a horse but my dad said no, not now. So I will keep asking so I can have a horse of my own."

"If you are wondering what kind of horse I am going to have, it is an Icelandic Pony because they are small and nice and sweet. I looked at their pictures in my grandma's horse book after I returned from a visit with Grandma-great at her friend Darlene Kiser's place. She showed me a picture of a beautiful Icelandic horse she used to own."

"Last summer, I took lessons from Grandma Win. I enjoyed riding in the big pasture on a horse that **I controlled**. Grandma often gave me an A+ for the session we had. It was fun."

"One of my favorite movies is *Flicka*. She is a pretty horse and ran so fast like a lightening strike. I loved her so much. Someday I may have a horse just like her when I get too big for the pony. I write stories about owning a horse just like Flicka. I know that someday my mom and I will be riding some horses of our own. My mom was raised with horses and once this has been in your life, you can't get over them."

+++++

Renee Mobley Maher: Boise
3rd daughter

Maker of Beautiful Quilts and Helpful Hearts

The Stars at Night Shine Big and Bright—especially at hunting camps as overhead the night hunter brandished a blazing sword while all around it constellations danced with white and blue fire. Is this scene why most hunters love to go to the high mountains to camp? I believe it is. For it's at the late night campfire, just before it is about to go out, that a person can see the stars so clearly. Maybe it's to watch the V of migrating geese flying across the sky unafraid, swooping over the quiet canyon. Or is it watching and listening to the wind trying to twist the tops off the tall pines telling of a coming storm? Maybe it's standing on the edge of a steep cliff and feeling like you're the only one there within miles. Then I heard Renee say, "It's the sound of my heart beating fast as we view a wild herd of elk that dad and I were able to sneak up on."

This is who Renee is.

"Raising two sons, I knew I needed to include this outdoor lifestyle for they both enjoy the activities we can enjoy in Idaho. One is the adventure of the hunt and a continuing desire to go to the mountains—spring, summer, fall and winter. Our family vacationed and played in the Fairfield area."

Sean, Renee's son, has enjoyed riding horseback since he was in grade school. This is why I choose his picture to be on the front cover of my second novel titled, The Journey Series—Star Dancers Summer Journey. Her older son, Brandon, has helped us build fence and we enjoy them both. They are fun grandsons.

At the age of sixteen Renee had climbed Mt. Borah, the highest mountain in Idaho. With more than thirty years of snow skiing under her belt, she has seen how beautiful the mountains look with their sparkling, white covering and can't stay away. However, the fall is one of her favorite times—seeing the change of colors adorning the mountain side. It's the best time to take pictures (which she loves to do) as well as ride her mother's horses, like the one named Bingo.

"The last time I went to support the hunt, I was glad I did. One of my nephews got an elk down in an area where it took three of us to get it out. Dad was having trouble with his knee and just being there as a helper to him was rewarding. That same week, Dad and I used our steeds to out run a nice bull elk before he disappeared into the trees. These fine horses we use are our work animals **carrying out our kill** as we lead them back to camp."

"I did not ride much when I was young. I didn't have much of an opportunity; I guess it was because most of my friends didn't ride. My music was important to me as well as being on the tennis team in high school. I love skiing and then fly fishing and now quilting—these are other activities I enjoy."

"Horseback riding, unfortunately, only happened when I went hunting. Maybe a middle child, like me grows up too fast. But the older I get the more I wish the experience would have been greater. However, I will never forget the times I saddled up and led the command. Bingo, an Arabian cross, was the horse that I learned to ride as it seemed anyone could ride him. He seemed to have a sense of knowing the rider's capabilities. And thank goodness for that. He could travel with me on trail-less rides to and from my *wanderers* needs."

The following is one of my stories.

A Tribute to a Horse Named Bingo

"One October morning, we were in the Fairfield area near Willow Creek. While still in camp we heard shots. Hoping it was from *our* mighty hunters that were out there trying to bring home their ultimate prize, we tried to get them on the walkie-talkie, but had no response. The horses were saddled earlier and the children were outside 'tending' the bonfire. Mom suggested that I take the horses up the ridge in case our hunters got something down. I pulled on my boots, made a light lunch, filled the water bottles and started out the door when I saw that Amber, my niece, was seated on Bingo and **my son, Sean**, on Braddo, the other horse and looking very much ready to ride. The nine year olds were grinning ear to ear. Thus, I went back inside, put on my hiking boots and made more lunch, grabbing more carrots and apples for them all."

"Alright kids," I said, acknowledging the ready riders, "Let's go experience the great outdoors."

"An hour out, up the steep incline we rode when I heard a faint sound from Amber. 'Aunt Renee, shouldn't we get off and walk?' she asked looking down at a steep drop-off."

"No. Your horses have better footing than you or I do!" When I replied this, she agreed and hung on while Bingo came up to me and nudged me as I slipped toward him as if to say—get going. Sean just gave me a trusting look and then grinned. It was then that I remembered what surefooted animals they were. Bingo has guided me through thick timber that he jumped, walked over round rocks and all the time taught me to stay on him. He knew who he had on his back then just as he does now. And he knew he would get the reward I had in my pack when we got to the top."

"Then, coming to, I stopped on a small out-cropping, patted the horses as I talked to them and told the children what a good job they did. We all had a good treat before we went on in search of the unknown. Unfortunately we didn't see any deer or hunters. I led them back to a safe point in the trail where I knew the children would be comfortable in the lead. I watched them head for camp and thanked God for the safety he provided for them to go by themselves down the mountain. The horses performed well. What an accomplishment for two small children to see the view we saw from the top of the mountain and hear the small creek laughing at us as we wandered beside it. It was a beautiful thing to have this experience. And years later, the two young riders continued to go on rides with their grandmother."

"After Bingo died, on later hunts there were younger horses who took Bingo's lead. I miss him a lot, but young Braddo taught me how to take control. He stood still as I held him and Dad's horse as Dad went around the corner to shoot at an elk. We heard the shots and felt the vibrations of the big rifle. However, a presence in the wind whispered, 'Be still.' Later when Dad showed up, I felt a couple **familiar nudges on my pack**."

"How did they know? Bingo was that you whispering? Your presence will always be everywhere that we go in these mountains. You understood our needs and our thankfulness. You had provided numerous safe rides for all of us—especially for the children from ages four to eight as often they rode on top with a deer in the pack bags. At times like this I still feel you nudging me knowing I'd give in, a treat **worth remembering**."

+++++

The little bay Mustang had entered the world of the domestic horse—a far cry from what he had known in the Nevada desert where the land left to the Mustangs is typically rugged, arid and rocky. Life there is often hard and grazing meager.

Sara Mobley Hoy:
4th daughter
Boise; now Nevada

New Life

2010 event:

"What is this in the corral?" Sara asked Beth.

"Your Little Harley, or the nearest thing to it," was her reply.

"When we first saw him we were sure he was orphaned. The wild horse herd was not near where the colt was standing along the highway fence. He seemed so alone and by his condition we could tell he hadn't had much nourishment."

"We went home and called the BLM about seeing him there. They said they were aware of him and asked if we were interested in adopting him. I said yes, and he agreed to deliver him to the ranch that week."

Sara's story: "I don't remember when I began riding and only remember bits of my first horse show. At seven years of age my mother bought me a new western shirt and straw hat. We borrowed a pair of chaps from a friend and atop Scout, our trusty quarter horse, into the arena I rode. I didn't place that day, but I knew **I had found something I was passionate about.** Most of my favorite horse experiences revolve around Jake—Chief Jake Dewey, an Appaloosa-Arabian cross. He was gelded late and therefore retained many of his stallion-like qualities such as, his thick neck and the way he acted up around mares. Joe Dawkins green-broke him and I was there most every afternoon while Joe worked with him. Jake was the first horse I 'finished'. We were best friends. Together we won several awards at 4-H, Idaho-Oregon-Nevada (ION) and Magic Valley Appaloosa Club events."

"At one such show we had to really work for the ribbons we received. Our first event, Showmanship at Halter, was truly a battle of the wills. Jake would stand still for only a few minutes at a time. He was preoccupied by the two mares we were between. While other contestants stood there smiling with perfectly still horses I had to constantly pull Jake out of the line, circle him, and set him back up—all while making sure I knew where the judge was and being in proper position myself. Frustrating as the class was for me, **Jake and I won**. This brought protests from some of the competitors' parents. The judge simply told them that the class was Showmanship at Halter and I had to work the hardest to show my horse at his best. I wasn't as mad at him after that. We finished the day Hi-Point Youth for our age group." (Jake is the horse in the picture.) At the time, what I didn't understand was the parents' display of unsportsmanlike conduct. Youth classes are supposed to be fun and a learning experience. I wonder, even now, if those parents realized what they were teaching their young horseman."

"I showed many horses—my mother's Arabian, the neighbors registered Quarter Horse and Bourbon—an Appaloosa-Thoroughbred cross that I used for Rodeo Club as well as Trail and English classes, to mention just a few. But Jake was always my favorite. Showing wasn't everything. I loved to ride, whether it was around my parent's farm, out through the nearby desert or on trail rides with my family. Besides, Dad wouldn't have a horse around that couldn't pack a deer or elk during hunting season. I guess the horses had their 'chores' just like us kids growing up on a farm did."

"After high school I moved away and put horses aside until recently. A few years ago I moved to my sister Beth's hay farm in central Nevada, where I currently live. My interest in riding and working with horses was renewed. I take Poncho, my sister's Paint horse out for a 'tricky-tour' around the farm, mostly just bareback as he is quite old. It is a good way to unwind after haying all day. About two years ago Beth acquired Eclipse, a Paso mare. Eclipse likes to GO. Every chance I get, she and I take off for a jaunt. It felt good to be riding again but I still didn't have a horse of my own. Then, in November 2009, my parents found me an Arabian cross named Chadow, a beautiful bay. I loved his spirit as it was much like Jake's. When it snowed on the farm, Chadow would race around the corral, rear, and kick up his hind quarters. He would try to get the two older horses to play, which they found quite annoying. He was quite enjoyable to watch prancing around the corral. Chadow and I began working really well together and the last time the folks were here at the ranch, mom and I took Chadow and Eclipse out for a two hour ride. Unfortunately, it was short lived. In May 2010, **Chadow died suddenly**. It was heartbreaking. I have only a few memories with him."

"Ah, but the memories of riding all the wonderful horses in my life abound. Traveling to horse shows all around the West, including a national event in Montana, where I may not have placed but was proud to have made the final cuts. I am grateful to have had such opportunities to develop my love for horses. Thank you, Mom and Dad. I love you both. There will never be another Jake, but maybe in the near future I will be fortunate enough to have a similar relationship with another such wonderful horse."

Footnote: "Shortly after writing this for mother, I adopted a two week old mustang colt whose mother had died. We fed him milk from a bucket several times a day and he is growing and acting like a kid in the corral. I'm not sure what will become of this union. He still possesses some of the instincts of the wild horse with an acute sense of his own importance when I fuss over him. I have hi-hopes for Harley being a good riding horse. We can only work, wait, and see."

+++++

Paige Hoy: Boise
Age 19 Sara's daughter

Maintain Saddle Repairs

In June of 2001, Paige at age ten, my youngest granddaughter, rode her favorite horse, Bingo, on a desert ride with me. When we got back to the barn, she was taking the saddle off when the stirrup came sliding over the horse and hit her on her head causing a cut deep enough that it took **eight stitches** to close up the wound. Her sister Amber got sick looking at the wound. The next day we wrapped the stirrups with soft leather and repaired some of the other tack. This is the year we learned to maintain good repairs on old saddles. Amber had just returned from Ketchum church camp and commented that she was going back to camp as nothing like this happened there. We laughed about Amber's reaction and reminded her that her little sister that was injured.

However, this accident did not keep Paige off of the horse that summer, as two weeks later, Paige, Grandma and Grandpa, rode horses out to the desert until sunset.

The following year, Paige rode into Marshall Lake near Stanley. She rode the five mile ride on "her" horse with Grandpa, Bill and I and my friend, Lonna Smith and her teenage neighbor, Hailey. It was a beautiful summer day for riding. The sky was a clear blue above the tall trees as we rode through them on the way to the ridge that overlooked Redfish Lake. When we got to the top, we stopped often to take pictures of us on horseback, with the rugged Sawtooth Mountains in the background.

Excitement grew as we began the switchbacks down to beautiful Marshall Lake. The view of the lake held us in awe. It was nestled against the tree lined mountains on three sides the blue water gave out a silver laced glow. The waterfall at the far end of the lake fell nearly fifty feet and created a fast moving creek that fed the lake with fresh water. There was an island near the middle that had blooming fireweed growing on it. **It was such a beautiful sight.** We settled near the lake to have our lunch and rest the horses.

Taking the same way back, when on the ridge, Paige asked me if she could ride Braddo, my horse, the rest of the way. I agreed. When Paige was settled into the saddle, she reached for a pretty branch of wood with a lot of moss on it to take home with her. When she put the reins down on Braddo's neck he took off down the trail at a fast pace—heading for home.

Alarmed, Paige cried out. "Whoa, whoa, Grandma, help," as they disappeared in the trees on the way down the trail.

"Oh, Win!" Lonna yelled at me, "Go after them."

"No," I replied, "They will be back. Braddo is afraid to be by himself and he'll be back."

We waited, and soon heard the clippity-clop of a horse traveling in a hurry. It was Braddo coming back bringing our young, smiling granddaughter with him.

This is just one of many rides that Paige has taken with me. **She is a good rider and loves horses.**

+++++

Amber Hoy: Boise
Age 21, Sara's daughter

From Pony Club to Chasing Wild Things in the Desert

Elaine Dawkins of the Southwind Ranch, Jerome, said, "It's just a lot of fun."

My oldest granddaughter and I watched with interest as members of The Pony Club were galloping their horses through splashing water, across open fields, and over low log fences. It was a good day for us. On our way home, Amber Hoy, at age ten said she would like to take lessons and be a part of the younger beginning group. So we began a search for a flat saddle and bridle. Two weeks later, Amber unloaded Bingo, an Arabian Quarter Horse cross and saddled him up with English gear. She had already learned the parts of the English saddle and studied what the students do to prepare for the event of riding their animal. Even at ten, she was proficient in these requests.

Amber continues to tell her story.

"I enjoyed the new ways to ride in a flat saddle, as well as how to get Bingo to understand what I expected of him. But the most fun was the comraderie of the other girls my age. We studied the Pony Club books at club meetings to prepare for the 'Know Down'."

"Eleven years later I believe that today, **I am a better western rider because of my time with the Pony club members**. Paige, my sister, and I love to go to our grandparent's farm in Jerome, catch their horses, saddle up and ride the fields and canal banks for an hour and return 'all smiles', as Grandma Win said."

"My most fun ride with Grandma was when I was still in grade school. On our spring break we rode into the desert east just across the Snake River bridge. That day, I and three other girls my age, were guests at the Thursday Sage Riders desert ride. We had a fun lunch break where we all got acquainted. On the way back, we saw a small herd of deer that were on a sagebrush ridge. They were watching us with interest. We had wanted to gallop our horses all day, so we asked if we could go chase the watchful deer. Carol looked at her granddaughters Jamie and Jessica, and knowing they had the ability to ride well, said it was up to the rest of the responsible adults. They all agreed, but we were asked to watch out for possible rabbit holes in this part of the desert."

"With a hoop, we took off at a lope toward the watching deer. As we got to the top of the ridge we scared the deer off and I will never forget how they bound away from us. We continued to chase them until they were out of sight. What a ride—one I will never forget."

+++++

Willann Mobley Leckrone: Hailey
5th daughter

Willann was nicknamed Willie. She loved all animals and I was not surprised when she bonded so well with most any horse we linked her with. Her accomplishments were rewarding to me as I watched the many horses that came into her life prove to be very good saddle horses, several she trained from green-broke.

This is her story.

Gaining Satisfaction in Riding Many Types of Horses

"Being raised on a farm we had the good fortune to enjoy many cats, dogs, goats, calves and horses. My very own first horse was a black Shetland pony named Prince Dukey. He was my first memory in a parade as well as my first memory of a straw hat. He gave me my first **memory of a black and blue jaw** (from him kicking me) as well as my first serious accident. That was the day, with only a halter and rope on him I went riding him out in the pasture to open an electric wire gate. I was trying to pull back with my hand on the red wood handle when my hand slipped and slid on the hot wire. Needless to say, I screamed and recalled looking at Dukey like 'help me stupid' cause I couldn't let go of the hot wire. So he pulled back, not because of the blood curdling scream and not out of fear, but more like he wanted me to shut up!" Dukey and I went many places together around the neighborhood. When we went down to Marcia's we got a treat."

"My first big horse was a pretty colored Appaloosa named Ritzy Highspot. This horse had lots of black and white spots over his sorrel body, and two white spots on the tips of his ears. He was my first horse for showing in 4-H as well as the Magic Valley Appaloosa Horse Club shows.

He was a 'ritzy' horse easy to ride and show as he was well-trained by Patty Brown who my sister and I also took lessons from. I enjoyed Ritzy a lot. We could go anywhere together. One day I rode him down to my girlfriends house about two miles down the road from us. I tied him up on a log pole tie up then went inside. He managed to move the rope down the pole where he could reach a large mud hole. He must have pulled back when he slipped in the mud and fighting to regain his upright position, he broke his rear leg. This was the saddest day that I can remember having to do with horses."

"My sister and I had several nice Appaloosa's and went to the ION (Idaho, Oregon, Nevada) events and competed in most of the classes. The competition I enjoyed the most was held in Elko, Nevada when little Big Enough, my gelding and I won the high point youth award. (Horse in picture) He was a bay with a colorful blanket on his rump. He behaved perfectly and with me in my turquoise hat and matching chaps, we stood out like gold in a mountain stream—enough to catch the judge's eye that day. I also rode him in a three year old, snaffle bit class and we won the $50.00 prize."

"The most nervous I remember being was when I was ten. We were at the National Appaloosa show in Billings, Montana. There were more than 200 contestants in classes of the youth. We were just honored to be able to be a part of this **national event** so close to home. We rode in English, trail and western riding classes on a horse we called Bourbon that was a 15hh sorrel gelding with white flakes. He was without a doubt our most dependable horse—the one we used for rodeo club events. Although he was part Thoroughbred he never got high and we were always in control of him in the barrel and pole races. This horse was trained by Carol Pugh—what a horse trainer she was! Bourbon was a fun horse to take out on the trails and the desert with the Thursday Sage Riders. As a 5th grader I was always ready to skip school, saddle my horse and go off to the South Hills with those crazy, horse-addicted women."

"The time when I 'felt as one' with my horse would definitely be when we bought a 16hh, white Appaloosa/Thoroughbred gelding that was named Premo. He was related to a famous race horse that came out of Montana and had been entered in several races for three year olds. I worked with him myself. He was never sent to a trainer. When he was four, I rode him in many shows and entered the western and trail classes as well as English. He looked 'primo' when he was saddled with an English saddle and ridden in the arena and asked to walk, trot, and extend the trot and gallop. It was hard for any other contestant to beat him. Together, we learned to jump over three foot poles in the dressage class too. When Dad tore down an old cellar, he made us an arena where I could work this big friend and bond with him. You could always find me there after school until dark. Premo even let my big dog Jimmy, jump upon him and I placed the dog behind the saddle and the three of us went riding off. He was so much fun. I had him all through high school. We competed in the ION, Appaloosa Horse Club shows, 4-H, and rodeo team events."

"A registered Arabian named Macho came into our lives the year I was in junior high school. He was an oxy-moron to me, as I had never been around a horse that seemed afraid of so much that crossed his path. He was very beautiful—a dainty-dappled silver color, white main and tail. He was really good in an arena while ridden in English classes. I did enjoy this part of his tiny prancing as long as it brought me a blue ribbon because I loved English riding. He was good outside the arena too because my parents often took him to the mountain trails and rode him for nearly ten years before selling him to a girl who used him for a 4-H project. Ten years later the folks owned a very nice bay Arabian gelding named, Bingo Majerus, which even my young children could ride—it takes all kinds of horses that bring us companionships."

"As I conclude, I would like to say that winning trophies, plaques, money and belt buckles as definitely rewarding, however, I was more in the spirit for the satisfaction of seeing what I could do with the many breeds. Yes, I enjoyed the reward of getting that one horse over the fear of water that was noisily going under a bridge and for him to cross the bridge in trail class or teaching the horse to jump into the trailer—just doing many things without a fuss. I can't say I was a Horse Whisper, but I was definitely an **avid Horse Lover**!"

"Thanks Dad and Mom for those lovely times."

+++++

Melissa Leckrone: Hailey
Age 19: Willann's daughter

Bingo was my Favorite

Melissa enjoyed riding at a very young age just like her mother did. The pictures I have of her when she was five in an oversized, western hat and wearing jeans and tennis shoes tells all. She still could not reach the stirrups of the children's saddle for two years since she was not very tall. This still did not stop her from riding every chance she got. Today, at age 19, Melissa comes to the farm with her younger brother, Andrew, ready to ride at any time of the year. A picture of her on Braddo and Andrew on Callie was taken at Christmas time last year even with snow in the fields. Melissa often puts her daughter Hillarie (age 3) in the saddle with her and off they go, smiling all the way.

The following is her story—enjoy.

"My favorite ride with Grandmother, when I was eleven, occurred during the summer when we rode in the South Hills south of Twin Falls. We unloaded near the ski lodge and began our ride up a fun trail in the trees, then up a slight climb to Deadline Ridge. I was riding Bingo as he was my favorite. Mandy and Paige, my cousins, were also riding my grandparents horses, Braddo and Calypso that were very well broke horses for trail riding. Grandmother was riding Charla, a nice Paso mare. Arriving at the top, we tied up for lunch in some trees and sat down to enjoy the view of Magic Valley to the northwest. Then we rode across the top just above where the lift lets off the skiers. As we entered the heavily wooded area we scared up some deer. They bound down in front of us and our horses stopped to watch them disappear. Going back down the mountain, we watched for them again but saw only tracks. **It was a fun uneventful day**, unless you call stopping at the Rock Creek store for double dip ice cream cones uneventful. Yum, yes, it was all good."

+++++

In conclusion, I would like to add that most people keep their dreams and desires inside. Some of these women that I have written about have let their God given courage inside them bloom, as they undertake to live their dream and enjoy a horse of their own. I thank God for their memoirs that they have so freely given to me.

This book is dedicated to my five wonderful daughters.

Love,
Mother